COGNITIVE-EXPERIENTIAL THERAPY:

An Integrative Ego Psychotherapy

COGNITIVE-EXPERIENTIAL THERAPY:

An Integrative Ego Psychotherapy

by

Melvin L. Weiner, Ph.D.

Clinical Professor of Psychiatry
University of California School of Medicine, Davis

and

Langley Porter Psychiatric Institute
University of California, San Francisco

BRUNNER/MAZEL *Publishers* • New York

Library of Congress Cataloging in Publication Data

Weiner, Melvin L.
  Cognitive-experiential therapy.

  Bibliography: pp. 220–224
  Includes index.
  1. Cognitive-experiential psychotherapy.
I. Title. [DNLM: 1. Cognition. 2. Psychotherapy—
methods. WM 420 W425c]
RC489.C62W45 1985   616.89′14   85-11030
ISBN 0-87630-382-3

Copyright © 1985 by Melvin L. Weiner

Published by
Brunner/Mazel, Inc.
19 Union Square West
New York, New York 10003

MANUFACTURED IN THE UNITED STATES OF AMERICA

Nothing ever becomes real till it is experienced. Even a Proverb is no Proverb to you till Life has illustrated it.

John Keats

I am always doing *what I can't do yet* in order to learn how to do it.

Vincent van Gogh

Foreword

Dr. Melvin Weiner has written a welcome and unusual book. It is welcome because it introduces two new psychotherapy techniques that promote effective problem solving in therapy and in the patient's life. His book is unusual in that it advances novel ideas and techniques while remaining grounded in the best of traditional theory and therapeutic practice.

Dr. Weiner's primary innovation is a set of tasks and puzzles carefully introduced by the therapist into the hour. In extensive verbatim transcripts and in pilot clinical trials, he demonstrates how these tasks can help patients to mobilize their ego functions for active mastery instead of resignation, retreat, and repression. In a second innovation, Weiner describes the therapeutic use of audiotapes made by patients in the course of their love and work relationships. Both techniques encourage therapists and patients to collaborate in making connections between therapy and "real life."

The enterprise of psychodynamic psychotherapy has always seemed to me to strain the credulity of our patients. They come to us because they have problems that they feel unable to solve. We convince them that exploring their feelings and working through the therapeutic relationship in the consulting room will somehow help them to feel better and behave differently. In *Cognitive-Experiential Therapy* there is explicit recognition of the fact that therapy is a problem-solving enterprise.

The new name for this therapy does not imply that the author claims to have discovered a new theory of human nature and its vicissitudes. The approach presented in the book is grounded in the work of two grand theorists of human behavior and development—Piaget and Freud. It represents a serious attempt to bring together these approaches usually characterized too quickly as theories of cognition (Piaget) or emotion (Freud). As the title of the book suggests, the therapy attempts to mobilize healthy cognitive and ego processes, but gives equal time to the dynamic forces in the patient and in his or her relationships that interfere with the application of the ego to the resolution of central life issues.

In traditional psychodynamically oriented therapy, therapists adopt a "blank screen" persona to encourage free association and provide a safe environment for the emergence of anxiety-laden material. The therapeutic stance is justified by its goal of helping patients to move from victim to master of internal conflict. From a Piagetian perspective, these are ideal conditions for the patient's exercise of *assimilation*. As part of an organism's adaptive capacity, assimilation is a biological and psychological Procrustean tendency to cut the world to fit our own system of meanings. But assimilation is only one of two necessary adaptive functions. Piaget also believed, and I think Freud would have agreed, that *accommodation* is necessary for adaptation and growth. That is, we must at times modify our structures, behaviors, and meanings in response to challenges perpetually presented by the physical and social world. While the therapy hour occasionally provides opportunities for disequilibration and accommodation, it is the assimilative side of the adaptation process that usually holds center stage. Patients may be grappling actively with long-standing personal issues, but they rarely have the chance to react to new problems; and therapists rarely have a chance to observe patients' problem-solving skills in action. Thus, therapists are usually limited by their interpretations of patients' interpretations of how they cope with daily life.

Consider the merits of adding to the usual verbal interchange between patient and therapist a task or puzzle that the patient attempts to solve. In addition to the focus on problem solution (the cognitive focus), the therapist pays careful attention to feelings and free associations aroused as the patient attempts to cope with frustration through guided explorations (the experiential focus). Just as Piaget vastly increased the power and replicability of his methods once he switched from interviews about natural phenomena to probing questions while the child worked on laboratory tasks, Weiner shows that it is possible for therapist and patient to use tasks to grapple with a shared reality.

Using Weiner's techniques, therapists can open two direct windows on transference—one looking out on patients' interactions with them and another examining what patients bring from the past and present to their interaction with the tasks. These same two windows allow a multiple perspective on countertransference. Therapists' tendencies to filter patients' behavior toward them through idiosyncratic lenses can be reduced by the opportunity to observe patients engaged in other meaningful transactions. Like the surveyor recording data from at least two vantage points, the therapist *and* the patient can map the territory through a process of triangulation. Diagnosis (differentiated assessment) and therapy go hand in hand.

Weiner warns the reader that this book does not provide simple techniques that can be immediately applied to revitalize a therapy that has reached a point of stagnation. He is right. First and foremost, the user of problem-solving tasks and the audiotapes must be a fine therapist. Weiner's own verbatim accounts of therapy hours with a variety of patients, along with thoughtful annotation and comments, demonstrate his own qualifications on this score; these accounts themselves provide an excellent reason to read this book. Though it does not adopt a "how to do it" approach, one chapter does present a helpful therapist's manual. There is also a complete description of the tasks, and guidelines for systematic evaluation of the therapy for those who wish to explore the techniques in their own practice.

I believe that Dr. Weiner has done admirably what he set out to do. He has provided a stimulating approach to therapy that focuses both on cognitive and affective/experiential aspects of ego functioning. He integrates psychodynamic and cognitive approaches in a developmental framework that gives promise of helping a wide variety of patients. Whether or not readers are moved to try the new techniques, they will be challenged to develop new perspectives on their work and to keep their eye on helping patients develop solutions for the problems that brought them into therapy.

Philip A. Cowan, Ph.D.
Professor of Psychology
University of California, Berkeley

Contents

List of Tables

About the Author

MELVIN L. WEINER, Ph.D., is currently Clinical Professor of Psychiatry at both the University of California School of Medicine, Davis, and the Langley Porter Psychiatric Institute, University of California, San Francisco. Dr. Weiner, who is both a psychotherapist and an experimental psychologist, trained at the Menninger Foundation, the Worcester State Hospital, and the Albert Einstein College of Medicine of Yeshiva University, and completed analytic training in New York City. After collaborating with Jean Piaget at the Institut Rousseau of the University of Geneva, he served on the faculties of the Albert Einstein College of Medicine; City College (CUNY); and the New School for Social Research. In addition, he has engaged in the private practice of psychotherapy since 1960.

Dr. Weiner has published extensively on ego development and psychotherapy and is the author of two previous books, *Personality: The Human Potential* and *The Cognitive Unconscious: A Piagetian Approach to Psychotherapy*.

Preface

This book aims to increase the therapist's effectiveness through the application of an innovative psychotherapeutic approach, Cognitive-Experiential Therapy (CET). Readily integrated into approaches of diverse orientations, CET has been applied both in short- and long-term treatment of a broad range of emotional problems of children and adults.

The roots of CET can be traced back to experimental research the author initiated in 1950. That research (1975) attempted to delineate the growth processes leading to improved adaptation and contact with reality. This new volume arises out of extensive clinical studies that led to the identification of six growth-inducing principles that expedite therapeutic progress. These principles, which will be detailed in Chapter III, suggested that a patient's improvement in therapy requires:

1. Experience as well as understanding
2. Thought balanced with action
3. Increased contact with reality
4. Corrective feedback

CET is thus anchored in *experience* and *action*. In order to balance understanding with experience, specially devised experiences and slices of reality from outside the therapy session are superimposed on and integrated into the traditional therapist-patient interactions. These experiences consist of over 200 verbal, nonverbal and three-dimensional problem-solving tasks and numerous audiorecordings of the patient's interpersonal relationships. In response to the clinical material presented by the patient, the therapist systematically selects those experiences that most appropriately address the patient's problems and needs.

To balance thought with action, the patient is required to respond not only by thinking, free associating and talking about these experiences, but by acting upon them and actually doing things in the session with the goal of mastering them. Although the patient's actions and accompanying interaction with the therapist clearly reveal the patient's unique coping style, defensive structure and underlying conflicts, the focus is not on diagnostic evaluation. Rather, the goal is to help the patient to rise above his conflicts and use the session in a novel therapeutic way.* The CET session is transformed, in part, into an experiential-developmental laboratory where corrective feedback obtained from the consequences of the patient's actions and from the therapist helps the patient to develop more adaptive cognitive and defensive processes and a more effective behavioral repertoire.

A major portion of this volume is devoted to a treatment manual to provide practical techniques and guidelines for conducting CET. To avoid the ambiguities that arise from abstract discussion of cases and to make the therapeutic process come alive, the book is unusually detailed in its case presentations and revealing of the therapeutic process. Excerpts of transcripts of audiorecorded therapy sessions with a broad range of patients and emotional problems are presented to demonstrate the CET method. In addition to being clinically instructive, such detailed description of a CET therapist's activities affords the scientific community with the raw data for evaluating the method and provides a more solid basis for clarifying, amending and validating the approach.

While the clinical presentations and analyses of the therapeutic interactions illustrate how CET can implement the therapeutic process, a therapist can gain most by supplementing these guidelines for practice with supervision by therapists trained in CET and by participation in intensive CET training seminars. Such additional training is especially important for beginning therapists who may be tempted to

---

*Because our language lacks a true generic pronoun, "he," "his," etc., are used as a shorthand for both male and female individuals.

append this seemingly simple technique to an undeveloped therapeutic style, producing a gimmicky and potentially harmful misapplication of the treatment approach. Listening to audiotapes and/or viewing videotapes of CET sessions has also proved helpful in learning to integrate CET into a therapist's repertoire. Maximum benefit can be achieved with a flexible, comprehensive treatment plan based on an integration of CET, biologic and social approaches. While I do not propose CET as a blueprint for all psychotherapeutic endeavors, it can serve as a useful adjunct for therapists with various theoretical orientations.

Even if the reader does not find the CET method and techniques compatible with his clinical style, I urge him or her to evaluate on their own merits the growth-inducing processes which form the conceptual framework for CET. These growth-inducing processes have been identified as essential ingredients in therapeutic change. They have been derived from over sixty years of research in cognitive development by Jean Piaget and his colleagues and from over thirty years of the author's experience as a psychodynamic therapist and an experimental developmental psychologist. The growth-inducing processes can serve as points of departure for independent development and reformulation of therapeutic method and technique, and leave room for the individual practitioner to apply the processes creatively and to develop a unique style. These issues of exploring new directions and extending the limits and applicability of CET are addressed in the concluding chapter, *The Future of CET*.

However reasonable and compelling the theory and methods of CET may be, their usefulness and chief test of success will be determined ultimately by the degree to which they improve the outcome of therapy and extend the range of patients who can be effectively treated. Efficacy is the prime criterion by which any new approach is judged. Because of the promising results obtained in the clinical trials reported in Chapter VI, *The Effectiveness of CET*, research is continuing to evaluate CET more thoroughly with a larger sample.

The basic tenet of CET is that there exists an intimate relationship between the cognitive and emotional organizations in an individual. Cognitive life and emotional life are inseparable, although distinct. There is no separate cognitive behavior and emotional behavior— behavior is always both. Cognitive and emotional behavior simultaneously and mutually influence and define each other.

Although CET evolved within a cognitive developmental framework, it goes beyond consideration of only cognitive functioning by always placing it in the context of the dynamics of the patient's emotional development. In CET, the patient travels a path which leads from the cognitive problems that are presented to him to his emotional problems, and vice versa. When the patient's ego functions are brought to the foreground of the therapeutic endeavor in CET, they in no way become an intellectualized study of cognitive processes viewed out of their emotional context. On the contrary, although the patient's ego functions, adaptational repertoire, reality orientation and states of consciousness are explicitly identified and considered in detail, they are understood in the context of the patient's conflict, defense, transference, regression and fixation. In essence, then, CET represents a synthesis of cognitive, behavioral and adaptational processes with psychodynamic processes; i.e., what can be called an "integrative ego psychotherapy."

We should emphasize, therefore, that in formulating a new integration of developmental, psychodynamic and behavioral approaches, CET does not intend to brush aside or replace other theories or techniques. On the contrary, because of its unifying, multidisciplinary framework, CET can serve to supplement a therapist's particular approach. It can be effectively integrated into approaches of diverse orientations in various disciplines, such as psychiatry, clinical psychology, psychiatric social work, psychiatric nursing, school and counseling psychology, marriage, family and child counseling, occupational therapy and speech therapy. It is hoped that the theoretical framework and clinical research and examples presented in this volume will stimulate clinicians and researchers from these disciplines to test the approach, report their experiences and continue in the spirit of exploration.

COGNITIVE-
EXPERIENTIAL
THERAPY:
An Integrative
Ego Psychotherapy

CHAPTER I

What Is Cognitive-Experiential Therapy?

CET is an experimentally grounded psychotherapeutic approach directed both toward short- and long-term treatment of a broad range of emotional problems and patient populations (Weiner, 1975, 1979, 1980a, 1982, 1983, 1984, 1985). It has been used in the treatment of:

1. Acute anxiety states
2. Childhood behavior disorders
3. Obsessive-compulsive neuroses
4. Hysterical neuroses
5. Acute nonbipolar depressions (outpatient)
6. Acute schizophrenic episodes (inpatient and outpatient)
7. Acute manic-depressive episodes (inpatient)
8. Nonbipolar psychotic depressions (inpatient)
9. Borderline disturbances
10. Narcissistic personality disorders

Our basic premise is that the most profitable therapeutic experience derives from implementing a balance between thought and action so that the patient can gain maximal corrective feedback from the consequences of his actions and increasingly make more adaptive accommodations. For this purpose, in response to the clinical material presented by the patient, CET systematically superimposes on and integrates into the traditional therapist-patient interactions a series of specially devised experiences that require the patient to respond not only by thinking and talking about them, but by acting upon them. From the consequences of his actions and the accompanying interaction with the therapist, the patient obtains corrective feedback.

Since there is a relationship between getting to know objects in a more differentiated way and getting to know the self (cf. Piaget, 1936, 1937; Witkin et al., 1962), a CET therapist provides a balance of experiences by introducing into the sessions events from both the world of objects and the world of people. Different experiential procedures are used to address these different aspects of physical and interpersonal reality: (1) "therapeutic tasks" focus on solving problems with objects and with aspects of physical reality not usually present in therapy; (2) audiorecordings of the patient's current relationships with people illuminate aspects of his daily interpersonal behavior.

Over 200 therapeutic tasks are currently used in CET. The tasks have been either specifically designed for CET or adapted from diverse sources which can be traced as far back as seventeenth-century designs. The tasks involve two- and three-dimensional objects where visual, spatial, auditory and other sensory modalities are required to master the problem. A number of verbal problems are also employed. The Jug Problem (p. 205) is a typical problem-solving task. The solution to this problem requires an integration of seeing, hearing, touching and mechanical and manipulative skills. The patient must explore, experience and use his sensory and mental powers to solve the problem and master the task. Equally important is *how* he does it, his mental process and feelings in arriving at the solution and "in doing what he can't do yet in order to learn how to do it."

With the audiotape technique, recordings are made by the patient of his real-life interactions with people. The patient brings these tapes to the sessions for playback. He and the therapist then listen and respond to what actually transpired in the patient's interpersonal relations. We will elaborate on the method and rationale of the therapeutic tasks and the audiotape technique, illustrated with case studies, in Chapter II, *Therapeutic Method*.

It is important to emphasize that these experiential activities are not intended as diagnostic assessment instruments nor merely as cognitive exercises within a free-associational field. These procedures, integrated into a session in response to the patient's problems and needs, are designed to expedite and deepen the therapeutic process by spurring the patient into action *in* the session. Through these actions and their consequences, the patient experiences and demonstrates an authentic view of his cognitive and defensive style. He is enabled to examine himself, to reflect upon his own transactions and, most important, to transcend simply understanding the experience by initiating adaptive and accommodative actions. The CET session is, therefore, transformed, in part, into an experiential-developmental laboratory where feedback from the consequences of the patient's actions and from the therapist helps the patient to explore and develop more adaptive cognitive and defensive processes and a more effective behavioral repertoire.

1. THEORETICAL FRAMEWORK

The basic tenet of CET is that there exists an intimate relationship between the cognitive and emotional organizations in an individual. Cognitive life and emotional life are inseparable, although distinct. There is no cognitive behavior and emotional behavior; behavior always reflects both cognitive and emotional aspects. Cognitive and emotional behavior simultaneously and mutually influence and define each other.

The term "cognitive" has a broad scope as used in CET. Attending to the patient's ideas, percepts, world- and self-view and memory is, of course, central to any cognitive therapy. But CET goes further by attempting to capture and analyze the processes underlying the cognitive behavior. Therapists have always taken into account the patient's perceptual, thought, language and memory processes, but the methods of CET enable the therapist to be more explicit and precise and to grasp the patient's underlying cognitive processes in a more systematic way. The work of Piaget (see Gruber and Vonèche, 1977), Rapaport (1967), Schafer (1954), Werner (1957) and Witkin et al. (1954, 1962) in explicating the cognitive operations of the individual have influenced our cognitive analyses.

As we will discuss more fully in Section 2 on *Historical Roots* and in Chapter III, *Growth-Inducing Processes,* CET has been profoundly influenced by cognitive developmental theories, especially those of Piaget (1936, 1937, 1945, 1954, 1975) and Werner (1957). A number of therapists have addressed various aspects of therapy within this developmental framework, e.g., Anthony (1956, 1976), Basch (1977),

Feuerstein (1980), Friedman (1978), Gouin-Décarie (1962), Greenspan (1979), Sandler (1975), Schmid-Kitsikis (1973), Wachtel (1981), Wolff (1960), and especially Cowan (1978), who has suggested various ways of applying developmental concepts to child therapy.

Although CET evolved within a cognitive developmental framework, it goes beyond consideration of only cognitive functioning by always placing it in the context of the patient's emotional development. For this purpose, contemporary ego developmental theory has provided us with the psychodynamic context for understanding the emotional complexities of the patient's intrapsychic and interpersonal life (see Weiner, 1975, 1979, 1980b).

In CET, the patient travels a path which leads from the cognitive problems that are presented to him to his emotional problems, and vice versa. When ego functions are brought to the foreground of the therapeutic endeavor in CET, they do not in any way become an intellectualized and remote study of cognitive processes considered out of their emotional context. On the contrary, although the patient's ego functions, adaptational repertoire, reality orientation and states of consciousness are explicitly identified and considered in detail, they are understood in the context of the patient's conflict, defense, transference, regression and fixation. In essence, then, CET represents a synthesis of cognitive, behavioral, and adaptational processes with psychodynamic processes; i.e., what can be called an "integrative ego psychotherapy."

Although CET is related to and has been receptive to the findings and concepts of other approaches, at the same time it is distinguished from them in several important ways. For example, we share with Beck (1976, 1979), Ellis (1973), Goldfried and Goldfried (1980), Mahoney (1974), and Meichenbaum (1977) their emphasis on the relationship between cognition and behavior and action. In a similar vein, Sherman (1979) and Sherman and Levine (1979) review a number of approaches that help the patient to learn new problem-solving skills and coping strategies. However, CET places these emphases in the context of developmental and psychodynamic processes. Moreover, our cognitive approach focuses not only on cognitive behavior such as the thoughts, assumptions and belief systems or coping responses which the cognitive-behavioral theorists emphasize, but on the processes underlying the behavior. In addition to helping the patient to develop new cognitive behaviors, our goal is to assist him in reorganizing his overall cognitive structure and the operations which organize, regulate, articulate and coordinate the raw sensory data and which give rise to the cognitive behavior, such as discussed by Piaget (1950),

Weiner (1975) and Werner (1957). Bieber's work (1980), although sharing with CET its psychodynamic context, does not emphasize underlying cognitive processes, but focuses on the "extinction of irrational beliefs" (p. 16).

Similarly, CET is related to a number of approaches which stress the here-and-now, experiential component in therapy. For example, group therapy, couples therapy, Gestalt therapy, transactional analysis, psychodrama, play therapy, bioenergetic therapy and assertiveness training groups have all emphasized the actual living through of feelings and events in the here-and-now of the therapy sessions.

What distinguishes CET from these approaches is that real challenges from outside the therapy session in real time entailing real risks are introduced into the sessions. These "extra-session realities" are not aimed primarily at eliciting emotional or symbolic expression, as in play therapy, nor are they "as if" exercises introduced into the sessions like role playing or speaking to an empty chair. Rather, the patient must commit himself to goal-directed action for which he is held accountable. He risks exposing his strengths and weaknesses. There is a real chance of frustration and failure as well as opportunity for success and gratification from mastering these events. Our experiential-developmental laboratory goes beyond making manifest hidden feelings and thoughts. It provides the patient with a tangible medium for reorganizing his cognitive and defensive style and for enhancing veridical and accommodative contact with the environment.

2. HISTORICAL ROOTS

CET is an experimentally grounded approach with roots that can be traced back to research the author initiated in 1950 in H. A. Witkin's Perception Laboratory. This series of investigations, conducted with normal adult subjects, addressed the psychological mechanisms at work in perceptual change (Weiner, 1951, 1955a). We explored a fundamental dimension of a person's relationship to the world—his orientation in space. Subjects were placed in a tilted position in a totally darkened room and instructed to determine whether a tilted luminous rod surrounded by a tilted luminous cubic frame was upright. With no visible objects available as reference points for spatial orientation, the subjects encountered considerable difficulty in gauging the true vertical, having instead to use their estimated body tilt as the standard of verticality to determine the orientation of the rod and frame.

The need for real-world reference points became even more evident with prolonged observation. The longer the subjects' access to real-world objects was restricted, the more disoriented they became and the more their perceptual judgments deteriorated. Thus, limiting an individual's interactions with real-world events induces perceptual change, but in the wrong direction; that is, the person moves in the direction of distortion and maladaptation.

In 1951, this research was carried forward by exploring the mechanisms that would help individuals to develop more adaptive perceptions (Weiner, 1952, 1955b). Using the same experimental set-up, we found that introducing special experiences designed to increase awareness of their bodies and surroundings was critical in helping subjects to improve their perceptual performance. A related experiment by Witkin showed that merely explaining these experiences, in the absence of the concrete experiences themselves, was ineffective in producing change and "rarely altered the subject's perception of the situation. Its effect was rather to enable him to interpret his perceptual experiences in an intellectual way" (1948, pp. 32-33).

In 1952, as part of the Perceptual Learning Project at the Menninger Foundation, we isolated some of the processes necessary for adaptive cognitive development (Weiner, 1954, 1956). In this key set of experiments, we focused on the cognitive processes as well as the final product. A modified Ames Distorted Room was designed and constructed for this series of experiments. When subjects looked into this room, they encountered a number of disturbing illusions: It looked like an ordinary square room when, in reality, not only was it trapezoidal in shape, but a person walking into the room appeared to walk right through a solid wall; a person walking around in the room appeared to grow or shrink in size when, in actuality, he moved toward or away from the observer; marbles in the room appeared to roll uphill when actually they rolled downhill; and so on.

The results indicated that: (1) systematically introducing real-world events or slices of reality in the form of objects and people into the room was necessary to enable the subjects to develop the cognitive processes essential to surmount the illusions and perceive reality; (2) the subject's active involvement in doing things and conducting experiments with these real-world events was necessary for perceptual development; and (3) helping to modify the subject's cognitions (perceptions, ideas and beliefs) was of limited value unless the cognitive processes from which these cognitions were derived were also reorganized and modified. This conclusion was derived through having the subjects view a second, differently designed distorted room which, unbeknownst to them, had been substituted for the first distorted room. We found that the perceptions and beliefs developed in the first distorted room were of limited value and actually worked against the subjects. These new cognitions were adaptive only in the specific room in which they were developed. In the new room, the subjects succumbed to illusion all over again, perceiving this room as no different from the first.

In striking contrast, the new cognitive processes developed in the first room were of generalizable value and could be flexibly applied to the second room and quickly used to enable the subjects to develop new adaptive cognitions. These new cognitive processes engendered a general capacity to overcome illusion and perceive reality in all kinds of distorted rooms.

This research, which attempted to delineate the developmental processes leading to improved adaptation and contact with reality in adults, led us to question whether these same developmental processes could be found to foster growth in the child's natural evolution from infancy to adulthood (compare Weiner, 1956, with Piaget, 1936, 1937, 1945). Our plan was to isolate the general learning experiences which play a central role in development in both children and adults and then apply these processes to the therapeutic process. We hoped to be able to induce growth in individuals where the developmental processes have been arrested. Although Jean Piaget was not a clinician, he was intrigued with this idea and, in 1955, invited the author to collaborate with him to pursue these hypotheses in Geneva (see Piaget and Weiner, 1957-1958).

This comparative developmental research revealed that children and adults do indeed develop in parallel ways. It proved possible to identify six *growth-inducing principles* which could be applied to the therapeutic process. These principles, which will be explored in detail in Chapter III, suggested that a patient's improvement in therapy requires:

1. Experience as well as understanding
2. Thought balanced with action
3. Increased contact with reality
4. Corrective feedback

From 1960 to 1967, these guiding principles were refined and made operational by incorporating them into therapeutic practice. After experimental use of CET from 1967 to 1979 with a broad range of diagnostic categories and patient populations, intensive clinical trials were conducted from 1979 to 1983 on a random population of ten patients (Weiner, 1984). This research is discussed in detail in Chapter

VI, *The Effectiveness of CET*. The approach has been taught to a multidisciplinary group of therapists in the fields of psychiatry, clinical psychology, social work, psychiatric nursing and occupational therapy in the Department of Psychiatry at the University of California, Davis.

3. THE IMMEDIATE GOALS OF CET

(1) Foster the Patient's Motivation

The motivation of the patient is probably the most important single ingredient ensuring therapeutic success. Without a highly motivated patient, all therapeutic efforts are doomed. Negativism, withdrawal and lassitude can defeat any therapeutic effort. Attempts to motivate the patient have relied mainly on the force of the therapist's personality and his capacity for compassion and rapport to build a strong bond with the patient. Although these are vital prerequisites for all good therapy, there is a risk of motivating the patient to seek only to please the therapist, resulting in short-lived and illusory therapeutic success. CET's method emphasizes long-term psychological growth by stirring the patient's *intrinsic* motivations.

From the very beginning, CET provides the patient with a glimpse of the rewards obtained through success. The patient is given a challenging, tangible problem and sees that he can solve it. He experiences that he is capable, worthy, in control and that he can manage himself. By thus mastering the problem, the patient starts to believe in himself. He is afforded an immensely healing and gratifying experience in its own right. This hard-won, meaningful and genuine achievement presents the patient with a highly charged, seldom experienced sense of creative mastery. It catalyzes that priceless motivator—hope—and fosters the patient's persistence, dedication and commitment to the therapeutic work.

(2) Promote the Therapeutic Alliance

If our desire is to make contact with our patients, to be trusted by them, to let them know we want to understand and help them, then establishing a therapeutic alliance is vital. It overrides all other technical considerations. Without a working therapeutic alliance, even the best of techniques will founder. Successful therapy depends on a solid therapeutic relationship which sustains the patient's motivation to enter into and work effectively in therapy.

CET's method builds on and goes beyond expressing compassion and developing rapport with the patient. The therapist's active role in working on the real-world events with the patient demonstrates in a tangible way that he is a reliable, concerned, caretaking, involved and accepting person.

Equally important, doing something productive together emphasizes mutuality in the therapeutic encounter. This reciprocal patient-therapist relationship plays an important role in implementing the therapeutic alliance. The activities express concretely the cooperative nature of the therapeutic relationship and communicate that the therapist and the patient are actively engaged in a mutual quest for solutions to the patient's problems.

(3) Empower and Restore the Patient's Integrity

CET provides an antidote to the patient's low self-esteem and damaged integrity. Mastery of the events introduces the patient to a sense of his power and self-worth. The patient gains strength from experiencing his capacity to overcome conflict and frustration and to contend with problems successfully. He is shown that he is not trapped. He becomes a believer in himself and his integrity. He discovers the power to reshape his life.

(4) Empower and Augment the Therapist's Integrity

CET broadens and expedites the scope of the therapist's professional interventions. Whereas traditional therapy enables the therapist to seize opportunities for growth, CET interventions enable the therapist to become a moving force and more systematically channel his best energy toward *creating* opportunities for patient growth. This active engagement places the therapist in a new light as a professional who need not only sit and wait, but who can take a more creative and active role in directing the course of therapy.

(5) Objectify the Therapeutic Interaction

Patients often accuse therapists of being insensitive and biased in their views. They argue with the therapist about the truth of his observations and interpretations. It may be easier, therefore, for a patient to assimilate information about himself and the world when he is the initiator of that information than when it is offered by the therapist, who may be accused of being biased. As a consequence, CET sessions are structured so that the patient can discover the truth himself and stop struggling with the therapist. The patient can argue with the therapist, but he cannot argue with reality. The real challenges presented in the tasks and the patient's audiorecordings of his interpersonal interactions are the media for obtaining an objective view of himself and his relationship to the world. This form of sensory-based reality testing is an invaluable ally in overcoming the patient's resistances and surmounting narcissistic distortions, both of which can impede or destroy therapeutic success.

(6) Experience Tangible Progress Within the Therapy Session

Patients engaging in therapy are often overwhelmed by a feeling that they are confronted with a big, hopeless, and unknowable task. Contending with the real-world events in the sessions, however, acts like a psychological mirror which enables the patient to see how he is doing. As the patient contends with the tasks and the audiotapes in the sessions, he obtains tangible evidence of his progression from the beginning of therapy, where he struggled fearfully, distortedly and maladaptively, to later stages in therapy where he deals with events more courageously, objectively and successfully. He can see himself growing and getting better. His efforts "pay off."

Discovery of his real accomplishments and improved perspective with the events in the session not only fuel his intrinsic motivation to continue to grow, but foster the development of a realistic self-image. This self-discovery of change is vital for helping the patient to develop a new self-concept of his growing competence and effectiveness.

(7) Provide a Balanced View of the Patient

A therapist wants to understand his patients, discover who they are, what their problems are and what they want from therapy. Especially with more seriously disturbed patients and in crisis intervention, a therapist needs to "size the patient up" to determine how he can best be helped. Because many patients have succeeded only too well in assuming an adaptive front and are aware mainly of their misery but oblivious to the reasons their life is conflictful and ungratifying, it can take months or years for the therapist to help the patient obtain the clarity of focus necessary for him to resolve why things never seem to go right. Anna Freud observed:

> We are all familiar with the accusation not infrequently made against analysts—that they may have a good knowledge of a

patient's unconscious but are bad judges of his ego. There is probably a certain amount of justification in this criticism, for the analyst lacks opportunities of observing the patient's whole ego in action. (1936, p. 23)

CET quickly provides both the therapist and the patient with a more representative view of what the patient is truly like. While dreams, associations, slips of the tongue and historical reconstructions or projective tests probe deeply, the patient's actions in dealing with the slices of reality in the here-and-now are a microcosm of his way of dealing with daily life. This behavioral view adds balance and perspective to the view obtained in the confines of the consultation room.

The advantages of this slice of life perspective led Erik Erikson in his therapy practice to visit prospective patients in their homes and have dinner with them and their families before accepting them for psychotherapy. He recounted (1983) that he wanted to balance his view of the patient as seen inside the therapeutic situation with a more representative view of the patient in his natural environment.

CET induces the patient to view himself outside of his carefully protected illusions. It cuts through the denials, rationalizations and pretenses that often surround and invade the patient's presentation and gets to the heart of the matter. For example, when asked what he thought and felt about his action on a task, a patient responded with uncanny candor, "That sounds like a depressed little boy!" He was right. Underneath the adaptive front, there was a lonely man who felt and acted like a little boy abandoned by his parents when he was six years old. CET thus counteracts the insularity of the patient-therapist relationship, enabling the therapist and the patient to engage the therapeutic endeavor with fresh eyes and ears.

In addition, whereas therapy typically focuses on the darker side of life, CET, with its focus on problem solving, contending with challenge and discovery, enables the therapist to gain a perspective which reveals a side of the patient's life frequently obscured in therapy—the patient's wit, perceptiveness, resourcefulness, creativity and imagination. He sees the active, inventive and goal-directed ego at work. Are we not impressed when we hear a patient play a musical instrument with professional competence, or write with humor, insight or irony, or when we witness his skills and dexterity in other endeavors? CET helps the therapist to see the patient's pathology in perspective and to appreciate his adaptive potentialities. He understands not only where the patient has come from, but also where he can go.

However, the fact that CET adds a diagnostic perspective to therapy does not mean its projective or assessment dimensions are its principal purpose or use. Moreover, although contending with the tasks does serve to enrich the patient's associations, CET is not merely a cognitive exercise within a free-associational field. How the patient learns to surmount the real-world challenges and gains therapeutically from the experience is the main goal of CET. With the therapy session becoming a "live" experience, a therapeutic laboratory, the patient uses the tasks as a springboard for developing adaptive ways to contend with his problems.

There are other important therapeutic goals that CET addresses which we will consider in the following chapters describing its therapeutic strategies and theoretical framework. We now turn to a discussion of the therapeutic method and its rationale, illustrated with clinical examples.

CHAPTER II

Therapeutic Method

All psychotherapy tries to seize opportunities for growth; CET makes them as well. Beginning with the first session, CET transforms the sessions into a testing ground for new adaptations. The real-world events and "extra-session realities" introduced into the sessions help the patient not only to learn the truth about himself but, in contending with the events, to do "what he can't do yet in order to learn how to do it."

The real-world events counteract the patient's egocentricity and isolation and help him to discover his inappropriate and/or distorted affective and cognitive reactions. In this way, the patient develops a counter-solipsistic perspective from the experience itself and from the therapist's objective interpretation of the experience. By being confronted with the conflicts and contradictions between his self-view and the perspective-view obtained in the sessions, the patient becomes aware of his rigidly held fictions, carefully protected illusions and inappropriate interpersonal behaviors. He can begin to overcome his distortions and deceptions of perception, thought, memory and language when he is challenged with the here-and-now realities in the sessions.

This process illumination of the patient's cognitive and affective reactions is but one stage in the therapeutic experience. Effective use of the events requires a coordination of three stages: action in the here-and-now, process illumination and reflection, and change in behavior.

Simply acting in the here-and-now is insufficient. The therapeutic potency of the real-world events derives from the corrective feedback obtained from the patient's actions which enables him to transcend simply having the experience and translate it into behavioral change.

1. THE RELATION OF CET PROCEDURES TO TRADITIONAL METHODS

There are two main processes in psychic functioning: regression and progression. Day and night, a person's level of regression and progression varies depending on inner states and environmental conditions. For example, in dreaming and daydreaming, the person becomes more primitive in functioning and more primary-process oriented, autistic and infantile in a developmental sense. On the other hand, progression is fostered through commitment to goals, solving problems, resolving conflicts and inventing and creating things. Under these conditions, the person is more oriented toward secondary-process thinking and behavior is adaptive and adult in a developmental sense.

Regression and progression are necessary, complementary, interdependent components of development: neither can exist without or dominate the other for the growth process to proceed. If growth is to be implemented through therapy, a balance must be struck between these processes. When either gains precedence over the other and dominates the therapeutic process, growth is impaired. For example, if the therapeutic procedures inordinately minimize reality considerations, invite fantasy and encourage acting out, primitive, impulse-ridden, regressive behavior results and the therapy can be jeopardized, producing abruptly terminated or protracted therapy or psychotic regression.

On the other hand, therapeutic procedures overemphasizing cognitive controls, reality testing and explanations can inhibit the patient from exploring his anxieties, guilt and vulnerabilities, which would enable him to become acquainted with his most crippling internal difficulties. Any gains are likely to be superficial, intellectualized and short-lived.

When the therapeutic procedures are structured to help the patient to shift between, reconcile and balance these two bipolar regressive and progressive processes, he can overcome his developmental arrests and imbalances and achieve a better adaptation.

Different components of the therapeutic setting and procedures promote either regression into the fantasy world, the irrational primary process and distortions of the transference, or progression into improved contact with reality, the reasonable secondary process and the resolution of the transference. The ways in which different therapeutic procedures focus on and implement regression or progression are summarized in Table 1.

CET aims to improve the balance between and coordinate regressive and progressive procedures. In addition to incorporating standard procedures for promoting regression, as noted in Table 1, it also provides a new medium for promoting progression by developing systematic progressive procedures that can be readily integrated into traditional technique.

We recognize, of course, that traditional therapy does not limit itself to regressive procedures, nor is the idea of balancing regressive and progressive procedures something new. This is something that is surely done by experienced therapists. However, progressive procedures have heretofore been dependent on the resourcefulness of the therapist in focusing on cognitive controls and aspects of reality which induce ego-integration and adaptation. CET, in contrast, provides a systematic method and therapeutic structure for promoting these essential synthetic, secondary-process functions. CET thereby facilitates the coordination of regressive and progressive processes.

Contending with the tasks of CET provides the patient with stable physical and interpersonal (i.e., the therapist) anchor points in the real world. The patient must mobilize his ego-integrative resources and strengthen his relationship to reality. Because of his enhanced strength and resources and more secure foothold in reality, he has found a safe place. He is able to deal with the fear, risk and uncertainty of sinking into the more primitive and irrational aspects of regression because, if need be, he has the strength and resiliency to rebound and pull himself out.

For example, at the end of a session, he can pull himself together, drive home or go back to work and make decisions and carry on with his life. The patient can, consequently, dare to loosen controls and ease reality testing and authentically experience his anxieties, vulnerabilities and guilt and all the deeper layers of his crippling problems, including the transference.

At the same time, increasing the patient's ego resources not only provides him with the ego strength to enter into a therapeutic regression, but with the cognitive organization and controls to surmount it. Despite his being in the throes of a regressive reaction, the patient can disengage and contain his irrational primary process, interrupt and hold in abeyance his regressive and disruptive feelings and flexibly shift to the rational secondary process. He is thus provided with the

TABLE 1
The Role of Therapeutic Procedures in Promoting Regression or
Progression

Regressive Procedures	Progressive Procedures
1. *Sensory impoverishment* Sessions are relatively objectless and involve minimal sensory stimulation or physical movement.	1. *Sensory enhancement* Sessions contain tasks which provide sensory stimulation. Manipulation is encouraged.
2. *Passive* The patient drifts along in a random, timeless and goalless manner.	2. *Active* The patient takes the initiative and contends with tasks in a goal-directed, inventive way.
3. *Primary-process thinking* Free association, reverie, dreams: the patient says everything without order, logic or discrimination.	3. *Secondary-process thinking* Mastery of tasks: the patient is logical, organized and reality-oriented and makes decisions.
4. *Give up control* The patient genuinely experiences and expresses his feelings without censoring. Nothing is too trivial or far-fetched. Unreflective.	4. *Gain control* The patient modulates his expression of feelings. He is purposeful and responsible and verifies the consequences of his thoughts and actions. Self-critical and reflective.
5. *Renounce reality testing* Idiosyncratically symbolic and not concerned with consensual validation. The patient explores his inner world of fantasy. He recalls and reveals all material without appraising their realistic implications.	5. *Promote reality testing* Tasks require the patient to focus on reality and obtain consensual validation through testing hypotheses and checking on the consequences of actions. He must be discriminating and solve problems.

capacity to work productively in therapy, assimilate interpretations and work through the transference.

CET thereby promotes creative regression or "regression in the service of the ego." The patient can genuinely replicate in the therapeutic relationship the regressive forces which are destroying him while simultaneously addressing the complementary and essential task of summoning up the progressive synthetic processes which enable the patient to deal with and resolve these regressive forces. He can overcome his fixations and pathological regression, and rise above himself and progress to new forms of adaptation with adult gratification.

2. PROGRESSIVE PROCEDURES

(1) Real-World Problem Solving: Therapeutic Tasks

With this experiential procedure, the patient explores how he actually contends with and masters or fails to master the therapeutic tasks. The goal here is to simulate a broad range of psychological events which will not only tap the patient's cognitive approach to problems, but also touch upon and evoke his emotional and fantasy life in the process of contending with the tasks. A critical feature in eliciting this emotional expression is that the tasks and the supportive therapeutic relationship make it safe and pleasing to confront problems that otherwise would be considered too threatening and so would be kept in fragmented obscurity through defensive measures. The actions represent expressions of the patient's basic self which he may, deep down, have always known, but never dared to express.

(a) Therapeutic technique

Over 200 therapeutic tasks have been developed. These tasks are not just paper-and-pencil tests of the type encountered in diagnostic and projective assessment procedures. Rather, they include a variety of perceptual, problem-solving and conflict-resolution tasks, utilizing the visual, auditory, tactile, olfactory and kinesthetic-proprioceptive modalities.

So that the reader can obtain experience with the actual tasks, thirteen representative tasks, illustrated with photographs and drawings, are presented in the *Tasks and Resource Materials* in the *Appendix*. The clinical examples described throughout this volume demonstrate how these tasks are used in CET.

The tasks represent aspects of physical reality not usually present in therapy. They require the patient to make and maintain contact with reality. They force him to come to grips with matter, substances, facts, workable ideas and procedures and rules that are externally verifiable and necessary to solve the problem. They curb the primary-process tendency and enhance the important function of reality testing. They harness energies, provide them with objects and allow the sublimation of erotic drives and the neutralization of aggressive forces into activities that are constructive, if not creative. They help to create an orderly division between the physical and interpersonal, setting up distinct spheres of experiences, making relating to them more manageable. They help the patient to structure time, for the tasks are solvable in *real* time rather than in an amorphous stretch of time that stimulates primary-process activity.

It cannot be stressed too much that the 200 tasks so far developed are not *"the"* 200 tasks or the only 200 tasks that can be effectively utilized in CET. The particular tasks are not as important as the *concept* of experiential intervention, i.e., of introducing challenges and problems from everyday reality into the therapy sessions. The practicing CET therapist should, therefore, feel free to introduce and adapt other tasks of his own choosing or creation into the therapy sessions. In the final chapter, *The Future of CET,* we show how and why a new task is developed and integrated into a patient's treatment.

The tasks are designed to engage different aspects of the patient's interpersonal and problem-solving behavior; different tasks highlight different aspects. Therefore, a wide repertoire of tasks is employed to gain a coherent picture of the patient and his problems and to provide the patient with a broad arena for developing new adaptations.

In actual practice, the therapist selects a problem-solving task or an audiotape of the patient's interpersonal relations (discussed in the next section) and integrates it into a particular session because of its relevance to the ongoing therapeutic process. We will present extensive clinical examples illustrating how these real-world experiences are integrated into the therapeutic plan with a broad range of patients and problems.

The therapeutic value of a task derives not from a "quick success" in solving the problem, but from the process of awareness and understanding emerging from the engagement with it. Therefore, if a patient is productively working on a task but has not mastered it in a particular session, it can be continued in the following sessions. This emphasizes the continuity of the therapeutic work from session to session.

During a typical therapy session, the patient expresses his feelings about a recent incident with another person, relates a dream or remembers an event with his family. The therapist and the patient discuss these issues as they would in a standard therapy session. Then, to help the patient gain a deeper understanding of the issues raised and to expedite resolution of these issues, the therapist engages the patient in an appropriate here-and-now experience. For example, with a task, in addition to thinking out loud and talking about the task, the patient must cope with and master it. The patient also expresses his feelings, ideas and sensations and recalls events or feelings in his past which the task evokes. He continues a running dialogue with the therapist, blending his work on the task with his feelings and associations. The therapist "works both sides of the street," continually juxtaposing a focus on the outer world and the demands of the task with the inner world of the patient's thoughts and feelings, clarifying and interpreting defensive and characterological operations, coping processes and reality considerations, as well as transferential considerations.

In words suitable to the therapist's style and the patient's age and socioeducational background, the therapist introduces a task by saying:

I have some tasks which will shed more light on your problems and how you go about solving them. Here's a task that I'd like you to work on. Think out loud and tell me what you're experiencing and trying to do and everything that goes through your mind, including even the small details that you ordinarily might think irrelevant or too trivial to mention. If you find the going difficult, stop what you are doing for a while and tell me what it reminds you of. What feelings, sensations, memories or images are you experiencing, even if they seem to have nothing to do with the task? There is no hurry. Take your time. Your approach is as important as solving the problem.

In working on the tasks, the patient displays the full range of his positive and negative affective and cognitive tendencies. The therapist and the patient see exactly how he behaves, feels and copes in his here-and-now actions. For example, as the patient tries to solve the task, he may express his frustration and anger when he does not find an easy solution. Or he may feel that the task involves a trick, bringing to the surface his lack of trust in the therapist. Or he could ask for hints or give up easily, expressing his passive longings. He might recall events or feelings in his past of which the task reminds him. He often then reverts to memories related to problem-solving difficulties in general and may relate these memories to his current problems.

We anticipate that some therapists may experience varying degrees of discomfort by employing interventions which their training has excluded. The therapist may be concerned that introducing tasks or other real-world events, such as the audiorecordings, into the sessions will interfere with the therapist's technical neutrality and contaminate the transference. Gill's comments on the relation of the therapist's activity to neutrality are appropriate here. He notes:

> Inactivity must not be confused with neutrality. Neutrality does not mean an avoidance of doing anything, but rather giving equal attention to *all the patient's productions,* without prior weighting of one kind of material over another, and confining oneself to the analytic task, that is, abstaining from deliberate suggestion. (1982, p. 63; italics added)

Moreover, introducing these real-world experiences into the sessions does not have to dilute the transference or diminish the importance of insight, the working through of the patient's unconscious dynamics, or even the unconscious meaning of the new experiences and actions. On the contrary, the following clinical examples demonstrate how CET intensifies and expedites the therapeutic process and heightens intrapsychic and interpersonal consciousness. It can deepen the therapeutic process by helping to bring transferential issues to the surface. Working through can take place in the affectively meaningful present where experience and insight are an intrinsic unity. It is important, therefore, for the therapist to explore the patient's reactions to the introduction of the events and their effects on the transference. The therapist should ask the patient what he thinks and feels about these interventions and inquire into the fantasies and expectations which they elicit.

The same therapist, the author, conducted the therapy for all the patients in the clinical examples. It is important to note that the therapist's technique with different patients or even with a particular patient at different stages in therapy was not always the same, but varied depending on the patient's personal characteristics and problems presented at the time. As we note in the annotations to the clinical presentations, the therapist must adopt a flexible perspective in applying CET. For example, an approach that is appropriate for a hospitalized psychotic, depressed or schizophrenic patient would not be suitable for an outpatient neurotic patient.

Several conventions are used in presenting the transcripts. Something indecipherable is indicated by "inaudible." A silence of from one to three seconds is indicated by "...," from four to six seconds by *"pause,"* from seven to twelve seconds by *"long pause,"* and from thirteen seconds to two minutes by "*very long pause.*" It is noteworthy that, except when a patient was directly working on a task, there were no silences of over two minutes, a result consistent with our finding that the approach counteracts withdrawal and resistance and stimulates more active therapeutic interactions. To preserve confidentiality, names and other identifying details have been disguised.

Although the clinical examples provide numerous opportunities to comment on patient psychodynamics, our annotations of the therapist-patient dialogue, interspersed throughout the presentations, for the most part focus on technical issues and on clarifying how to apply the method. The commentaries discuss the rationale for the strategies used in a case, illustrate how the method is best employed through effective technique and point out pitfalls and lapses in good technique. To provide a basis for improving technique, we also indicate how the therapist could have intervened more effectively and what could have been done or said at any given point.

Clinical Example: Erik—Jug Problem*

This case demonstrates how a task, the Jug Problem, is integrated into a typical initial interview. Erik, a divorced man in his late forties, had ten years previously put a pistol to his ear and shot himself. Miraculously, he survived, sustaining minimal brain damage, although the bullet is still lodged near a vital area of his brain. After lengthy rehabilitative measures, Erik was able to return to functioning. Lithium therapy was initiated. He was admitted to the hospital for a second time with severe depression and for adjustment of his lithium medication. While in the hospital, Erik was referred to the therapist for evaluation.

(The first ten minutes of this interview, during which the patient's background and events leading up to his present hospitalization were discussed, are deleted.)
Therapist: Were you making out pretty well on your own?
Patient: Yes. I was making out pretty well on my own. It was good business, conducting seminars for executives from all over the country.
T: So what happened all of a sudden? Where was your fall?
P: Well, about '72 I had a big depression and attempted suicide by shooting.

---

*Because Erik was interviewed after the clinical trials were completed, he is the only patient presented in the clinical examples who is not included in the efficacy study described in Chapter VI.

T: What happened then?

P: I just didn't see any way out. Everything was black and so I decided to commit suicide.

T: Couldn't see any way out from what?

P: From all the problems that I had. Personal problems and . . .

T: What personal problems did you have?

P: Well, the business wasn't going well and I was doing some drinking and my love life was very bad. I was living with a lady and that was very bad. *(Pause)* Everything seemed to go black.

T: What happened just then?

P: Pardon? *(As a result of his suicide attempt, the patient's hearing is impaired.)*

T: What did you think of just then when you were reminiscing?

P: What was I thinking when I was, it's hard to say. I was just trying to reconstruct in my own mind how it was, how it actually was that I took such a drastic step.

T: What do you think?

P: Everything was black and it had rained for weeks on end and. . . . Oh, I know. Another thing was that I had been on Antabuse and I was drinking in spite of it and that was making me very ill. *(Pause)*

T: You thought of something?

P: Pardon me?

T: You thought of something then?

P: Yeah. I thought of, I was just thinking of how different my life might have been if I hadn't tried to commit suicide because after that I had to go into fairly extensive treatment and *(pause)* I could trace my manic-depressive condition back at least until then. And then I had it ever since.

T: You got kind of sad thinking of it.

P: Yeah.

T: It was a turning point in your life.

P: Yes. *(Pause)*

T: What are you thinking now?

P: I'm just trying to think back on that whole situation. *(Pause)* Whether I'd been manic-depressive before then, whether I could think of any episodes. I'd always been a very gregarious kind of person. And then on the other hand, from time to time they would call me very moody. But nobody ever called me a manic-depressive.

T: What I'd like to do with you now, Erik, is I have some tasks. You've seen these around the table here.

P: You have some what?

T: Tasks. It's like a problem. I'd like you to work on it with me right here now. The problem is written right on the jug. Why don't you read it?

The therapist is not dodging the patient's feelings. We have found that an indirect approach is sometimes more effective in exploring very frightening feelings that play such a drastic role in a patient's life. Mobilizing the patient's ego resources by introducing one of our goal-directed, ego-integrative tasks enables the patient to develop the necessary security and control so that he is not overwhelmed when he comes back to his feelings. We are as much concerned with the affective aspects of the patient as with his cognitive functioning. "Cognitive" in the CET approach derives from the idea that it focuses, broadly speaking, on helping the patient to become more aware of himself through these different interventions.

P: (Reads) "This jug was made to try your skill. Drink if you can but do not spill." That looks like a formidable task.

T: It is. I'd like you to work on it now.

P: You want me to actually try to drink from this without spilling?

T: Right.

P: Look, I'm an engineer and I would say that this is impossible.

This "impossible" is the typical pathognomic sign of somebody who is depressed. The hopelessness of meeting challenges is paramount. The task evokes the patient's characteristic response to stress and frustration. He is confronted with his avoidance of anxiety as he runs from the problem. The therapist attempts to introduce the patient to a sense of his capacity, to show him that he can meet the challenges by contending with the tasks. He can be strong again.

T: Why?

P: Well, because when I go to drink, I have to drink from one of those other holes, not from one of these upper holes or something. But if I try to drink from the upper hole, obviously I am going to get wet.

T: Well, maybe there is a way you can figure out to do it. Use your engineering skill.

P: Okay.

In spite of his depression and anxiety, the patient becomes actively engaged in the task. His mood changes noticeably. His body movements are now lively, his face brightens and is expressive, his voice pattern changes and he leans toward the therapist as he talks.

P: (Erik attempts to suck the water from the holes in the side of the jug, although considerable water leaks from the holes as he does so.) Okay?

T: Well, that's pretty good. You got it out of one of the holes all right. But I wonder if you can think of another way without getting it out of the holes. It gets so messy that way.

P: No, I don't mind. (Laughs)

T: Let me put some more water in because a lot of it leaked out. (The therapist refills the jug.) Okay.

P: Now you want me to drink out of that and not spill anything and not drink out of the bottom holes like I just did?

T: Yeah. (Pause) What are you thinking?

P: I'm thinking that it's impossible, but I'm investigating.

T: Good.

P: (Chuckles)

T: Why do you smile? Are you enjoying it?

P: Well, because you seem to be enjoying my chagrin.

T: I'm enjoying your working on it.

P: (Laughs) Well, it's clear that if I do that . . . Wait a minute. (The patient sucks from the spigot of the jug.)

T: What happened then?

P: I was sucking on it to see if I could, maybe there was a way to suck up from the low end. (Sucking and whistling sounds)

T: What happened then?

P: Nothing.

T: And?

P: I thought maybe the handle was a trick handle, but it is hollow.

T: So what do you think now?

It is very important here that the therapist interact with the patient and provide this kind of cognitive and emotional feedback. The purpose of asking these things is not only to elicit the patient's feelings and thoughts, but to affirm for him what is happening. The therapist focuses on the whistling sound to help the patient develop his sensory awareness and gain from the feedback obtained from this awareness. Especially with regressed patients, becoming more aware of the surroundings as well as inner feelings is very important for reality testing.

In addition to enhancing the therapeutic alliance, the task fosters reality testing because a real object is presented. We say that regressed people have "lost their contact with objects" and that they need more development of object relationships. Here is a concrete instance in which they can contact reality, grapple with it and see themselves in relation to it. This becomes a source for development.

P: I think the problem is getting tougher. *(Sucking at holes)*
T: You are trying all those spigot holes.
P: Uh-huh. *(Pause. The patient wipes up the water that has spilled onto him.)* That's all right. It was raining today anyway.
T: Right. What are you thinking now?
P: I don't think that there is any way that I can do it without spilling it other than the way I did it the first time. Is it imperative that I find a way?

This is the metaphor of his life. Withdrawal. Giving up. In his life, he is divorced and, although he has three children, he has very little contact with them or with his ex-wife. He is estranged from life. In the session, the patient can see what he is actually doing with his life. It becomes a source of objective feedback.

T: Yeah, because if you are very thirsty, how are you going to get the water out?
P: Oh, that'd be simple. I'd just quickly pour it into that container there.
T: But that's just it. What if you tried to pour it in the container? What happens?
P: Well, if I do it quickly, I'll salvage some of it.
T: That's just it. Without spilling a drop.
P: Uh. *(Pause)*
T: What were you doing then?
P: I'm blowing in. I want to see what the physics of this little configuration is.

The task requires that the patient use secondary-process thinking. The therapist encourages this by interacting with the patient and trying to elicit the causal reasoning behind his actions.

T: Did you notice something?
P: (Continues blowing) I don't know. I give up.
T: Why do you give up?
P: Because there doesn't seem to be any way.

T: What do you feel when you say you give up? You just want to push
    it away?
P: No. I know that if I keep after it, I'll just get frustrated.
T: And you don't want to get frustrated?
P: Well, certainly not.
T: Why not?
P: *(Said with a twinkle in his eye)* Because I'm already frustrated
    enough with my problems.
T: And this will make it even worse?
P: This is a little passing problem.
T: Uh-huh. Could that be the way things are with you, that when you
    come upon something that is seemingly difficult, the first response
    you had was, "It's impossible." Remember?
P: The first thing what?
T: The first thing you said was, "It's impossible." Then you tried it and
    you said, "Well, I could get it out of that little hole a little bit."
P: Yeah.
T: And now you try to investigate and you say, "I give up." Is that like
    your life?

The therapist provides the patient with an objective picture of himself,
using his actions with the task as a metaphor.

P: I don't think that is necessarily characteristic of my life, but maybe
    it is. Maybe I've never had it so simply displayed. I tend to think
    of myself as pretty much of a digger and getting things together
    and working out puzzles even.

The patient thinks of himself as a digger, yet he has been running
from life his whole life. His actions vividly demonstrate what is not
easily explained. The key is that the patient can argue with the therapist's interpretations, but he cannot argue with reality. The task
confronts Erik with who he is and the kinds of defenses that have
created problems in his life.

T: Yeah.
P: I think this is a remarkable puzzle. It's just that I can't think of any
    way that, I think I have exhausted the possibilities of getting
    water out of the . . .
T: But you are a creative person. Why give up so easily? I mean, in
    engineering do you think [aerospace company] would have done
    all those things if some engineer would have said, "It's tough, too
    frustrating"?

The therapist is supportive by emphasizing his belief in the patient and his resources.

P: We would have gotten a straw.
T: Yeah, but what if you didn't have a straw? Before a straw was invented. Just you and the puzzle.
P: Just me and the puzzle, huh? *(Pause)*
T: Does it remind you of anything in your life, doing this?

The therapist bridges the gap between therapy and daily life, using the patient's behavior on the task as a metaphor.

P: No.
T: Doesn't bring back any memories?
P: Oh, I guess I've been faced with problems that are tough to solve.
T: What happens then?
P: Well, very often I solve them because when I was an engineer, why, that was my job, to solve problems.
T: How about personal problems?
P: Well, maybe I have put them off, you know, and not solved them adequately . . . This handle is hollow.

The patient's secondary-process thinking is mobilized and he discovers the hollow handle.

T: It is?
P: That's what it looks like. There's a hole in the bottom there.
T: So?
P: So I ought to be able to suck it out.
T: Right.
P: *(Loud sucking)*
T: Why didn't it work?
P: It did work. I got a whole mouthful of it. (*The patient shows the therapist a few drops of water on his tongue.*)
T: Oh, you did . . .
P: It's true. Look. There's still water there. *(Loud sucking)*
T: It should be easy, not using tremendous force.
P: You didn't say it had to be easy.
T: I'm telling you now.
P: All right. So far I've shown you two ways of getting water out of here without spilling it and you don't like either way. You like only your way.

T: Try the hole way, the first way.
P: This side hole way?
T: Yes. You see, it spills out all over.

The patient can get water out of the jug if he spills it all over himself. All his life, this may have been his style; namely, that he allowed himself to "get by" with partial and inadequate solutions to problems. What the therapist is doing here is saying, "No, you can go beyond that. I believe in you."

P: It's so full, just my jittering here will make it spill.
T: That's what I mean. It is a messy way.
P: Okay. But sucking on this with holding this and bringing it up through the handle, you have to admit, is a . . .
T: But why do you think you hear all that whistling sound?

Pointing out the connection between the whistling sound and the result fosters the secondary-process thinking necessary to solve the problem. This will also help the patient in reintegrating and dealing with his daily problems.

P: Because it's a harder way of doing it. It requires energy to do it and the sound is a manifestation of the energy. So anyway, there's one-and-a-half ways.
T: Yeah. I'm not saying you're not creative. But try to explore it more. I think you give up too easily. *(Pause)* I mean it should work if this were a straw, right? It should come up with a siphoning action.
P: Yeah.
T: Why doesn't it come right up?
P: It does come up.
T: But if it were like a straw action, you would just suck it and it would just spout right out. You wouldn't have to use such force that you're breathless. Something must be missing.
P: It's possible, perhaps, for me to cover up these holes [on the sides] *(pause)* like that.
T: Yeah, except that's going to be messy, too. There's going to be leakage someplace.
P: *(Laughs)* You just don't like my work.

The patient covers several holes but, when he sucks on the remaining ones, the water spills all over him.

T: That's what I mean. I don't want you to get wet, Erik.
P: (Jokingly) Yes, you do.
T: (Laughs) No. If you were working on an engineering problem, some kind of space thing, there would be no room for leakage.
P: Right. *(Pause)*
T: What are you thinking?
P: (Pause) I'm wondering whether there really is a way.
T: Why would I give you something that is insoluble?
P: So as to make me frustrated.
T: Why would I want to make you frustrated?
P: Just to see how quickly I do or whether I do or . . .
T: You mean what happens when you get frustrated?
P: What happens when I get frustrated. Right.
T: What happens when you get frustrated? Tell me.
P: (Laughs) Well, I'm not going to smash your little pot.

The patient expresses his anger and frustration through denial.

T: You thought of it, though. You get pretty pissed off.
P: (Laughs) Yeah. *(Pause)* Aw, there's a hole under here! *(Erik discovers the hidden hole and solves the problem.)*

It is fascinating to note that immediately after the patient expresses his anger, he is freed to mobilize his secondary-process thinking which enables him to expand his awareness and effectively explore the jug and master the task.

T: What do you think now?
P: That's a way.
T: That's a way. The hidden hole.
P: Yeah. It's hard to look underneath when you are spilling water all over the place, but I should have done that.
T: What are you thinking now?
P: It's a lot less work when you cover up the hole.
T: How does it make you feel?
P: Good! *(Beaming)* Solved the problem.
T: Uh-huh.
P: Got another one? *(Laughs)*

The patient's response here is very important because it indicates the healing effect of mastering the task. After grappling with and finally solving the problem, he looks forward to more challenges. He is no longer depressed. He is hopeful and looks to the future. There is nothing like a demonstration of the patient's competence, that he is self-directed and can take control of his life, to enhance his involvement and motivation. Now we can see the virtue of not jumping in and prematurely providing clues or solving the problem for the patient, for that would rob him of the gratification of self-discovery and mastery and undermine his feelings of self-worthiness. Through his own activity, he discovered that he is capable of effectively dealing with reality. This is a living demonstration which, unlike many interpretations that just go in one ear and out the other, is something that the patient can take with him and that can assist him in developing a more effective self-image.

T: Yeah, I have plenty. Any other thoughts come to mind about that when you solved it?
P: Well, with a more thorough investigation, you know, I'm embarrassed that, as an engineer, I didn't turn it upside down or look at it from underneath there and I didn't feel that hole.
T: Does that bring to mind anything?
P: Not specifically, but perhaps it is indicative of the way I handle some of my problems.
T: How?
P: Slipshod.
T: Do you have an example?

To generalize the therapeutic experience to the patient's daily life, the therapist focuses on the metaphor evoked by the patient's actions in the session.

P: Oh, just not taking care of things on time, letting things slip. Procrastination. *(Pause)*
T: Is that what was happening back in '72?
P: Possibly. Yeah. It's hard for me to remember the specifics. Because that was something I don't . . .
T: But you might have let things slip away from you?
P: Yes.
T: Can you recall anything now?
P: No, not specifically. But generally. There was a case of not handling my affairs.
T: How about your personal affairs?
P: Very bad.
T: How were they bad?

P: Just let them slip and not take care of things.

T: Do you have an example?

P: (Pause) No, I don't have any specific examples. Just everything was bad.

T: In other words, this feeling reminds you of that.

P: Right.

T: The same feeling.

P: Right.

T: Things slipping away, not taking care of things. Not taking care of yourself.

P: Right.

T: Maybe that's when you get depressed. You get overwhelmed and things slip away and, before you know it, it is difficult to get things together again.

P: Yeah. Well, there's a question of whether that's when I get depressed or when I get depressed, I let things slip away. I don't know which of those two it is.

T: Right. At least you know now that if you don't let things slip away, you do have the resources to solve your own problems.

P: Right.

T: It's not that you can't do it. You've got the stuff. You say, "I should have solved it as an engineer." You've got the stuff, once you are able to get things together, explore, look at it from different angles, get a different perspective on it. Maybe that is something that can help you to even things out so you don't go through these total swings. Keep on top of things. Does it ring a bell?

P: Uh-huh.

The therapist focuses on and supports the patient's adaptive assets *("You've got the stuff")* and points out how he can use his resources to gain greater control and stabilize his life.

T: What are you thinking?

P: I just think I gotta do that more.

T: Some particular thing you are thinking of, some plan?

P: Pardon?

T: Do you have a plan, something special?

P: No, I don't have a plan yet. I've been working on a plan for weeks.

T: You have been working on a plan?

P: Right.

T: What kind of plan?

P: A living plan. What I am going to do, how I'm going to get my life squared away. How I'm going to handle my depressions.

T: You think this has any connection?

P: Sure.

T: What's the connection?

P: Oh, giving up or letting things go, not following through.

T: Now you have some handle, something that you could see really works if you make a plan, follow through, don't let things slip away. You can control things. You say you don't know which came first. But if you short-circuit this vicious circle, you can stop things from overwhelming you and then you could climb out of the pit that you're in.

P: *(Pause)* Right.

T: What were you thinking then?

P: Nothing. Just what you're saying is true.

T: You're not saying it just to please me, are you?

P: No. *(Said smilingly)* Why would I do that after you frustrate me with the bottle here?

T: *(Laughs)* Are you still pissed off at me?

P: Oh, no. *(Laughs)* As a matter of fact, it was kind of fun.

T: It's more fun when you can overcome the frustration. If you just solve it right off, where's the fun?

P: Yeah.

T: You don't sound too convincing, though.

P: No. I was thinking it should have been a fairly straightforward problem, but I made it tough.

During the last few minutes of this interview, Erik expressed a desire to explore these issues further with the therapist and to work out a plan for starting psychotherapy.

Summary

We all know that one of the most difficult things to get across to a patient is a sense of his own responsibility for the predicament he is in. If a patient can see how he contributed to his problems, then he is also enabled to find a way to solve them. What was important in this interview, therefore, was that the patient's activities with the task helped him to see his contribution to his problems and that the problem-solving approach he used in mastering the task (exploring, experimenting and looking at the problem from a different perspective) could serve as a metaphor for an adaptive approach to solve his problems in daily life.

(2) Real-World Interpersonal Experiences: Audiotape Technique

This second experiential procedure implements understanding of what is really happening in the patient's interpersonal behavior. The technique consists of exploring in the sessions audiorecordings made by the patient of his real-life interactions with people. The patient is provided with a powerful medium to counteract his insularity and learn the truth about his interpersonal reactions.

Not infrequently, patients will absorb feedback offered by the tapes more readily than when provided by the therapist. To many patients, especially in the beginning of therapy, transference distortions impede the value of the therapist's observations. The tapes, however, can be counted on to hold up an undistorted "psychological mirror" to the patient, and provide spontaneous and truthful feedback in a variety of interpersonal settings which he will find hard to deny.

Bringing the real world into the sessions permits the patient to see himself with fresh eyes. He can become more self-observing as well as other-observing. The major forces which shape the patient's life are viewed not only through memories and psychological reconstructions of his life, but are exposed through his actual daily behavior. By seeing the realities of his interactions, he discovers his denials, distorted self-perceptions and inappropriate interpersonal behaviors.

Since the recordings reflect the true picture and rhythm of the patient's life, the therapist and the patient can ask daring and fundamental questions about his life, questions that could not have been formulated previously. After ignoring or rationalizing away whatever did not accord with his distorted self-image, the patient starts to become aware of a part of his life he never dared confront. He begins to overcome the distortions and deceptions of perception, memory and language when he is challenged with the realities of his interpersonal relationships. The outer reality and the inner, psychic reality can be brought into focus, like the split image in a camera's viewfinder.

The audiotape technique provides the patient with a powerful curative tool for interpersonal learning. Each taping session enables the patient to obtain corrective feedback which can be integrated into new interpersonal behavior. He can then see the results of his therapeutic work when he subsequently tapes new interpersonal encounters. The application of the audiotape technique to a variety of interpersonal settings will be further explored in the concluding chapter, *The Future of CET*.

Consequently, in addition to interacting with the patient through discussion of his problems and associations, the therapist explores the patient's real interpersonal life through the recordings that the latter brings into the session.

(a) Therapeutic technique

The patient is asked to tape conversations of his daily dealings with people by setting up a recorder at home, at the office and on the telephone, thereby capturing segments of his current interactions with people. The patient then brings the tapes into the session as soon as possible after the experience for playback. The therapist and the patient listen to and confront objectively what actually transpires in the patient's interpersonal relations. The patient thereby obtains a powerful self-observatory experience where once-cherished self-images are challenged.

For ethical considerations, the patient is instructed to notify other persons that they are being recorded. Moreover, to maintain strict confidentiality, the patient is asked to enter into an irrevocable agreement with the therapist never, under any circumstances, to let the tapes get out of his hands and never to make a copy of the tapes or to play the tapes outside of therapy other than for therapeutic purposes. The patient must explicitly acknowledge and agree that the tapes are to be employed for one purpose only: as privileged communications to be used only as a tool for his own psychotherapy. He also must agree either to tape over his recordings or to erase them completely within one month.

Through this approach, the patient can more clearly come to perceive what is really happening in his interpersonal behavior and what he is actually feeling and doing with other people. Is the patient passive, needy, warm, seductive, aloof, exploitative, sarcastic, competitive, caring, obsequious, rejecting, controlling, childish, etc.? What does the patient want from and do with other men and women?

Just as with the tasks, to be most effective the audiotape technique is not used in isolation or as a gimmick, but is integrated into the mainstream of the total therapeutic endeavor. A tape, therefore, is introduced either by the therapist or the patient to focus on particular issues. For example, after discussing a patient's relationship with his spouse, the therapist can ask the patient if he has a tape of a recent interaction with him or her by saying, "I think a tape will help us to understand how you actually feel and do things with your spouse. Do you have a tape for us to listen to?" On his part, the patient can also assume responsibility. He can take the initiative and bring in recordings to clarify a problem. In addition, a tape is often helpful in addressing the resistance. For example, the therapist can ask the patient to play a tape when the flow of his associations appears to be obstructed and when confusion and inconsistencies in the patient's account are compounded by further obfuscations. Similarly, when the patient is obviously evading exploration of his feelings and seems doggedly intent on escaping the here-and-now into the seemingly intimate details of past experiences, the therapist can ask the patient for a recent tape.

Although introduced usually after the first few sessions and used throughout the course of therapy, the audiotape technique also has been used effectively when first presented during later stages in therapy. The following clinical example illustrates how the technique expedited therapeutic progress even when introduced after three years of therapy (because the technique had been developed during the course of this patient's therapy). It should be stressed, however, that the audiotape technique, like the other real-world interventions, should be employed in the context of the patient's total treatment plan and that it is not intended to serve as a crutch to circumvent confronting and dealing with a difficult or intractable case through appropriately applying standard therapeutic techniques.

A tape should not be used merely to breach a temporary impasse or to avoid dealing with the resistance and the perplexities of inner life that are always natural parts of any therapeutic endeavor. The exigencies of a patient's life and the flow of the therapeutic material are always primary. A flexible audiotape technique is called for. The therapist should not rigidly follow a routine program of incorporating a tape into every session or of introducing a tape at a predetermined time.

Because the audiotape technique is relatively simple to incorporate into the sessions and does not require any special therapeutic materials other than a tape recorder, we will present only one case example to demonstrate how the technique is integrated into CET. The major portion of the book will, therefore, be devoted to demonstrating how a variety of therapeutic tasks are employed in addressing different problems.

Clinical Example: Sara—Audiotape Technique*

Although Sara had made substantial gains in the work area and had grown from being financially dependent on her parents to self-sufficiency during the first three years of her therapy, she still related to

---

*The reader can refer to the brief case reports presented on pp. 179–191 to obtain information on each patient's problems and background.

her parents and people in general in a child-like, dependent way. She was able to develop only superficial, immature relationships with men and dated only infrequently.

The audiotape technique is particularly suitable for focusing on these interpersonal problems and would have been introduced within the first few sessions of her treatment had the technique been ready for clinical use at that time. However, three years had elapsed before it was first used in her treatment. At that time, it played a vital role in helping to resolve her fundamental interpersonal issues, issues which heretofore were addressed but never explored in such clarity and depth.

First, we obtained fresh and penetrating views of the patient's relationship with her family: her father, mother and sister. Second, we saw precisely how the patient related on the job and how her deeply entrenched, self-hurtful, masochistic behavior patterns constantly sabotaged her business dealings. Third, rarely had the therapist and the patient been so acutely aware of the depth of the anger that lay behind her persistent obsequious and conciliatory behavior. Fourth, we gained access to the developmental roots of her masochistic character structure through exposing her infantile, sexualized relationship with her father. Fifth, although many aspects of the transference had been previously explored, the tapes played an important role in bringing to life the central dimensions of the transference and helping to resolve them.

Most important, concurrent with these intrapsychic insights, over the course of the first six weeks during which the audiotape technique was instituted, the patient evidenced significant improvement in her interpersonal relationships, especially with men.

The following presentation is based on recordings of eight therapy sessions.

In this first session, the patient relates that the tapes are more revealing of her authentic feelings and ways of interacting with people than simply talking about these interactions: *"I don't know what you're looking for, so I won't be able to manipulate the things I'm saying."*

T: Isn't it interesting that in all these years, you haven't recounted anything personal? This makes you excited and frightened. Then all that you've talked about has been relatively impersonal.
P: Some things. Well, this is very personal. You get to know what I sound like when I talk to other people when I'm not in here and have everything planned out.
T: So this is more revealing than anything you can talk about here.
P: Yeah. I sound like a real jerk. Yes, it's revealing. That's why I don't want to [play the tapes].

In the following session, the roots of the patient's deeply entrenched stubbornness and anger are traced to her feelings of being displaced by her sister.

P: I'm still afraid of major criticism in doing this [playing the tapes], though.

T: Yeah.

P: I'm afraid I'll bring it in here and it'll get picked about to shreds.

T: What do you think that indicates?

P: That I'm afraid of punishment. Parental punishment. Disapproval.

T: But you were excited about the idea last time. Almost as if you want that parental disapproval. That's what's familiar.

P: The parental attention is familiar.

T: And also the disapproval.

P: I keep sounding like I'm such a, you know, I've had such a hard childhood. It wasn't that bad. I mean, I have these negative feelings about it, but I wasn't mistreated.

T: Yeah. So what do you think happened?

P: Somewhere along the line I got on the wrong track.

T: Where?

P: When I was really little, you know, four or five or something. I think maybe I got mad because I had a new sister and just kept staying angry for some reason. Never really knew how to get rid of it or handle that. It wasn't really that bad. I had a lot of opportunities. I just needed to reach out and take them and I didn't want to. I wanted to stay and be stubborn about something, about staying a child or something.

T: You mean you just never grew up.

P: That was the major thing. I just didn't want to grow up. I dug in my heels from the time I was little.

T: Why do you think you don't want to grow up?

P: I thought I'd be loved more if I was a baby.

T: Mmm-hmm. And now, do you still believe that?

P: Obviously, I act like it.

T: Here?

P: Yeah, I goof up and do babyish, dumb things. I think that's going to get me something.

T: What?

P: Some kind of love or attention or care.

T: Criticism.

P: I hate criticism. I don't respond well to it.

T: Yeah, but is it you're doing things for that?

P: Because I think that the criticism will stop and I will get something else, some babying.

T: But first you get the criticism.

P: That's the way the world works, I guess.

T: That's the price of getting the attention from being a baby.

P: Maybe that's why the criticism is exciting. I can't believe I'd really like the criticism, 'cause I don't.

T: Mmm-hmm.

P: That's why doing things right seems so empty and dull and dreadful.

T: Look what you lose. You won't have the criticism, you won't have the parenting.

P: Yeah, we've talked about that. Risk. It really frightened me to not be a person who can change though. Maybe I will never change. I'll just stay the same. And want that, you know, continuing paying the price and getting the criticism. *(Ten minutes later the patient picks up on this subject.)* So I get these messages and believe them. Where does that leave me? Well, back to being a child. I'm supposed to be miserable and not succeed and so on and so forth. She's [the patient's mother] happy with me. No wonder she's happy with me. 'Cause I'm doing it.

T: Mmm-hmm.

P: I'm doing what she wanted. Maybe, maybe. She'd rather I did it closer to her, I guess, so she can enjoy it.

In this session, the patient realizes that one of her central defense mechanisms is escape into fantasy. She wants to talk about a dream she had recorded: *"It's more harmless."* The therapist points out that the tapes are *"an exercise in reality. . . . You can go on for years and years, and the therapist can be completely snowed because he has no idea what reality is."* She distorts her presentation in therapy not merely through acts of commission, but through omission. *"I just kind of don't give it all out."*

P: (Listening to the tape) This is really depressing.

T: What do you mean?

P: I'm always trying to escape. I don't like it.

T: What is this reality like?

P: This reality is a pretty incompetent person.

T: How?

P: In my personal relations.

T: What do you mean by incompetent?

P: I really don't know how to recognize another person and talk to them like they're another person. Just bound up in my own little insecurities. . . . Well? . . . Pretty horrible. That person is not real. It's not fully human. Well, these are the worst ones. I might try to play the dream. It's more harmless. It's just the most awful experience listening to these. It's, it's kind of like swallowing acid or something, what I imagine that would be like. Well, that's the conversation with Bill. Bill woke me up.

T: It's an exercise in reality, a mirror, a mirror. You can go on for years and years and years, and the therapist can be completely snowed because he has no idea what reality is. And since you don't want to see what reality is, it becomes a *folie à deux.* Now, we have a little reality here. You can bullshit all the way you want, but you can't bullshit what's going on in your life from these tapes.

P: No, that's why it's very unpleasant to listen to.

T: I know. It's better unpleasant now than to end up a total failure. *(Pause)* The issue is that you don't really want to see yourself.

P: Yeah. *(Softly)* I don't like this part. . . . How do you tell if you're a success at therapy?

T: Well, one thing is that you see yourself pretty accurately.

P: I kind of fall in and out of it. How can I snow you, though? All I do is I just don't tell you enough.

T: Precisely.

P: It's not that I'm trying to fool you. I just kind of don't give it all out.

T: Precisely. Well, we're beginning to see what the reality of your life is like with these tapes.

For two years, the patient had been unsuccessful in opening a much-needed second store to meet the growing competition in her business. At the very beginning of this session, the patient excitedly told the therapist that within the past two weeks she had finally mobilized herself and entered a winning bid and successfully negotiated a very favorable ten-year lease on a new store. Later in this session, the tapes enabled the patient to address an area of disturbance that had been walled off from effective exploration; i.e., her fundamental problem with anger.

T: (After several minutes of listening to the tape) Maybe you're a much more angry person than you are willing to admit.

P: I'm always willing to admit I'm angry.

T: Yeah, but not, I mean just being angry is one thing, but maybe you're a nasty person.

P: Oh, I certainly don't let it get out very much.

T: That's just it, maybe there's a lot of stuff inside.

P: I wish I were nasty, I wouldn't have anything to worry about.

T: What do you mean?

P: Maybe my motive is to be nasty but I have no nasty skills. *(Pause)* Except for a few.

T: What few are those?

P: (Pause) Well, I don't know. I was going to say obsequiousness but that's not, only it's nasty to some people.

T: Maybe this obsequiousness is the reaction, the disguise, the smoke screen for the nastiness.

P: Well, maybe it is. I much prefer to just be nasty, but you just can't do that. *(Blows nose)* You get no cooperation. Everyone hates you openly instead of covertly.

In this session, playing a tape of a telephone conversation with her family helps the patient to overcome her egocentric view of them and obtain a clearer perception of her behavior. She becomes more self-observing as well as other-observing: *"I don't sound like a very nice sister. I always thought she sounded bad. I sounded even worse. I wouldn't like to have me for a sister."* She also is able to explore her anger toward her father. Although she loves him dearly and *"would kiss his feet,"* she cuts him down.

P: So, which one do you want to hear?

T: What do you want to hear?

P: (Pause) I don't know. It doesn't matter. *(Pause)* Whatever you want.

T: It's your tape.

P: My tape. I'll play the tape of my family. *(Listening to tape)* I guess I'm putting her [her sister] down.

T: You didn't realize it before? *(Listening to tape)*

P: I don't recognize my own voice. I don't think I sound like that.

T: Why don't you turn it [the recorder] off. *(Click)* What do you mean?

P: I don't think I sound like that. That person I don't recognize.

T: What's different?

P: She sounds jolly and sort of forced. I didn't think I sounded like that with my family.

T: What did you think you sounded?

P: More honest. . . . I didn't realize I was putting her [her sister] down. I thought I was responding to her own, well, she put herself down. *(Sighs)* . . . It just doesn't sound like what I think I sound like.

T: What's going through your mind?

P: I sound like the same jerk who's on all the other phone calls.

T: What do you mean?

P: I thought that my family, I was different with them. I thought that I was what I really thought I was with them. That I knew how I sounded with them.

T: How did you think you really were with them?

P: A lot nicer sounding. A little bit less hostile. More honest. Somehow. *(Pause)* She sounds the same. . . . I don't sound like a very nice sister. I always thought she sounded bad. I sound even worse. I wouldn't like to have me for a sister.

T: You'd like to have what?

P: I said, "I wouldn't like to have me for a sister."

T: Why?

P: I don't like that person. Talking to my sister, putting her down.

T: Mmm-hmm. How did you put her down?

P: Well, I kept telling her it's okay, it's okay, you got to start somewhere. And she's telling me about this job. I just didn't think it was that bad. *(Pause)* I didn't realize I was that unpleasant. *(Listening to tape of the patient's father)* I'm putting him [her father] down here too.

T: Well.

P: He puts me down in the end.

T: How are you putting him down?

P: I'm putting him down because I'm saying, oh, you really need these [management training] sessions, I think you better go. Well, listen to what I say. *(Listening to tape)* I'm treating him terribly. I'm really treating him terribly.

T: How?

P: I just sound terrible. I'm really, well, listen to him, he sounds like he's being wounded or something. He's all fumbling around.

T: How, is that the way he usually is?

P: No, he's usually very forthright. Well, he's a little bit waffly, but . . .

T: Throughout the whole conversation, he's kind of depressed.

P I know. I thought it's 'cause I was cutting him down about the management training. . . . *(With emphasis)* I would kiss his feet and I treat him like that!!

T: What?

P: I just find that very upsetting.

T: Why is it upsetting?

P: That I'm behaving in this way. *(Sniffles, pause)* But I'm mad at him too. I must be pretty angry at him to treat him like that. *(Listening to tape)*

T: There's not much emotion there in that conversation.

P: Yeah, well, I'm just wanting him to say something to me, like I love you or something like that. And I'm just . . . he just isn't doing it and so that's it. *(Listening to tape)* Oh, you know what else I did today? I sold one of those big machines I've been trying to sell for seven, eight months now. I'm just, things are busting out all over.

In this session, we explore the roots of the patient's self-destructive and masochistic behavior in her childhood relationship with her parents: *"They didn't like me, period. . . . They wanted me to be a failure."*

T: *(After listening to a tape)* You acted apologetic [with that reporter].

P: I know that.

T: I don't think you know.

P: You don't think I know it?

T: Why did you act like you're sucking up to him?

P: I do that to everybody. *(Crying, blows nose)*

T: Why?

P: Because that's the way I feel.

T: What do you mean?

P: That's the way I feel about myself. Apologetic.

T: What are you apologizing for?

P: Myself.

T: What about yourself?

P: I don't like myself. What else do you want to know?

T: What is it you don't like about yourself?

P: The fact that I don't, I let people walk all over me.

T: Why do you do that?

P: I don't know. Maybe I feel I'm basically dumb or something.

T: You have no rights?

P: I certainly act like I don't.

T: Of course, what you get out of it is that you then humiliate yourself, you feel badly, you feel like a child, you feel stepped over.

P: No, I feel helpless and out of control and I don't like that feeling.

T: But you get something out of it because otherwise you wouldn't constantly see yourself . . .

P: I don't like that logic.

T: Well, but there must be a payoff.

P: Somewhere. Yeah, we got to find it.

T: Well, you continually get . . .

P: Not in this humiliation stuff.

T: . . . yourself into this because there's something that it does to you or for you that keeps reinforcing it.

P: Yeah, it reinforces my idea of myself. As not good. That is what not good people do.

T: So you've got to live up to the image.

P: Down to it. Yeah.

T: You don't dare change that image?

P: Maybe I'm too afraid of another way to be.

T: What were you afraid of the other way?

P: I don't know. The successful part.

T: You mean, if you dare change it, that maybe your parents won't like you because you're not living up to their image?

P: No, because they like seeing me wealthy.

T: But, not when you were a kid, they didn't like you being outspoken then.

P: They didn't like me, period. They didn't care what I did. They didn't like me to be successful or not successful. They just . . . I think . . . No, they wanted me to be a failure 'cause they felt like they were failures for some reason. And they wanted the good comparison. To them.

In this session, the patient discusses how the tapes have been helpful.

P: They've [the tapes] been helpful.

T: How?

P: 'Cause I hear myself when I'm talking on the phone. And I hear how I sound a little bit more. And I try to change it. I'm a little more active. There are some things I would have handled a little differently if I hadn't listened to myself on tape. Some conversations with Johnny [her boss] for example, I would have been, it would have been fifteen yeses instead of eight or ten.

T: Mmm-hmm.

P: If that makes sense. Instead, you know, yeses meaning, you know, obsequious part.

The patient's infantile relationship with her father is explored in greater detail in this session.

P: Well, I've been constantly late, a couple minutes late the last two or three months. And I was a little early today.

T: Mmm-hmm.

P: I think the difference is I'm looking forward to this. I have a tape of myself talking to my father and it's going to make me feel good. I want to hear it again. I want to hear his voice. Um. Alex turned down the [offer to] run the other store today and I took it a little bit personally. I'm feeling kind of disappointed and kind of like, what am I going to do next and what am I going to tell Johnny, so I felt lonely, so I called a couple of people and I made tapes, and I called my father. I called my family. So that's what I do. *(Sighs)* And then thinking to myself, what am I doing, you know, why am I calling him? What is wrong with me? Why am I stuck on my father? This sounds like this has some sort of textbook case or something.

T: Uh-huh.

P: And why don't I start getting normal and dating and all this kind of stuff? And then I sort of usually stop thinking about it at that point. So, anyway, that's why I'm early. *(Listening to tape)* I had to stop it [the tape]. It's very pleasant listening to this.

T: What's pleasant about it?

P: It's just wonderful listening to the sound of his [her father] voice. It's just, I'm sitting here feeling wonderful. It's sort of scarey.

T: Scarey?

P: It's sort of sick. . . . He's the one person I'm letting make me feel good. You know, sort of idolizing him. . . . And I don't really want to even get into why. I just don't know. 'Cause it sounds like that textbook case again. *(Listening to tape)*

T: In describing [to your father] where the store was, you described it like a child would describe it. In relation to where you used to live, the back alley.

P: He doesn't know the streets in Fairfield.

T: What's the essential factor of the location?

P: *(Sighs)* Two Hundred 8th Street.

T: No, what's the essential *quality* of the location?

P: Next to the university.

T: Next to the university.

P: I said, that's what I said. I said, "Remember that road that goes right next to the university."

T: But you didn't say, you didn't highlight it. Where is it located? It's adjacent, right adjacent to the university. You said next to, you remember 8th Street, you remember this, you remember that one-way street, it didn't sound like a person who's describing a business location. You became very much a child.

P: Yeah. That's why I like talking to him.

T: Why?

P: 'Cause I can be a child. And he doesn't call me on it. *(Pause)* My mother is different. That's why I don't idolize her. What she does is, ah, she acts like she's being this, you know, loving parent, but actually she does treat me like an adult but she sort of hides it a little bit. Like if I were to say that to her, she'd say, oh, but surely you've looked at the fact that you're competing with yourself. And, you know, she'd look worried, like, wait a minute, didn't you check that. That's what she's really saying.

T: Mmm-hmm.

P: That's why I didn't talk to her. . . . It's kind of awful, I can't really talk to anybody except him. Even then, they're just these long . . .

T: Yeah, you talk to him but you become the child. No wonder you don't do things in a grown-up way because that's what your yearning is.

P: What do you mean, don't do things?

T: You have this tremendous pull to remain a child with your father. So it's difficult for you with Johnny and Bob and Alex Peters and Alex Bromberg and Hughes and all the employees to be an adult because there's this pull.

P: Yes. Well.

T: A struggle. It's like struggle against, kind of a magnetic pull.

P: To be a child or to talk to my father?

T: Yeah.

P: There's a pull to be a child but it's more ingrained than anything. The pull is when I start feeling lonely and I want to talk to my parents and I want someone to take care of me. That's where the pull is. But I'm always acting a little bit like a child. I'm just too naive not to.

T: You act like a child because the pull overwhelms you. The pull gains the greater weight than the other things. Than the adult things. You give in to the pulls, you yearn for the wanting to feel good. You said, "I want to listen to my father. It makes me feel good."

P: That's right. That's exactly right.

T: So now you know why it's difficult for you to do things in an adult way because this makes you feel good. Being the child. If you were really grown up, you wouldn't feel good.

Summary

These excerpts indicate that in addition to gaining a clearer view of why she did what she did, the patient also came to understand the genesis of her patterns of behavior. Through associations to the tapes and recollections of the past, she explored the developmental history of her present behavior. Although previous use of the therapeutic tasks had facilitated improvement in the patient's life, introduction of the audiotape technique struck at the very core of her problems and resulted in significant therapeutic gain.

We now turn to a discussion of the growth-inducing principles that form the theoretical foundation for CET and which are implemented through the therapeutic methods just discussed. We will demonstrate each of the principles and how they facilitate treatment, and indicate the relationship between a particular intervention and its positive effects with specific clinical problems.

CHAPTER III

Growth-Inducing Processes

Although it is generally agreed that new experience is essential to psychological growth and that psychotherapy is a special method for providing that experience, the challenge to the therapist is to discover the kinds of experiences which are most effective in generating the patient's development. Various therapies have, of course, identified a number of experiences which assist the patient in his development. For example, clarification, confrontation, interpretation and analysis of the transference are considered important experiences for inducing growth.

CET expands the scope and quality of the experiences provided in therapy by isolating the learning experiences that play a central role in inducing growth in both children and adults. We have identified the following six growth-inducing processes which form the theoretical foundation for CET and which we incorporated into its therapeutic method.

1. Balancing the patient's interactions with reality
2. Augmenting feedback
    (1) Taking responsibility: owning up to one's behavior
    (2) Testing reality
3. Fostering exploration and experimentation
    (1) The experiential-developmental laboratory
4. Promoting activity

5. Contending with challenge
6. Balancing verbal with nonverbal communication

1. BALANCING THE PATIENT'S INTERACTIONS WITH REALITY

The key to a patient's development derives from the active interplay between his schemes and the world of reality. Growth is impeded when one withdraws, as Proust did, into the hermetic sanctum of his cork-lined room.

A scheme has a double nature: it is a mobile, evolving product of interaction and represents the structure that adapts; when the functioning within the structure is under consideration, it is also the internal psychological apparatus, a mechanism or tool which develops.

A patient develops when his schemes develop. A scheme is the active, organizing process within the individual which defines what an individual is capable of doing, perceiving, thinking and feeling. His style of interacting with the world, his psychological repertoire, is an expression of his schemes. As a scheme develops, it extends the individual's repertoire and permits new kinds of mental operations to occur.

Developmental theory formulates a genuinely interactionist view of the individual. Schemes develop through the simultaneous interaction of two complementary processes: *assimilation and accommodation*. The individual relates to the world not only as his intrapsychic processes dictate (i.e., the assimilation of the environment to schemes), but as he transforms himself to the external reality (i.e., the accommodation of schemes to meet the demands of reality). Both processes are reciprocally dependent. In trying to bend and fit new information into existing schemes (assimilation), schemes are bent and modified in the process (accommodation).

Development is a cyclical process. Consider the child who can pick up large objects, but lacks the dexterity to hold small ones. Small objects are novel features of the environment to which he must adapt. When he encounters a small object, he finds that it is almost, but not quite assimilable. By interacting with the object, his grasping scheme accommodates to its smallness. It develops slightly and extends his capacity to hold the object. Slightly smaller objects now come within range of his newly developed assimilative capacity which, in turn, enables the child to make new accommodations. Within the first year, the cycle is repeated again and again until the child's transformed grasping scheme has developed new adaptive capacities (i.e., holding objects of all sizes) which did not previously exist.

Imbalance between these two processes impedes growth. If assimilative processes dominate and become the individual's primary means of interacting, his relationships to people and things are egocentric, distorted and subject to blind spots. He relates to the world primarily through trying to impose his schemes on others without making compensatory accommodations to theirs. Nothing new is ever learned. On the other hand, if accommodative processes dominate the individual's interactions, he acts on pretense. Constantly attempting to conform, chameleon-like, to outer demands, he imitates but seldom initiates. He is plagued by problems of identity and passivity.

Maximal growth takes place when assimilative and accommodative processes are activated together. Although we can conceptualize assimilation and accommodation as separate processes, they are not separated from one another in an adaptive act. An individual cannot effectively assimilate now and accommodate later; coordinated interaction is necessary. When they function disjointedly with one or the other process dominating the interaction, growth is impaired.

These insights are critical for psychotherapy as an agent for change. To produce change, one must employ methods which help patients to interact with the world in a more balanced way. For this purpose, CET invites, even requires, that the patient act upon and accommodate to real events presented in the session during the very act of trying to assimilate them. Otherwise, the patient may try to mold the new information to what he already thinks he knows rather than change his behavior to fit the new requirements of reality. Without an anchoring to reality, the patient may fall prey to accommodating his words rather than his schemes. Nothing will change except the words. The patient may develop a more sophisticated language and become the best-informed neurotic on the block, but awareness and insight will be split off, intellectualized and rendered ineffective. Little improvement in adaptive capacity will be achieved.

The crux of treatment is *equilibration*. If we give wrong or incomplete interpretations, we can correct them in the light of later information. If opportunities to interpret escape us, they will present themselves again and again. But if we mishandle the equilibration, the treatment is in trouble. The failure to establish and maintain a therapeutic balance between assimilative and accommodative processes within the session is, like mishandling the transference, a vital mistake, for it perpetuates and reinforces the patient's current inadequate, imbalanced interactions. (For further discussion of equilibration in therapy, see Cowan, 1978; Weiner, 1980c.)

CET provides a variety of therapeutic media to develop an equilibrated *modus operandi* for interacting. On the one hand, the therapeutic tasks enable the patient to experiment with and develop balanced interactions in contending with segments of reality presented in the sessions. On the other hand, the audiotape technique enables the patient to bring segments of his current interpersonal reality into the sessions to develop a more balanced repertoire in his interpersonal relations.

Balancing the patient's interpersonal interactions is also enhanced through broader opportunity for give-and-take interchange with the therapist during the task presentations and audiotape technique. The therapist gives instructions, sets goals and limits, provides clues and confronts and interprets the patient's actions. This interpersonal component of the patient's responses enables him to experience his characteristic and socially disadvantageous ways of relating to people in general and, through the therapist's unexpected responses, to discover his unrealistic assumptions. By being confronted with the discrepancy between his distorted expectations and what actually occurs in the therapist's real-world behavior, the patient is faced with the inappropriateness of his behavior and offered the means for correcting and altering his behavior. This reality, based on immediate cognitive and emotional feedback, provides a powerful means for enabling the patient to accommodate and resolve his interpersonal and transferential problems.

Gill points out that: "It is becoming increasingly recognized in our literature that the effects of an analysis are due not merely to insight but to the experience of a new relationship" (1982, p. 119). Even Glover, the staunch advocate of uncontaminated analysis of the transference, asserts, *"The main function of the positive transference is indeed to permit a re-experience in non-ambivalent form of earlier ambivalent attitudes to the parents"* (1955, p. 128; his italics). (For further discussion of interpersonal processes in relationship to the transference, see Blum, 1971; Loewald, 1960; Weiner, 1979.)

Our enhancement of the therapist-patient interactions is, however, a very different matter from the deliberately engaged-in "corrective emotional experience" of Alexander (1946), for the interaction is not an end in itself with its goal of providing "good" experiences to rectify the mistakes of childhood. Our "therapeutic experience" entails exploring and developing new equilibrated interactions whereby a more adaptive *modus operandi* unfolds.

2. AUGMENTING FEEDBACK

To gain from interacting with the world, the patient must obtain corrective feedback. Feedback is the relationship between action and reaction, which provides a necessary corrective to imbalanced interactions. Without corrective feedback, behavior is rigid and self-perpetuating rather than flexible and accommodating.

Change and growth are implemented when the person is provided with circumstances whereby he can obtain feedback based on the consequences of his own behavior. The effects of feedback start with the infant's earliest relationship to his mother. Reporting on his studies in infant development, Bettelheim observes:

> This is why artificial feeding times, arranged according to the clock, can dehumanize the infant. The reason is not just that time-clock feeding is contrary to the natural rhythms of the body. . . . More important here is that it prevents the infant from feeling *his* actions (crying, smiling) have a significant effect on this important life experience of being fed.
>
> What humanizes the infant is not being fed, changed, or picked up when he feels the need for it, though they add greatly to his comfort and feeling of well-being. Nor does irregular care necessarily dehumanize, though it will tend to make him dissatisfied with life or may cause poor development or sickness. It is rather the experience that *his* crying for food brings about *his* satiation by others according to *his* timing that makes it a socializing and humanizing experience. It is that *his* smile, or facial grimacing, evokes a parallel or otherwise appropriate response in the mother. (1967, p. 25)

For development to proceed effectively, it is, therefore, important that the child experience that his actions have an impact on the environment and that they make a difference. Growth is implemented when the infant becomes aware that the consequences of his self-generated actions (for example, his smile or facial grimacing) evoke an appropriate response from his mother. Each action has the potential for enriching the child by evoking a response from the environment —feedback—which provides the necessary corrective to evaluate his behavior and on which the next action sequence can be based. Feedback provides for "modifications of the scheme to accommodate it to the initially disturbing element" (Piaget, 1975, p. 26).

Applied to the psychotherapeutic context, to implement change, one must provide the patient with opportunities for obtaining corrective and enriching feedback from the consequences of his self-initiated actions. Although feedback provided by the therapist's interpretations, confrontations, etc., is important, it is not as convincing as the information the patient can discover for himself through self-initiated actions. CET procedures often provide profound self-confrontations. One cannot hide from oneself when one is the initiator of the feedback obtained. A patient may have been told some truth about himself, but without impact, until he discovers it through his own actions. The self-initiated feedback provided by CET engages the patient in vital self-observatory experiences which may be a necessary first step in the therapeutic process.

Although feedback derived from the tasks and the audiotape technique may facilitate therapeutic change, it is not synonymous with change. Feedback promotes growth through (1) taking responsibility, and (2) testing reality.

(1) Taking Responsibility: Owning Up to One's Behavior

Growth depends on a person taking responsibility for everything in his life. One of the central problems for a patient is that he cannot comprehend how he is the architect of his own misery. He is largely neither aware of nor in control of how his emotions and cognition affect his behavior or how his behavior affects other people. Blinded to how the consequences of his behavior are of his own doing, he is oblivious to how he contributes to his own dilemmas and how he is more the victim of his own distortion and denials in cognition, emotion, and choices than he is of his environment. Without a clear sense of responsibility for what he does to contribute to his problems, is there any wonder that he repeatedly gets himself into the same old predicaments and cannot find a way out?

Dealing with the tasks in the auspicious environment of the sessions, insulated from the usual chaos and problems around him, enables the patient to experience what he and his problems are really like and what he does to contribute to them. The sessions afford the patient that necessary new perspective that enables him to attempt new and positive action to resolve his problems.

When the patient is confronted by the realities of his performance, his behavior is not merely explained to him, but demonstrated by reference to his actions in the here-and-now. In committing himself to action on a task, the patient is not only made aware of his behavior, but becomes accountable for it since it is *his* self-initiated actions and *his* feelings that are directly related to and account for the success and/or failure of his performance. He cannot as readily disavow or disown his behavior and feelings.

Gaining responsibility for disclaimed action and cognition and disowned feelings is critical to growth and therapeutic effectiveness. As Loewald notes:

The patient is not merely to be made aware of the existence of such contents [unconscious patterns] in his psyche, but he is asked . . . to own up to them as *his* wishes and conflicts and defences, and to re-experience them as psychic activity of a non-automatic nature. (1971, p. 62)

By seeing how he is the writer of his own script, as reflected in his actions on the tasks, the patient can begin to surmount "suffered" events in which he feels he is the passive recipient of thoughts, feelings, and actions which "control him" and can replace them with conscious choices, thoughts, and feelings with which he controls his life. By grasping that he has the ability to "cause things to happen," with the locus of control placed more firmly in himself, the patient can begin to take control in directing his life and making more productive choices.

A patient can deny responsibility for his behavior in three ways:

1. He can deny the existence of the problem.
2. He can deny the significance and personal implications of the problem.
3. He can deny the solvability of the problem.

Only when a patient accepts responsibility for his behavior on these three levels can therapy truly proceed. The tasks make an important contribution by providing a powerful medium for addressing and resolving the patient's resistance on all three levels.

Interpreting a patient's denial is often insufficient because he will deny the very interpretation that attempts to bring about awareness of that denial. CET enables the therapist to breach these most tenacious of resistances by confronting the patient with his task behavior in the sessions, thus revealing the denied aspects of his problems. Those feelings and ideas which the patient was unable or unwilling to express and own up to are spontaneously exposed and captured through his task behavior. The therapist can then point directly to the behavior and confront the patient with the feelings that are expressed through the task. The patient cannot as readily deny these feelings because they are reflected back to him by the therapist in the observable moment of their occurrence.

Clinical Example: Anna—Horseshoe-and-Ring Problem

In the following case, therapeutic progress was obstructed because Anna's major problem was her denial of feelings. She acted, but rarely was aware of what she felt, except for an almost constant undertone of diffuse anger which she expressed toward almost everything in her environment. The most she would allow herself was that she was "upset." During one of her therapy sessions, the Horseshoe-and-Ring Problem helped to bring the denied aspects of her feelings to light.

P: I can never do that [the task].

T: Why not?

P: Greasy.

T: What does that make you feel?

P: It feels dirty.

T: Could it be that when you feel a challenge, that you're overwhelmed by it, your first instinct is to strike out and criticize the thing itself and find some fault? So you have to find that it's greasy, dirty. Could it be that's how you react to frustration? We've talked about this many times, but you can see a living example right now.

P: *(Long pause while the patient continues to work on the problem)* It seems impossible. I don't know what to do.

T: What do you feel like doing?

P: Just aimlessly doing the same thing over and over again.

T: Any feelings you're experiencing?

P: No. *(Pause)* Sort of futile. *(The patient placed the horseshoes together so that they looked like a gun, and pointed them at the therapist.)* Could shoot you.

T: You're pretty angry. What you don't say in words, you express in actions.

P: I don't feel angry though.

T: That's exactly it. One of the things you can strive for is to be more in contact with your feelings so you don't express it in action. Like in the old days, you used to hit Ernie [her ex-husband], and the other ways that you indirectly get at Ira [her current boyfriend].

P: I don't feel angry though. I'm not sure what I feel. All my imagery is hostile though.

T: Like what?

P: Like hanging myself. *(The patient had made a suicide attempt prior to starting therapy and was very depressed during her first therapy sessions.)*

T: What you block from taking out on another person, you take out on yourself.

P: Mmm-hmm.

T: Is that what you do a lot?

P: Yeah.

T: Like what?

P: Get depressed, feel that nobody likes me. *(The patient then talked at length about the anger she had for her mother for rejecting her, which she had rarely dared to express.)*

Summary

The patient's typical pattern of denial, which was responsible for many of her problems, was brought to light through her task behavior. During the course of the session, different levels of her denial were revealed. Her feelings of inadequacy *("I can never do that")* were defensively projected onto the tasks and expressed through her perceiving the task in a negative, repulsive light *("greasy; it feels dirty")*, and then expressed in her anger toward the therapist *("could shoot you")*. Her denied anger *("I don't feel angry; I'm not sure what I feel")* is bottled up and redirected toward herself *("get depressed")*, which leads to feelings of self-hatred *("feel nobody likes me")* which, we later find out, have their roots in her being rejected by her mother.

Whereas the therapist's dialogue had not previously succeeded in revealing the self-destructive pattern and exposing the underlying defensive denial, the tasks brought this whole pattern to light in a way that the patient could perceive and accept. Further, after seeing this pattern repeated in task after task, the patient began to own up to her feelings and get in better touch with them.

As her mechanisms of denial were worked through, she also became more aware of the parallels between her feelings expressed in her task behavior and her feelings toward the therapist. In working through the roots of these feelings in her childhood rejection, she began to build a new and more positive image of herself. As a consequence, she no longer had to react defensively with anger. As she became less angry and depressed, the quality of her interpersonal relationships also improved considerably.

(2) Testing Reality

Reality testing is the most important ally a patient will ever have to surmount his egocentricity. It is the antidote to narcissism and self-absorption.

The key to effective reality testing is not to have someone tell a person the truth about the world and his relationship to it, but to arrange the circumstances so he can discover the truth himself.

When a person is isolated from reality, he does not have the opportunity to obtain objective feedback and learn how to distinguish what is real from what is not. By introducing extra-session realities into the sessions, CET provides the patient with a safe place where he can contact reality and learn the process of testing it. Confronted with real challenges in real time which simulate real-world stresses, the patient obtains objective, focused feedback both from the consequences of his actions on the task and from the therapist. The patient can gain a realistic view of himself and his capacities outside of his carefully protected fantasies and illusions.

The tasks enable the patient to develop his perceptual and cognitive skills and the capacity to communicate in consensually validated terms. The tasks entail making discerning observations, sorting out useful and irrelevant things, taking things "as they are" in their substance without being diverted by their symbolic significance, keeping perceptual and cognitive errors to a minimum and, when they occur, correcting them, and exercising judgment and making decisions that have adaptive value in solving problems.

Because the patient can test reality buffered by a favorable, protective therapeutic alliance, he can contend with the demands and challenges without the denials and withdrawals which set up an impenetrable defense against change. The patient is offered multiple opportunities to learn how to take the initiative, make investigations and explorations, exercise curiosity, be analytical, logical and organized, and make comparisons and judgments based on discerning observations of essential and unessential elements in a problem. In short, he can develop a *modus operandi* for testing reality.

The structure of the sessions alternates between "looking inward"—exploration of the patient's feelings through standard therapeutic methods—and "looking outward"—engaging in reality testing while coping with the tasks. Integrating internally perceived insights with learning how to contend with the tasks of reality enables the patient to resume development from that stage in his life where his poor reality testing and withdrawal from the world undermined his ego development. Whereas reality was experienced in childhood as overwhelming, too demanding, dangerous or oppressive and was met with failure and discouragement, now the patient can counteract his developmental arrests with a nurturing, challenging and diversified environment which provides him with the salutary opportunities to develop his ego apparatuses and skills in using them.

The following clinical examples demonstrate how the problem-solving tasks help the patient to test reality and strengthen his ego-integrative capacities in dealing with it. Although the case illustrations are of a schizophrenic patient with a tenuous hold on reality, all patients, especially during times of stress and ego disorganization, benefit from the shoring up of defenses and strengthening of their contact with reality which the therapeutic tasks provide. The Ping-Pong and Ruler Problems used in the following examples, both of which focus on reality testing, are particularly helpful at these times.

Clinical Example: Hal—Ping-Pong Problem

The following excerpt is taken from Hal's therapy session immediately after he was discharged from the hospital. (See pp. 116-120 for a more complete description of his CET treatment during his hospitalization for an acute schizophrenic episode.)

During this session, the patient's tenuous hold on reality became increasingly evident. Instead of interpreting the patient's panic or exploring its dynamic meanings, which run the risk of opening the patient up to further regression, the therapist intervenes with a task, the Ping-Pong Problem, which was selected specifically because it injects concrete reality into the session. We see how the patient is helped to mobilize his ego resources and reintegrate during the session through contending with and mastering the task.

T: You can't just wander around in the street. *(On several occasions prior to his hospitalization, the patient had become disoriented and had difficulty finding his way home.)* You have no framework, you're totally in limbo.

P: Yeah, I'm letting myself be in limbo. I need the rest, the relaxation right now.

T: How long? You've been resting, relaxing for years.

P: No more than any other individual. No more than any other individual, and if you don't think so, look through my life and find out.

T: But are you responsible for any human being?

P: (Pause) Well, right now, I'm only responsible for one cat.

T: Human being.

P: No, I'm not. But I'm certainly not causing any damage to human beings.

T: What about Hal Frankle [the patient's pseudonym]?

P: I've been damaging him a bit, intentionally. *(Just prior to his hospitalization, the patient had engaged in several acts of severe self-mutilation.)*

T: What do you think that is? *(Pause)*

P: The reason I've been doing it is because my own concept of history and my own view of history has shown that civilization, because civilization periodically itself has thrown temper tantrums known as wars which I'm not happy about. My way of coping with the aggression of civilization and the craziness of civilization is my own business, which I will talk to you about.

T: You're wandering around. You don't even know what time of day it is.

P: I've got a watch on as far as earth time. If we're going to be honest. This is simply a sequencer for one particular reference temporal frame. I can invent time on the spot and invent a, and there's nothing wrong with that, or unethical about that. It's a . . .

T: Okay.

P: A right of any individual to invent a time and reference frame . . .

T: Let's do some real . . .

P: (Interrupting) Yeah, but listen to reality.

T: We'll have a reality, we'll have a little problem solving here. And we'll get down to reality. You said, "It connects you to part of yourself that is rational."

When the therapist came to see the patient during the first day of his eight-day hospitalization, he was curled up in bed, half-naked, lying in a fetal position. In spite of his severely regressed state of withdrawal and confusion, the patient asked the therapist whether he had any problem-solving tasks with him because *"it connects me with that part of myself that is rational."*

P: I like it. Fine, give me something.

T: (The therapist presents the Ping-Pong Problem.) The idea is, without tilting it, to get the ping-pong ball out, and without using the technique that you used last time. *(In the previous session, the patient had solved the Ping-Pong Problem using the "grabbing" technique.)*

P: Okay, without tilting it, by some other technique.

T: Mmm-hmm. And you can use anything in this room, without tearing it apart.

P: Okay. But wait a minute. I used this before and I used the string which is attached to it. Right?

T: Right.

P: So I have to use other tools than these two?

T: Than those, right.

P: Other tools than these two, okay, so take away these two. That's too easy, huh? So anything else in the room I can use? *(For ten minutes the patient tries various tools and odd objects lying about in the room.)* If I wait long enough, I'll use telekinesis. *(Pause)* Well, I don't even know if you have any specific concept in mind, but it's a reasonable test. It's a reasonable test. *(Long pause as the patient explores the office)* Well, I've looked at just about everything in the room. Just about. *(Pause)* And I'm not getting any new insights. I think I might be a little less anxious since I've taken action.

The reasonableness of the task makes contact with and mobilizes the reasonableness of the patient's ego. As he gains control over his primary-process, distorted thinking, he gives up using telekinesis, and starts to engage in realistic, adaptive actions by exploring the real world of the office. In addition, "taking [adaptive] action" and mobilizing his secondary-process functioning has the effect of helping him to contain his anxiety.

T: Maybe we should start thinking about ping-pong balls.

By focusing on the concrete aspects of a ping-pong ball, the therapist focuses on the concrete aspects of reality, rendering the problem more apprehensible.

P: Well, they're round, they roll, they bounce . . . they're light.
T: Mmm-hmm.
P: They're fairly white. There's only one thing I can think of that's a little different and that would cause some damage to the ping-pong ball a little bit.
T: What's that?
P: To take, somehow rig up something, attach one of these [a nail] to something and actually spike the ping-pong ball.
T: But that's a form of grabber.
P: In a way, it's a little different.
T: Yeah, but it still looks like a grabber. *(Pause)*
P: I'm stumped right now.
T: Well, think more about ping-pong balls.
P: They roll, they slide, they bounce, they're light.
T: Did you ever, do you play ping-pong?

The therapist helps the patient to contact reality by focusing on concrete personal experience.

P: I've played ping-pong, sure. *(Pause)* They can be spun.

T: Mmm-hmm.

P: And they bounce. They bounce very well.

T: What else? About them?

P: (Pause) Well, they're a very light kind of ball, they're filled with, I mean, they're hollow. *(Pause)* They float. Maybe this is the solution you're thinking of. To take the water from in there and float it up and out.

Once the patient perceived the ball's floatable qualities, he immediately saw the water in the vase in a new light and grasped how it could be used to solve the problem.

P: I don't know if there's enough water in there to do it, but, okay, so I got it eventually.

T: How did you get it?

P: Well, you said, "Think of their properties," and one of their properties is that they float because they're hollow. So their density is less than that of water.

T: How did you feel when you got it?

P: Pretty good. Fairly good. I'm surprised.

T: Surprised at what?

P: Well, it is sort of tricky, because there isn't enough, well, I don't think there's enough water in here to float it up.

T: Actually, first you can try to see if there's enough water. Secondly, you're not even seeing the broader aspects of it.

P: Which is what?

T: What if there isn't enough water in that container, then what?

P: Well, then the materials aren't at hand in the room.

T: Have you looked?

The therapist continues to address the patient's problem with reality testing by encouraging him to contact reality, to use his senses to test it, and to explore the environment's potentialities.

P: Well, there's water in there [the vase], but that's for the plant. You're not supposed to ruin anything. You mean, maybe there's a water faucet. I don't think there's a faucet.

T: There's also water in that orangeade jar.

With a psychotic patient, the therapist takes a more active role as a collaborator and makes direct suggestions in helping the patient with the problem, while at the same time being careful not to undermine his initiative and self-esteem.

P: Orangeade jar? Where is an orangeade jar?

T: Where the flower is sticking in.

P: Okay, but again you would be damaging something, you would be taking the water away from the flower.

T: For ten seconds.

P: Okay, that wouldn't make much difference. *(Pause)*

T: There are things in context that could be used. It's serving a purpose there, but you could empty it out and put it in there [the cylinder] and get the ping-pong ball out and put the water back in [the jar]. It's reversible. It doesn't destroy it. Like if you puncture a hole in the ping-pong ball, it destroys it. If you take a hammer, it's destroyed. If you cut something, it's destroyed, it can't be reversed. So taking water out and doing the job can be reversed without any damage.

Since reversibility is such a central process necessary for logical, secondary-process thinking, the therapist uses this occasion with the task to clarify the concept of reversibility and show the patient its value in testing reality and solving problems.

P: Yeah, it is. It's basically a reversible process, yeah. To do it that way. I see it. That makes sense. *(Pause)* This whole thing is okay.

Summary

In this session, we saw how the task served as a medium for contacting reality and for helping the patient to learn the process of reality testing. In mastering the task, he learned how to use perceptual exploration and manipulative activity as effective methods for testing reality, and to incorporate these methods into his repertoire of problem-solving processes. We also noted a marked improvement in the quality of the patient's verbalizations, reflecting less looseness in his thought processes.

Clinical Example: Hal—Ruler Problem

In the following example, the Ruler Problem enabled Hal to discover how many of his daily problems stem from his pervasive deficits in reality testing. Equally important, the task gave him concrete opportunities to develop his reality testing skills. For example, one of the central components in testing reality is learning how to consensually validate actions to provide a counterbalancing force to idiosyncratic thoughts. The task demonstrates the process of consensual validation, and helps the patient to apply it more effectively in contending with daily problems.

(The patient has worked on the problem for ten minutes.)

T: What has worked previously in finding out solutions to these problems? What is one of the ways to solve problems? Remember, we talked many times about how to go about solving problems?

P: Well, I'm not sure what you're trying to . . .

T: Is there a method, a *modus operandi?*

P: There's different methods at different times that work. I mean, it's hard to identify the elusive instant. I mean, what it is that triggers finally realizing something.

T: But we've talked about a method that seems to be applicable to many problems.

P: Well, trying different approaches . . . is what . . .

T: Yeah, trying. But isn't there something else? How do you try different approaches? *(Pause)* By trying, what does that mean?

P: Well, you try and come at the problem from a different angle. Do something different than what you have done before in terms of trying to solve it. *(Pause)* But here *(pause)* everything looks fine. I didn't count the centimeters. It seems to me if I were systematic, I would do that. *(Pause)* Of course, if it was a dramatic thing that was wrong, it shouldn't be something that was one piddly line or something. So maybe I shouldn't try that approach since you have given me that clue. *(Yawn)*

T: Why are you yawning?

P: Because I only had about five hours' sleep. I wanted to try to get up at least in time to look at the job board [to look for a new job] if I could, and I didn't get over there yesterday.

T: Yeah.

P: And I didn't get home until nine [in the morning], at least. It was after nine I think, a little bit, right around nine. *(The patient works as night-manager of a grocery store.)* Or nine-thirty, I forget. *(Long pause)*

T: Yeah, what are you thinking?

P: I was thinking about work. Thinking about the drop at work and what I have been doing lately.

T: The what at work?

P: The drop. The drop is . . .

T: Oh, the money drop [a hole in the floor through which money is dropped into a safe].

P: Yeah. What I have been doing so I don't have headaches at night is if I'm not sure if I dropped a twenty [dollar bill in the safe], I'll record it again, which means that if anything, my figures come out too high.

T: You checked your method against somebody else's point of view.

P: What do you mean?

T: With the drop. You checked the drop method with Nick [his supervisor]. Checking reality.

P: Yeah. Yeah.

T: Well, what could you do with this ruler?

The therapist draws upon the patient's daily experience in reality testing and focuses on the essential elements in testing reality that he could apply to the task.

P: Well, check reality.

T: How have you been checking reality?

P: I could check it against another ruler. That would be one way of checking reality, if there is another one around.

T: Well, there is no other ruler around, though.

P: By comparing it, that is one way.

T: How could you compare it?

P: Get something whose dimensions I roughly know. *(The patient measures his shoe.)*

T: Not roughly. I mean that's a ruler. You have to be exact. You can't check it against your shoe, because your shoe you don't know exactly what it is.

P: Well, still. *(Pause)* It's the dimensions of something that I know. What are the dimensions of something I know? *(Pause)* I see something that I can check it against.

T: What?

P: A standard sheet of paper. *(Pause)* Well, it's roughly correct, I guess. This sheet of paper is too short.

T: Why is it short? What's the size of the paper?

P: Well, the standard paper would be 8½ by 11.

T: Uh-huh. What is it there?

P: Eight and three-quarters by eleven and one-quarter. So everything comes out longer. It's consistently measuring something that's longer than it really is. Which means that the divisions are too close together. And the inches are too small. By some factor. So that's the solution to the problem. *(Pause)*

T: So what do you think of this? The problem?

P: It's interesting. *(Pause)*

T: How do you think it got that way?

P: This ruler?

T: Mmm-hmm.

P: It may have been made that way intentionally. Either as a joke or for purposes of use by psychologists, or something. *(Laughs)* Or it could have been a mistake, however they make this thing, the printing. I don't know. *(Pause)*

T: Once you got the idea of checking reality, then you finally looked around for another ruler, your shoe, and then you discovered the piece of paper. You had the resources, you knew that papers are a standard size. You didn't use it [his resources], you didn't think. You've got to check against another standard, just like you check your ideas against what Nick thinks, you check your ideas against what Brenda [his estranged wife] thinks about something. It's always a matter of checking. *(Pause)* To see what other people think. Not that you can't make a decision on the basis of your own feelings. But when it's involving things that you're not sure of, there's always a check. Feedback is another way. *(Pause)*

The therapist describes the process of reality testing and consensual validation.

P: That's interesting, but I'm wondering, I don't know why it is that I, I mean I do check on myself a lot.

T: But see, the way you checked here . . .

P: But I don't check with other people . . .

T: Right.

P: I can't check with other people, because there's no one I'm close enough with to have that kind of relationship with.

T: It's not only that. Here, you checked in your mind. You were going, just like all these ideas intrude in your mind, you give too much predominance to your mental images, things in your mind. You were thinking. You think too much. And, therefore, don't think *well,* because your thinking always needs a reference to reality, if it's to be effective thinking. And your thinking is an internalized, self-absorbed thinking. Like you say you don't have people to talk with. That's true. It's too much isolation, but it's your style to ruminate, and even in telling a story, to let your mind overweight things, rather than an interaction between your mind and the outside world. *(Pause)* It's a style.

The therapist points out that reality testing involves getting outside of one's private view of the world through testing and consensually validating one's views in an interpersonal context.

P: Yeah, I understand that.

T: Maybe because you were so isolated throughout your whole life that you developed this style.

P: Yeah. I think that's correct and I mean, I know it correlates with the physical problems that I had. *(The patient has suffered from congenital muscular-skeletal deformities which were corrected by a series of major surgeries taking place from ages twelve through eighteen.)*

T: It's what you called absorbed, locked in your body.

P: Yeah. *(Pause)* That's the only style I could develop. I was isolated. *(Pause)* I think that's unfortunately what happens to a lot of people who have a lot of static from their bodies or from something that keeps them from connecting with others or external environment.

T: Okay, that is past history.

P: I agree. I mean, in my case, fortunately, it's becoming more past history.

T: So you have to change your style of thinking.

P: Yeah, I do. *(Pause)*

T: It's difficult to do because it's been going on for so many years. But it's possible.

P: I did something recently along those lines that I'd never done before.

T: What's that?

P: My balance didn't come out right . . . okay. So I checked my figures and I couldn't find the error. So I called the bank and I talked to the customer service representative for a while. It turned out I had made a mistake. I hadn't recorded a check. But it took about a half an hour to get this straightened out, but normally I would have just let it go.

The patient relates the insights concerning testing reality to his daily life.

T: But finally you checked with the bank?

P: I checked, I wanted to make sure I knew. There's something else I've got to check on.

T: What?

P: I came back today and I got my paycheck. It has my raise on it. But it has no overtime for Memorial Day on it, which it should. *(Pause)* And I kept thinking I'll forget to check on that, and I'm trying to get myself to remember, but I should have time-and-a-half for Memorial Day and I don't think it's on there. And I get the feeling it's a hostile thing that Bill did, 'cause I think he was preparing the time sheets.

T: Whether it's hostile or not, all it requires is to check, and then right away you can settle it. Checking settles things and it settles whether your balance is right. It defuses anxiety and anger. *(Pause)* 'Cause otherwise it builds on itself.

The therapist points out how testing reality is valuable in containing anxiety and anger.

P: Yeah. *(Pause)*

T: Well, I think this could be a valuable starting point to use this as an example.

P: Yeah, as a metaphor.

Summary

This session helped Hal take a significant step forward. He grasped how testing reality with the task could serve as a model for a new way of coping with his problems in daily life.

3. FOSTERING EXPLORATION AND EXPERIMENTATION

Exploration and experimentation provide the enriching data to correct and modify the person's schemes, which then become the basis for new actions and explorations. CET, therefore, transforms and restructures the sessions into a testing ground for new adaptations. The patient is provided with a broad array of materials and circumstances to obtain feedback from his actions and emotional responses so that he can develop alternative approaches to his problems.

(1) The Experiential-Developmental Laboratory

It is difficult to change by thinking alone. Changes in entrenched behavior, affects, and cognition do not readily issue simply from awareness and understanding. Therefore, CET provides a medium for expediting the translation of insight into significant behavior change.

Freud was acutely aware of this problem of implementing change when he noted:

One can hardly master a phobia if one waits till the patient lets the analysis influence him to give it up. He will never in that case bring into the analysis the material indispensable for a convincing resolution of the phobia. One must proceed differently. Take the example of agoraphobia. . . . One succeeds only when one can induce [patients] by the influence of the analysis . . . to go into the street and to struggle with their anxiety while they make the attempt. (1919, pp. 165-166)

CET brings "the street" to the patient by creating a microcosm of his life in the sessions. The sessions are transformed into an experiential-developmental laboratory. In a nonthreatening, supportive environment, the patient experiments with new adaptations by dealing with the "slices" of reality that the tasks represent.

The task situations increase both the therapist's and the patient's awareness of just how he conceives of himself and tries to solve his problems. The patient demonstrates exactly what he is, what he feels, how he acts and reacts, and how he manages or mismanages his life in the subtle ways in which he flounders around in his attempts at solutions. Although the potential for revelation may imbue the task situations with considerable anxiety, this richly self-expressive material is capable of providing both the therapist and the patient with a more representative view of the patient's way of dealing with life.

The tasks serve as a psychological mirror, revealing the patient not only to the therapist, but to *himself*. By obtaining immediate feedback from the consequences of his responses to a task, the patient can experience the maladaptiveness of his strategies. Seeing that the consequences of his behavior and his feelings are of his own doing, the patient can become aware of his contribution to his problems. This immediate concrete feedback provides the patient with vital information for correcting and altering his cognitions and emotions, and for translating understanding into behavior change.

Within the experiential-developmental laboratory, the patient can explore new avenues of cognition and emotional expression without the danger of retribution or retaliation for daring to try new modes of behavior and without the risk of real negative consequences from trying new behaviors that are inappropriate and maladaptive. It is a safe, nonthreatening framework wherein the patient does not have to pay dearly for his mistakes. The structure of the sessions along with the therapist's encouragement and support enable the patient to free himself, to perceive in ways that could never even have occurred to him before, or to say or feel things that are extremely difficult for him to express.

He can test different ways of processing information and alternate cognitive and affective styles, to try one way and then reject it if it does not lead to a successful solution. He is urged to search for, experiment with and master different and more adaptive patterns of reacting. He is invited to seek out more effective ways of expressing feelings. The patient is shown that by acting, reflecting, feeling, reconsidering, and then correcting, he can discover a more effective behavioral repertoire. Experiencing the success and gratification of meeting challenges in a different, constructive way in the session inspires the patient to develop different, constructive approaches in contending with the dilemmas of his daily life.

Social inhibitions may be overcome, provided that the therapist maintains an atmosphere of acceptance and exploration. If the patient fears displeasure and resentment because of his accomplishments in the task situation, this too becomes grist for the mill and may be used as a learning experience.

The goal of CET is not merely to help the patient to understand himself, but to learn *how* to acquire understanding; not merely to master a task, but to discover how one attains mastery; not merely to arrive at a solution to a problem, but to comprehend how solutions are arrived at; not merely to develop particular feelings, but to experience how feelings develop. CET expands the medium for assisting the patient by developing ways of knowing how to know and learning how to feel.

4. PROMOTING ACTIVITY

By activity, we mean both motor behavior and doing something in the physical sense as well as doing something mentally which can catalyze the person to make decisions, take risks, choose, decide and commit himself to an idea or course of action. Activity is a vital precondition for growth, for without activity, the person is unable to obtain feedback, assume responsibility or test reality. In arguing for the centrality of activity in development, Piaget stressed:

All of my remarks today represent the child and the learning subject as active. An operation is an activity. Learning is possible only when there is active assimilation. It is that activity on the part of the subject which seems to be underplayed in the stimulus response schema. The presentation which I propose puts the emphasis on the idea of self-regulation, on assimilation. All the emphasis is placed on the activity of the subject himself, and I think that without this activity there is no possible didactic or pedagogy which significantly transforms the subject. (1964, p. 77)

Our research findings with adults and Piaget's developmental research with children consistently demonstrate that "the subject can know himself or herself only by acting on objects materially and mentally" (Piaget, 1978, p. 651).

In the clinical domain, Bettelheim observed that autistic children could be helped if they were induced to take action on their own behalf.

For our own part, we have found, as we worked more intensively with autistic children, that at the core of their disturbance was not . . . that they lacked for any passive satisfactions. Those satisfactions were very easy for us to provide. Some autistic children accepted the offered satisfactions and remained autistic; others rejected them. None moved out of the autistic position because of them. This they did only if and when we were able to *activate them*. . . . They came to life only when we were able to create the conditions, or otherwise be the catalysts, that *induced them to take action in their own behalf*. (1967, pp. 16-17; italics added)

The implications of these findings for CET are important: The therapist provides the patient with extensive opportunities within the therapeutic situation to invent and construct schemes through his own actions. Without inducing the patient to actively engage in the therapeutic field, we run the risk of reinforcing his false and destructive belief that life is a passive process, that thinking and reflecting on his problems are enough, and that he need mainly to absorb.

Since so many of a patient's problems derive from his archaic, passive approach to the world, our procedures are directed toward helping the patient to shift his ego state from a predominantly passive-reactive mode to an active-adaptive one. Introducing real-world, goal-directed challenges into the sessions induces the patient not simply to reenact his passive and maladaptive ways of functioning, but to experiment with and progress to a higher level of functioning. Rather than providing the patient with a license to act out his pathology or to indulge in passive-regressive gratification, the challenges of the task as well as the therapist's purposeful relation to the patient invite and demand that he shift his predominantly self-destructive, regressive, passive ego state to an ego-adaptive, adult, active mode of functioning.

In the final analysis, what brings CET to life is that it *activates* the patient. Our approach catalyzes the patient by creating the conditions wherein he is required to give up his passivity and inertia and take action on his own behalf. Instead of allowing himself to be the victim of his environment, the patient is shown, through concrete demonstrations with the tasks, how he can become a "moving force" in his life; i.e., assume more initiative and take an active stance in directing and gaining control over his life. CET induces the patient to *do* things differently, to try a new way of perceiving, thinking and feeling *in* the sessions, and to discover a new self-managing, competent repertoire which goes beyond awareness and understanding to behavioral change.

Clinical Example: Marj—Brook Problem*

The following example illustrates how assuming a more active role in contending with the Brook Problem helped Marj to adopt a concept of herself as a competent person who can cope and "control her destiny." As a result, she gained control over the self-destructive feelings which had driven her to the brink of suicide and returned to adaptive functioning, both at home and at work.

(After describing her suicide attempt and the events leading up to it, the patient talked about her family background. Then the therapist asked:)
T: What do you think that I can do? What do you want to do in therapy?
P: Wave a magic wand. *(Laughs)*
T: And? What should I do with the magic wand?
P: Get me to where I start taking care of myself without feeling guilty about it.

At this point, the therapist presented the Brook Problem to address the patient's passivity and demonstrate to her how she can take adaptive actions which would enable her to *"start taking care of myself without feeling guilty about it."*

P: Make like water skis.
T: But they'd sink. The idea is to get across and you don't get wet.

The therapist points out reality and clarifies the limitations imposed by the instructions.

---

*Portions of this section appeared in Weiner (1982) as part of a study on the treatment of outpatient depression.

P: That's impossible.

T: Why is it impossible? *(Pause)*

P: Are these like, big things or just little things?

T: Well, they're like planks of wood.

P: Planks of wood?

T: Yeah.

P: Okay. Are they about as long as the stream?

T: No. See, that's the idea.

Before resorting to pointing out the reality constraints in the task, the therapist could first have encouraged the patient to take the initiative and test reality by saying, "How can you tell?" or "How can you find out?" or even "Try it out and see," which would foster active, adaptive action and serve an ego-building function.

P: Oh, I see. *(Pause)*

T: Yeah, that's the idea. That they're too short to just stretch over the stream. *(Pause)*

P: And they're too short to stick up like that?

T: How would you stick them up like that? You mean as stilts?

P: Yeah.

T: You can't use them as stilts.

P: You can't use them as stilts?

T: No. *(Pause)* Because it's a very deep stream.

P: You wouldn't chop them up and fill up the hole?

T: Oh, no, it's a very deep stream. What are you thinking? What's going through your mind?

P: I'm trying to figure it out. There's got to be a trick to it.

T: What kind of trick?

P: I don't know. It's probably something really simple. *(Laughs)* I feel really dumb.

T: Why?

P: I don't know, 'cause it seems like I should be able to figure that out.

T: You mean, it seems that it should be simple, but it isn't?

P: Mmm-hmm. That's all I'm feeling right now is kind of stupid.

T: Yeah?

P: It's not long enough to make a bridge, to hold it up like that?

T: No. Because there'd be nothing to hold it up.

Instead of fostering the patient's passivity and doing the work for her by too readily clarifying reality, the therapist might again have encouraged the development of adaptive ego functions by requiring her to do more of the work. He could have asked her to switch from her experiencing to her observing ego with questions like, "What do you think of that?" or "How would that work?"

P: That's true.
T: How would you get it to the other side? You're only on one side.
P: That's true. You can't get your feet wet?
T: No. What were you thinking?
P: I was thinking it's impossible.
T: How does it make you feel?
P: Stupid.
T: What goes through your mind?
P: That I won't be able to figure it out.
T: Why is that? *(Pause)*
P: Because there's probably a real simple solution.
T: You thought that you should get it sort of right off?
P: Yeah.
T: But figuring it takes time sometimes.
P: Can I lie down on these, hold my feet up, and paddle myself across?
T: No, you can't get wet.

Since the therapist had already repeated that the solution required her to remain dry, he might have facilitated a more active, self-responsible approach to the problem by simply asking, "What do you think?" However, since the patient was suffering from intense self-deprecatory feelings, the therapist was very careful not to exacerbate her feelings of aloneness and hopelessness. By answering her question directly, he demonstrated that, for the time being at least, he would provide the reality testing and ego supports which had been weakened by her depressive withdrawal.

P: Not anything can get wet?
T: No, that's the idea, otherwise you could swim.
P: Pole vault? *(Long pause)* I probably should stay here. *(Laughs)*
T: What are you going to do there?
P: Wish I could be on the other side. *(Sighs)* Yeah.
T: What do you usually do when you're in a situation like this?
P: Fix a drink. *(Laughs)*
T: Do you really?
P: Yeah, mmm-hmm.
T: You mean this is the time when you feel like a drink would help? Or you just feel like you'd like to have a drink?

P: Well, I think it would help me not worry about it. *(Pause)*

T: How would it do that?

P: It kind of, you know, relax and space out. Rather than sit and stew about it. *(Pause)*

T: You mean, drink enough after the first drink.

P: Mmm-hmm, I figure what the hell, I don't want to go anywhere anyways.

T: It doesn't matter?

P: It doesn't matter, yeah.

T: Do you feel good when you get high?

P: Mmm-hmm, usually. Sometimes I do it just so I can . . . if I need to cry or I need to, you know, do something, I'll do it just therapeutically.

T: And it lets you cry?

P: Mmm-hmm.

T: How many drinks do you need?

P: A lot. *(Laughs)* Quite a lot, yeah.

T: And then what happens?

P: Then I cry, then I feel better the next day. It's kind of like, I bottle up. I do that maybe once or twice a year. You know, when I've been under a lot of pressure.

T: What do you do instead of cry?

P: Well, I find myself getting really nervous and tense and kind of bottled up. So I think, well, it's time to do it.

T: Do you feel bottled up now?

P: No, 'cause I've been crying a lot this week 'cause I've been so upset.

T: With or without the drinks?

P: With, with . . . yeah.

T: With the drinks?

P: Mmm-hmm. Yeah, I can't do it without.

T: Even if things are pretty bad, you still need the drinks?

P: Mmm-hmm. To have a real good cry, I have to be somewhat smashed. *(Pause)* I can cry up a storm in sad movies. That's as long as I'm, you know, by myself. Then, that's crying about somebody else. See.

T: Mmm-hmm.

P: That's a thought that came to my mind. I'm very assertive and stick up for other people, but I never do myself. *(Very long pause)* Do I have any tools for anything? I don't have any tools to build something?

T: No. But what kind of tools were you thinking of?

P: Oh, hammer and nails, you know, cut them apart and make a little raft, and get across. Or sell the wood *(laughs)* to somebody and get enough money to get a little raft to go across.

T: Nobody around.

P: Nobody around? Make it into a helicopter.

T: Into a what?

P: Helicopter . . . Okay, I got it.

T: You got it?

P: Yeah. Make like a catapult thing, and then sit on it, then it flips, you know, like that.

T: Flip across?

P: Mmm-hmm.

T: How would you, who would be the catapulter?

P: You'd have to do it yourself.

T: How would you do it yourself?

P: I don't know, I don't know enough about a catapult to do it. . . . There's no beavers around?

T: What would they do?

P: Build a little dam. *(Laughs)* To get across. Or you could build a fire, dry up the water, start a forest fire. Hey, that'd be a way, you could start a forest fire with wood! Then it might dry up the stream.

T: You'd need quite a forest fire to dry up a stream.

P: Yeah.

T: You'd be roasted before you got across.

P: That's not a good idea. *(Long pause)* Can't think of any way to get *(long pause)* across there.

T: Yeah.

P: So I guess I'm just stuck on the other side.

T: What are you going to do then?

P: Just cope. *(Laughs)*

T: By cope, what would you do?

P: Oh, build a little house *(laughs)* with the sticks and just make do with what was there.

T: Yeah, but what if it's a *(pause)* you had to get across, you were starving. *(Long pause)*

P: Sure. I can't float on my stomach? *(Laughs)* *(Long pause)*

T: Yeah? Does this remind you of anything in your life? This predicament? *(Pause)*

P: I don't think so.

T: Being stuck in one situation and not being able to . . . *(Pause)*

P: You know, twenty years ago that would have gotten to me. I would probably have sat here and got hysterical 'cause I was really trapped. I don't get myself into situations where I'm really stuck. *(Pause)*

T: But how do you get out of them?

P: I always leave a little escape mechanism.

T: Like what?

P: I like to have my car always have gas in it. I always like to have a little money in the savings and, you know, and if necessary, I like to always have a little stash of pills in case things get too bad. You know, so there's always an escape route. 'Cause I can't handle being trapped. Staying single is a good way to keep from being trapped. *(Pause)* I can't figure out what to do so I sit here and wait it out.

T: What do you think would happen if you just wait it out? *(Pause)* Ultimately?

P: With what, getting across the stream?

T: No, life.

P: Without taking any action?

T: Yeah.

P: Be a very passive existence, and then . . . pretty much dependent on. . . . *(Pause)* Yeah, that's a bad place to be in. *(Pause)*

T: Is that how you feel? That you're sort of in a bad place now?

P: Today I don't feel like I'm in that bad place, but that's 'cause I, I knew I was coming down here and I thought, I did feel good about that because that's the first time I've done anything for myself, essentially for some time. And I have been thinking for some time that, you know, I probably needed to do something like this for like several years.

T: Uh-huh.

P: You know, 'cause things come up and I kind of fall apart. And get depressed and, and, ah, think suicidal thoughts as a way out. I felt considerably better. *(Pause)* That's going to drive me crazy. *(Laughs)*

T: I have the feeling that there are a lot of feelings that you are not expressing besides this feeling right now that you're, it's going to drive you crazy, that when you get upset, you don't express your feelings very much, just like you don't cry.

P: Mmm-hmm.

T: You sort of bottle up until it gets to a . . .

P: Mmm-hmm.

T: Till it explodes. *(Pause)*

P: Mmm-hmm. Yeah, that's why I have a "luncher" twice a year.

T: Mmm-hmm.

P: What I call my mini-breakdowns.

T: What are those?

P: That's when I get drunk and cry and sometimes beat on the rug and, you know, sometimes kick and scream. It's hard to schedule them, 'cause I've got to do it when the kid's not there. You know, 'cause she'd flip if she saw her mother, you know. I have to wait till real late at night so nobody's there. *(Pause)* So. *(Pause)*

T: What were you thinking?

P: I was just thinking maybe I decided I don't want to go across, at all, just that I like it here.

T: Maybe that's what you do, you sort of give up on doing anything good for yourself. You try to convince yourself that, well, having a good life really isn't, I'll just settle for what I've got.

The therapist uses the patient's task behavior as a metaphor for her behavior in life.

P: That could be.

T: If you don't try, you don't see what you're missing.

P: Mmm-hmm.

T: You save yourself from being disappointed.

P: It's like, I don't try to do things.

T: I notice, though, that you haven't really tried anything concrete. You had a lot of ideas in your mind, but you didn't actually take the sticks and use them and see what can be done with the sticks. Using the real stuff. You didn't even do it in the beginning. You didn't test out how long the sticks were to see whether they fit over the whole stream. It took maybe five minutes for you to do that. You didn't use the sticks and test, to feel them, see how long they are, what they are like, what you can do with them. It was all sort of sitting back in your mind. *(Pause)* You don't experiment and try out. You don't pick them up and hardly fiddle around with them.

The therapist promotes ego integration via action and exercise of function by showing the patient how she can take the initiative, venture out, exercise curiosity and test reality with concrete experiments using the materials provided her.

P: I think about it first.

T: But you didn't combine thinking with the stuff, the real thing, and doing something with the thoughts. Is it that you didn't want to show what you can do with the sticks, 'cause if you tried something and it didn't work out, then? . . .

P: It could be.

T: That you didn't want to show it, expose it, that you're a failure, open to ridicule? *(Very long pause)* What were you thinking?

P: Just what I was doing.

T: What were you doing?

P: Trying to figure out a way to get over there.

T: What were you actually doing with the sticks? You moved them around different ways.

P: Well, I was trying to, thinking of doing something weird. Like that, but that doesn't even make sense.

T: Why doesn't it?

Since the patient had discovered, but rejected, the correct solution, the therapist confronts her with her actions. He encourages her to take a self-critical attitude and justify her behavior, i.e., to switch from the experiencing ego to the observing ego.

P: I was trying to shorten the distance so that . . .

T: Yeah.

P: They would make it. *(Pause)* Here!

T: What do you think of that?

P: That would work.

T: Yeah! How come you got it now?

P: Is that it?

T: Yeah!

P: Really? *(Raises voice)* Oh!

T: You mean you didn't even know that's it?

P: Mmm-hmm.

T: Well, what does it look like?

P: It looks like a little bridge.

T: Yeah. So even when you had it, you didn't try it out. *(Pause)*

P: I wasn't sure of it.

T: What are you thinking?

P: I'm glad I got it, though.

T: How do you think it happened? *(Pause)*

P: By actually getting in there and playing with them. I wouldn't have figured it out just sitting and looking at them.

T: So what does this bring to mind?

P: Probably I need to take a more active role in things rather than sitting back and thinking about it.

T: I think this could be, is that something like your life?

The therapist relates the patient's way of approaching the task to her way of approaching problems in life.

P: Mmm-hmm.
T: That you spend a lot of time thinking, but you don't test it out?
P: Mmm-hmm.
T: You get a terrific idea, but you don't try it out and see what happens.
P: Mmm-hmm.
T: You can get into terrible trouble if you don't see what the results are. You get snowballing on and on and you never know whether you're right. If it's just in your mind, you don't change course and correct things.

The therapist points out the value of reality testing and of altering her behavior according to the information obtained from the consequences of her actions.

P: Mmm-hmm.
T: You don't check things out. *(Pause)* Until you tested it and virtually took it in your hand, you couldn't see this possibility. It's very difficult just to have a mental image of it, in terms of size and whether it's going to fit. *(Pause)* What are you thinking?
P: Do you have another puzzle?
T: Why do you want another puzzle?
P: I don't know. I like doing them.

During sessions two through eight, six additional tasks were introduced. After the eighth session (fourth week), the patient decided to terminate therapy because she felt considerably better and wanted to carry on by herself.

Summary

At termination of treatment, although many of the patient's characterological problems still remained, her depression had lifted and she was free of all suicidal ideation. As she assumed a more active and assertive role, she was able to cope with everyday stresses, take care of her thirteen-year-old daughter and return to productive work and social functioning.

5. CONTENDING WITH CHALLENGE

Challenge is one of the most basic mechanisms in the growth process. Challenge is "the driving force of development" (Piaget, 1975, p 13). Growth is facilitated when it is directed towards meeting and surmounting the challenges provided by conflict and contradiction. Piaget emphasized, "All development is composed of momentary conflicts and incompatibilities which must be overcome to reach a higher level of equilibrium" (1964, p. 78). Studies of Inhelder, Sinclair and Bovet (1974) indicated that children who were not offered challenges or who were not sensitive to contradiction made little progress in acquiring new structures. In fact, the children who made the greatest progress were those who initially appeared the most confused! Other studies (Turiel, 1966; Kuhn, 1972) suggest that if materials are structured at or below a child's developmental level, offering little challenge, there is little developmental change. Cowan (1978, p. 328) points out that optimal growth is attained when the challenge is just one stage above the child's predominant level. He states, "Children respond to material which is challenging, but not too challenging, and do not progress in response to material below their stage level."

These findings imply that therapeutic progress can be facilitated by deliberately challenging the patient and piquing his curiosity. More precisely, we apply the following two principles to the therapeutic context: (1) optimal mismatch between a task and a patient's existing level of development induces a temporary state of disequilibration; and (2) disequilibration is necessary for structural growth.

CET aims, therefore, not merely to relieve anxiety, but to induce structural growth by challenging the patient in optimally disequilibrating situations. Conflict, frustration and confusion are systematically introduced in the sessions in the form of nonthreatening, challenging tasks through which the patient can achieve clarity and resolution by taking risks and meeting the challenges.

Introducing challenges into the sessions induces the patient to experiment with and progress to a higher level of functioning. Rather than providing the patient with a license to act out his pathology or to indulge in regressive gratification, the challenges of the task as well as the therapist's purposive relation to the patient demand of the patient that he interrupt his self-destructive, regressive strategies and replace them with secondary-process, ego-adaptive functioning.

6. BALANCING VERBAL AND NONVERBAL COMMUNICATION

Piaget (1936, 1937) was acutely aware of the vital importance of the factors which implement growth before the acquisition of language.

He emphasized that nonverbal activity was critical for implementing the developmental process. This is not to say that he did not consider language as one of the primary vehicles for building schemes; however, language is not a sufficient condition for growth. To maximize the development of new schemes, it is necessary to complement and balance verbal interactions with sensorimotor and perceptual activity and other forms of nonverbal communication.

Translating this perspective into CET suggests that the greatest progress can be achieved by engaging the patient and communicating with him through nonverbal activities as well as through traditional verbal exchange.

We are aware of the critical role that nonverbal communication plays in child therapy and, establishing another "royal road" to the deepest layers of the child's unconscious, readily avail ourselves of this major source of therapeutic contact in play therapy. Therapists are, however, reluctant to incorporate nonverbal interventions into adult psychotherapy because of the tendency to equate nonverbal interactions with "hands-on" interventions, which could eroticize the transference. Therapists have, consequently, tended to assume a strictly verbal approach, neglecting acceptable "neutralized" forms of nonverbal interventions which can contribute to therapeutic success.

Kanzer has pointed to the downgrading that the nonverbal system has experienced in psychotherapy and remarked, "Only an intellectual bias and misunderstanding proposes that vocalized expressions must somehow be 'higher' or more therapeutic than other forms" (1961, p. 330).

The therapist's dilemma is that while his primary form of contact with the patient is verbal, the patient's very pathology can make this contact difficult. Especially at the beginning of treatment and during acute episodes where symptoms are exacerbated, verbal contacts are hard to make because the patient is withdrawn. The patient, absorbed in his private world, does not always succeed in finding words to express his feelings nor is the therapist able to reach that private world with words. Because the patient feels estranged from people and the world in general, efforts to communicate appear enormous to him and, what is more important, hopeless. He is overwhelmed by feelings of futility, helplessness, and desperation.

Freud was profoundly conscious of the powerful role of nonverbal communication. He commented:

He that has eyes to see and ears to hear may convince himself that no mortal can keep a secret. If his lips are silent, he chatters with his finger-tips; betrayal oozes out of him at every pore. And thus the task of making conscious the most hidden recesses of the mind is one which it is quite possible to accomplish. (1905, pp. 77-78)

The CET approach does not exclude or de-emphasize traditional avenues of verbal communication. However, the nonverbal, concrete, sensory, manipulative, motoric, and figural qualities of the tasks supplement and complement the verbal component of the interaction between the therapist and the patient. This broadened range of interaction forms a nonverbal bridge which helps to contact the nonverbal and preverbal components of the patient's schemes and intrapsychic life and is especially helpful in enabling the patient to make the shift from thinking, which emphasizes words, to experiencing, which encompasses nonverbal and affective processes as well. Not only can this nonverbal component initiate greater contact with the elusive elements of "the most hidden recesses of the mind," but it may be critical for reaching verbally uncommunicative and withdrawn patients.

To introduce nonverbal phenomena is, however, not necessarily to give them preference over verbal communication. Both provide clues to the patient's life and are necessary components in the therapist-patient interaction. Nor does providing a medium for nonverbal communication imply that preverbal phenomena are more important. Nevertheless, since nonverbal interactions are at the core of development and recapitulate the individual's earliest relationship to the world, which is long before the acquisition of language, and since serious disturbances are traceable to critical developmental deficits during infancy and early childhood, by communicating with the patient in the nonverbal mode, the therapist can more effectively help the patient on the level where repairs and growth can be implemented.

CHAPTER IV

Therapeutic Processes and Strategies

In the previous chapter, we discussed how the six growth-inducing processes served as a basis for CET's method and techniques. The incorporation of these principles into clinical practice has extended and refined the effectiveness of a range of standard therapeutic processes. Examination of our verbatim therapeutic protocols suggests that CET contributes to therapeutic effectiveness by reinforcing the following processes and strategies:

1. Enhancing the therapeutic alliance
2. Augmenting interpretive effectiveness and the tangible metaphor
3. Strengthening secondary-process thinking and ego integration
4. Resolving the transference
5. Promoting mastery and competence
6. Coordinating the past with the present

1. ENHANCING THE THERAPEUTIC ALLIANCE

A working alliance is central for therapeutic success. Effective therapy depends first on making contact with the patient and developing a durable therapeutic relationship. Arieti stresses:

The initial stage of treatment . . . is the most difficult and most crucial. As a matter of fact, we can say generally that unless an immediate and intense rapport is established at the beginning of the treatment, the likelihood of having a successful therapy is considerably reduced. (1978, p. 214)

(See also Frank, 1971; Greenson, 1967; Luborsky, 1976, 1984; Strupp, 1980 for further discussion of the therapeutic alliance.)

Our procedures are designed to enhance rapport and maintain a working relationship between the therapist and the patient. Working on the tasks together provides a soothing, nonthreatening relationship around which the other therapeutic processes can be maximized. In addition, by assuming a more conjoint role through the give-and-take of the task presentations, the therapist and the patient become more involved participant-collaborators. Emphasizing "we-ness" demonstrates to the patient in a concrete way the cooperative nature of the therapeutic relationship.

When the therapist acts as an "expert-authority" and "treater," he induces the patient to assume a submissive, dependent role, which can foster regression. In contrast, working on a task with the patient helps to place him in a more purposeful, adult, reciprocal relationship to the therapist, which fosters progression and adaptation. Moreover, the therapist becomes a "real" person who can serve as a stabilizing force throughout the course of therapy.

Through identification with the therapist's rationality, the patient reaches that part of himself which is rational. The patient employs this new-found rationality and clear-sightedness in the therapeutic situation to discover new ways of behaving and resolving his problems.

Here it is also important to emphasize that a productive working alliance is a two-way street and is equally helpful for the therapist. Any therapist, even a "well-analyzed" one, is not immune from the negative and destructive reactions encountered in patients during the course of regressive states. Moreover, severe negative transference reactions can become important obstacles to the therapist's alliance with a patient. However, since the tasks elicit a wider range of the patient's ego in action in the real world, the therapist is more readily able to perceive and appreciate the adaptive, positive aspects of his patient's overall behavior and develop a productive working alliance.

We do, after all, observe traits in our patients which we admire, such as charm, wit, verbal facility, forcefulness, and imaginativeness. These observations enable the therapist to appreciate characteristics in the patient's personality which indicate his personal, integrative efforts. The task situations bring to light a more balanced picture of the patient's total personality. They demonstrate the patient's competence when incompetence is often the focus. They sensitize both the therapist and the patient to the patient's resourcefulness and uniqueness and to how he can constructively use his resources in spite of the severe conflicts and contradictions in his life.

Therefore, despite being attacked by his patients for his insensitivity, forgetfulness, or greed, the therapist can more readily balance these distorted and regressive manifestations with his view of the patient's adaptive ego in action. Paradoxically, by reinforcing his reasonable object relationship with the patient, this kind of professional involvement can facilitate the therapist's objectivity. In this way, the therapist can more readily confront and resolve any countertransference problems and ensure that the working alliance takes precedence over all responses to the patient.

(1) Making Contact with the Patient

Asking for and receiving help are often difficult and painful for patients. Typically, the patient feels utterly baffled and defeated in his efforts to find a workable solution to his life problems. Filled with feelings of futility, he is tempted to give up the struggle, regress to an overtly passive and helpless position, and demand that some real or fantasy strong figure in the environment nurture and save him. At the same time, out of pathological pride and mistrust, he feels incapable of delegating such power to anyone. He therefore defends against these regressive impulses by denying them or by driving away potentially helpful persons through arrogant or rebellious provocation.

The therapist's nonthreatening, supportive but active presence enables the patient to reach out and overcome his feelings of isolation and intense despair that he will never attain solutions to the task or to the crises in his life. The therapist, however, should not be seduced by the patient's maneuvers into "taking over" and being a big, helpful, indulgent papa or mama.

The problem-solving tasks enable the patient who lacks the confidence to doubt and even to ask questions for fear that they will reveal his ineptness to develop a sense of wonder and curiosity about the world and to expand his flexibility in developing solutions. Instead of feeling overwhelmed, upset, confused, chaotic, and wanting to flee, the patient can learn how to contain these regressive feelings and develop new strategies for dealing with the unknown and the dilemmas facing him. Rather than feeling that all the forward motion has gone out of his life, he can initiate new behaviors and experience that he can make mistakes and still survive, that his last mistake may in fact be his best teacher. In addition, the purposeful, realistic, adaptive demands of the tasks can help to reverse the patient's regressive longings. He will find that the very doing of a task can be ego-building; it can enlarge his secondary-process functioning and shift the balance toward the ego-adaptive pole.

Clinical Example: Sue—Jug Problem

Sue was psychotically depressed, defiant, negativistic and withdrawn. She could not be reached through psychotherapy or pharmacotherapy. At the time of this session, Sue had been hospitalized approximately six months. This encounter enabled the therapist to make contact with her and establish a durable therapeutic alliance which made it possible for her to enter into and gain from a continuing therapeutic relationship with her therapist.

(The Jug Problem presented in this example was the third of four tasks used in the session.)
T: How can you get to drink out of the jug without spilling it out of the holes?
P: (Long pause) You can't. *(The patient sat back in her chair and folded her arms across her chest, as if withdrawing from the task.)*
T: It's a tough one. Why would I give you a puzzle if it's impossible to solve?

The therapist responds to the patient's withdrawal by empathizing with her feeling that it is a difficult task and reassuring her that it is indeed soluble.

P: If it's impossible to solve?
T: Uh-huh. *(Long pause)*

The patient attempts to plug up the holes on the sides of the jug by clasping her hands over them.

T: You're thinking of covering up the holes?
P: Yeah.
T: That's one possibility. It would be okay except that it's very difficult to cover up all the holes on all the sides, and it kind of leaks that way. Well, that was a good start. Try another possibility.

The therapist takes a more active, supportive role with this patient than with nonpsychotic ones by more freely interacting with her. He more readily provides immediate feedback concerning her attempted solution, pointing out and clarifying why her response was ineffective. He also encourages the patient's adaptive efforts and mobilizes her resources by suggesting she *"try another possibility."*

P: (Very long pause)
T: Are you thinking of some other possibility?
P: I don't see any possibility.
T: In other words, you can't get it out by plugging up the holes this way because it will leak. So there must be another way of doing it. Take a good look at the jug. Maybe there's some other way. *(Very long pause)* Are you thinking of doing something?

The therapist counteracts the patient's strong inclination to withdraw and give up by providing feedback to her actions. He helps her with her weakened deductive problem-solving processes *("There must be another way")* and reinforces sensory participation *("Take a good look")*.

P: No. I can't see any way.
T: What do you think these spigots are for here on the rim?

Allowing a severely depressed patient with low frustration tolerance to flounder in unsuccessful attempts only heightens her sense of failure and increases her tendency to withdraw. The therapist, therefore, more readily takes the initiative in providing clues early in the session by focusing on the relevant characteristics of the problem (the rim) needed for its solution.

P: I don't know.
T: What might they be?

Again, the therapist does not allow the patient to give in to her self-defeating negativism. He responds positively and, by focusing on the possible uses for the spigots, mobilizes her secondary-process thinking.

P: I don't know. Get a straw?
T: That's right. If you had a straw, you could suck it out. That's a good start because that's in the right direction except that we don't have a straw here. How could you do the same thing without a straw?

The therapist encourages the patient anew by providing immediate positive feedback for her partial solution.

P: Through the holes
T: How is that?
P: I don't know.
T: Well, maybe you got it. Through which holes?

Again, the therapist takes a positive, supportive stance.

P: These holes. *(The patient points to the holes on the side of the jug.)*
T: Well . . .
P: That still wouldn't work.
T: Yeah. Why wouldn't it work?
P: You'd still spill water.
T: Yeah. In other words, you could try sucking it out of a hole, but it would spill out of the other holes. How about the straw idea?

To facilitate the problem-solving process, the therapist assists the patient by again drawing attention to the relevant characteristics of the solution.

P: That would be perfect.
T: Uh-huh. *(Long pause)* Yeah. You've given up on it?
P: Yeah. *(After examining and handling the jug with her hands, the patient resolutely placed the jug on the table, sat back, and folded her arms across her chest.)*
T: It's tough to work on problems. If you don't get the solution, you give up.

The therapist responds to her nonverbal body language which indicated helplessness and futility. He communicates to the patient that he understands the difficulty of the challenge and that she feels overwhelmed by the problem.

P: *(Long pause)* What's the solution?
T: Well, that's what we'll try to work out together. It's a tough problem. It can't be solved easily by anybody.

The therapist is not simply supportive by acknowledging that the problem is difficult, but attempts to establish a therapeutic alliance by reinforcing "we-ness" and a helping relatedness. The therapist emphasizes his conjoint role in the therapeutic endeavor and demonstrates his desire to assist the patient in a concrete way by indicating, *"We'll try to work* [it] *out together."*

P: (Long pause) (Yawns)
T: You feel like going to sleep?
P: No, not really.
T: Well, what about these spigots. Does that remind you of anything?

The therapist again provides a clue by focusing the patient's attention on the spigots.

P: No. *(Long pause)* I don't have any ideas besides a straw.
T: Well, what do these holes look like?
P: Just holes.
T: They're holes. Where are the holes attached to? Where do they . . .
P: The brim.
T: Right. And then where does the brim go? *(Long pause)* See the brim goes around here, right?
P: Mmm-hmm.
T: And then what happens?

The therapist, serving as a more integrated alter ego, helps the patient by focusing on and delineating the step-by-step logical progression necessary for the solution.

P: It goes into the handle.
T: Mmm-hmm. And then?
P: Turns into the jug.
T: On the bottom here, right?
P: Yeah.
T: And then what happens?
P: Nothing. Oh, no, these holes don't go all the way through, do they? Is the handle hollow?
T: Well, how can you tell?
P: I don't know.
T: Well, what did you have in mind? Say it is hollow.
P: You can drink it through one of these holes. If the handle's hollow.
T: You mean like a straw?
P: Yeah.
T: You want to try it?

The therapist helps the patient learn how to test reality through adaptive action *("Try it")*.

P: (Sucking noise) Well, it . . .

T: What's happening?

P: Yeah, you can drink it through that [the spigot]. *(The patient smiles for the first time.)*

T: How did you figure it out?

The patient had correctly covered two of the spigot holes, but had fortuitously covered the hole hidden under the handle with her hand while tipping the jug. The therapist, recognizing the fragility of her ego, does not challenge her partial, accidental solution so as not to demean her very real accomplishment. Instead, he affirms the adaptiveness of her behavior by focusing on her achievement and addressing her thought processes.

P: I thought of it, but I didn't think it was made like that.

T: You mean you thought of it before?

P: Yeah.

T: But you didn't think it was made that way?

P: Uh-uh.

T: Why not?

P: I don't know. I just didn't think it was made like that.

T: So how did you figure it out? *(Pause)* At first you sucked on it and you just got air, right? So then what?

By reviewing the causal sequence used by the patient to master the problem, the therapist strengthens her sequential reasoning ability which is so essential for rational, secondary-process thinking.

P: Plugged these two up.

T: Why did you do that? *(Long pause)* Yeah? You want to try it again?

P: No.

T: Then you're satisfied that it works?

P: Yeah.

T: What does it make you think when you solved it? How do you feel?

P: Nothing.

The patient seems to have slipped backwards into her seemingly everlasting depression. Her fragile gain in ego functioning could have been threatened by her need to justify her behavior and by her fear that excessive demands could be made on her because of her success.

T: For a second there you seemed to brighten up a little bit. Like "Ah-ha! I got it." *(Long pause)* I have another puzzle for you.

The therapist attempts to counteract her regression by pointing out that she appeared to obtain genuine gratification derived from her accomplishment. In addition, by offering her another task, he indicates that he thinks she is a person capable of further success.

Summary

Having failed in so many aspects of life, including all therapeutic attempts, Sue seemed to have lost hope that she could ever be normal. She seemed to have stopped believing in herself and slipped into becoming a hard-core, chronic, resistant patient. The reason CET may have helped her to move out of her no-win impasse and to gain from therapy is that her mastery of the tasks demonstrated to her that she was capable of success and that she could do good things to take control of her life and care for herself. CET thus provided her with a healing experience which enabled her to begin to believe in herself again by introducing her to a sense of her power, self-worthiness and control.

2. AUGMENTING INTERPRETATIVE EFFECTIVENESS AND THE TANGIBLE METAPHOR

The patient's approach to the tasks and to the therapist while contending with them is an *in vivo* analogue of his approach to life. What he does, thinks and feels about a task is a tangible metaphor of what he does, thinks and feels in his natural environment. The patient's behavior and his cognitive and affective style in the sessions reflect the structure of his world. Key aspects of his problems that he may have evaded and which have escaped scrutiny are brought to the surface through the patient's analogous responses to the tasks. Warded off, deeply buried aspects of the patient's problems unfold in all their verity and can be brought into the mainstream of his mental functioning in the sessions.

The patient discovers that he relates to the task in the same way that he relates to people in his interpersonal relations. He experiences the concrete analogy between the tasks and his everyday life. He captures himself and his world in the tangible metaphor expressed through his actions on the tasks. He responds to difficulty and/or failure in the tasks with "That's the story of my life!" or "That's it exactly!" or "That says it all!"

Clinical Example: Judy—Horseshoe-and-Ring Problem

(As Judy worked on the Horseshoe-and-Ring Problem, she haphazardly moved the horseshoes around, ignoring the ring. She noted:)

P: There's not a whole lot of ways you can move these things. You can turn them. You can pass them through. I don't know if I can do anything different with this little guy [the ring].

T: As you pass it through, what do you do with the hoop [the horseshoe] or the ring?

P: Well, if I leave it in the middle, it gets turned. Maybe I need to take it out from the middle.

T: You're letting the ring flow where it may while you do the movement of the hoops of the horseshoe part.

P: Let it [the ring] fall as it may. *(Laughs)*

T: Yeah, it just goes while you move the others. Maybe you should do something with the ring and don't let it move where it bounces.

P: Sounds like an analogy to my life. *(Laughs)* Like just being impulsive and let it go as it goes and don't take steps to really look what I'm doing.

Summary

Contending with the Horseshoe-and-Ring Problem was instrumental in clarifying just what the patient's behavior was like. It crystallized the nature of her impulsive and disorganized behavior which interfered with her personal and professional life. After confronting these problems in task after task, she started to mobilize her secondary-process thinking and plan and "look what I'm doing" to help her more effectively contend with her daily problems.

In a similar vein, a patient with pervasive problems with passivity found that his passivity interfered with solving a task. After experiencing the consistency in his passive approach in task after task, he realized that this same passivity contributed to his problems in everyday life; e.g., to his two failed marriages, to conflicts in his relationship with his girlfriend, to his disturbances in sexual relations, to difficulties in working on his dissertation, to problems in teaching and relating to colleagues and the chairman of his department and, finally, to clashes with his parents.

Of course, a particular episode with a task did not change the patient. His experience with one task was but one step. However, after he saw the same problems in session after session, he began to explore the psychodynamic roots of what he "got out of" maintaining a passive life style. Cautiously, he tried a more active approach with different tasks and discovered that, not only was he capable of assuming an active role, but that it paid off in success and gratification.

After scores of experiences with different tasks, the patient became convinced that his actions had an impact on things and that a more active approach had a more favorable impact on the world. He then was gradually able to build up a new repertoire, incorporating more activity and control in his everyday behavior.

All the little insights derived from each task coalesce until a total picture gradually emerges. This coherent picture counteracts the fragmentary, conflicting and confusing view of their lives with which patients are frequently burdened. Lacking an effective focus, patients' efforts to change are undermined because without knowing more precisely what is wrong, they cannot know how and what to change. The tasks concretely and more definitively help the patient to experience what and how things go wrong.

Moreover, instead of waiting for big insights every once in a while, the patient encounters little insights in almost every session. This provides a strong motivational impact to the therapy: the patient and the therapist experience progress.

The patient's own actions in the here-and-now serve as a point of departure for understanding and changing his life. The therapist uses the tasks as a medium for interpreting what the patient is doing with his life and what his problems are. The tasks thus offer a broader base for interpretative intervention. These interventions are more comprehensible and effective because they can be concretely demonstrated in the patient's task behavior. Interpretations embedded in the patient's actions cannot as readily be evaded, intellectualized, distorted, denied or manipulated. For example, when the therapist says, "You are doing with the task (or perceive or feel or think about the task) just as you do with (or perceive or feel or think about) problems in your daily life," the patient is confronted by the reality of his life in the clinical microcosm.

Although he may try to deny and rationalize his feelings and behavior in the session, the patient cannot as readily argue with the reality as reflected by his behavior on a task. He is shown how he is the saboteur in his life by the way he sabotages his behavior on the task. The therapist's interpretations assume an air of emotional immediacy, directness, and concreteness. They can be directly and immediately checked against his actions. The insights obtained are not only cognitively represented, but "lived." They consequently take on a more personal, relevant and real quality and are less likely to pass through the mind like a mist. Because they help bridge the gap between therapy and the real world, these insights are more readily integrated into the patient's daily life and help to increase the overall effectiveness of therapy.

Clinical Example: Roy—Horse-and-Rider Problem

During his second therapy session, Roy encountered considerable difficulty with the Horse-and-Rider Problem. The therapist helped the patient to see how experimenting with and adopting an analytical problem-solving approach which was successful with the task could be applied to contending with his work. Thus, with the patient's task performance acting as a tangible metaphor of his approach to life, the therapist is provided with a broader and more effective base for analysis and interpretation.

P: I seem unable to get it [the task].
T: How does it make you feel?
P: A little bit angry at myself.
T: And you seem also depressed, like the possibility of failure has taken your energy. It's just sapped you.
P: Well, a little, yeah. *(Pause)*
T: Like you've almost given up trying.
P: Well, I have. I've run out of ideas. *(Laughs)*
T: What do you usually do when you run out of ideas?
P: Oh, I turn to something else.
T: Like what?
P: Oh, it depends, but . . . if there's another area of the problem I'm working on, turn to that. Or relax. Do something else.
T: How about trying a new approach? Experimenting?

The patient reveals that, when he reaches an impasse in attempting to solve a problem, his typical maladaptive style of dealing with it is avoiding it and assuming a passive attitude. The therapist points out an alternative approach: assuming an active, experimental attitude.

P: Well, I don't even know what else to do. I mean, this is very few pieces, and there aren't that many different arrangements I can think of.
T: But you don't actually use your hands and rearrange things.

The therapist points out that activity involves both "thinking" and physical actions.

P: No, I don't.
T: It's all in your mind.
P: That's right.

T: And your mind is limited. Because it's like your dissertation adviser who suggested specific cases.

P: Uh-huh.

T: The doing, the experimenting.

P: Yeah, it's like that a lot. That's what it feels like.

T: Well, move them around. Trying this, trying that, checking it. That's what experimentation is. Kind of playfully fooling around with it. *(Very long pause)* What are you trying now?

The therapist spells out just what "experimentation" consists of; namely, trying, checking, and assuming a playful approach.

P: Well, if these are transparent in front of the light, I could do it simultaneously. They're not transparent. Not enough. Unless I use a very strong light maybe.

T: Yeah.

P: Can I, I don't know if that's very close, can you turn that [a desk lamp] on?

T: Yes, but I don't think it's going to help that much. *(The therapist turns the desk lamp on to allow the patient to actively check the consequences of his experiment.)*

P: No. No, it doesn't.

T: What are you thinking?

P: *(Laughing)*

T: Why are you smiling?

P: *(Laughs)* It's bizarre. I mean, this seems like it should be such a simple problem. If it's got a solution. This has got to be facing that way. . . . I don't understand. This rider doesn't look like he's sitting on this horse. I mean, this doesn't look like it would be it anyway because the contour of the horse that he's sitting on doesn't fit this picture. No matter what I do with it.

T: Well, how could you make the contour fit? That's right, it doesn't superficially fit. How can you make it fit? *(Long pause)*

The therapist provides a cognitive clue by focusing on the articulation of the parts of the figures. Adoption of this analytical, perceptual attitude is necessary for the solution.

P: Oh, just trying to put them in different positions.

T: Uh-huh. *(Pause)* What's happening now?

P: Oh, for crying out loud! *(The patient discovers the solution, laughs.)* Ah-ha! Is that hysterical!

T: Yeah, what are you feeling?

The cognitive clue is successful in facilitating the solution. The therapist then addresses the emotional component of the problem-solving process.

P: Oh, I just solved the problem.
T: Uh-huh. How do you feel?
P: Well, I feel good about having solved the problem.
T: But?
P: But, I feel bad that I tried giving up.
T: Yeah?
P: (Softly) Why did I try to give up?
T: What are you thinking?
P: Well, this worries me. I mean, it does feel like what happens with
     my thesis. At least sometimes.
T: How?
P: (Sighs) Maybe just not having tried to play with it enough or some-
     thing. And something escaping me.

The patient explores the similarities between his problem-solving approach with the task and with his work on his dissertation.

T: What sort of things are going through your mind now?
P: (Pause) Well, I have an idea of what the same situation is right now
     with my work, but I don't see how to hold the pictures together
     to make it work.
T: On your thesis you mean?
P: Mmm-hmm.
T: How did you get it here? How did you do it?

By clarifying the patient's effective problem-solving process on the task, the therapist can then help the patient to apply this approach to his work.

P: How did I do it?
T: Yeah.
P: Well, I started to notice something about it, about the pictures. And
     then I asked you, I said it to you and you said, "How could you
     make it fit?" And then I started playing with it to try to make
     the curved part of the neck fit the horse. And I thought it was
     absurd because I had to hold the rider fully ninety degrees dif-

ferently than the way I was holding him before. But it worked, and then I realized both horses worked, and then I saw that symmetry, and I could put the other horse there and it would be perfect. That would be the solution.

T: So the first step towards the solution was really looking at it. The details.

The therapist stresses the adaptive role of active differentiation of the salient parts in contrast with the patient's less adaptive unanalytical, passive approach.

P: Mmm-hmm.
T: The parts.
P: The parts. Right. Looking at the parts.
T: Mmm-hmm.
P: Ah-ha!
T: Yeah?
P: So maybe that's what I have to do. At the details, huh?
T: Do you tend to look at the more general, theoretical, the grand theme?
P: Maybe, yeah. I do that. *(Pause)* I could, I guess I haven't exhausted everything that I could do [with my dissertation].
T: Yeah. How's that?
P: He's [his dissertation adviser] asked me to look at specific examples.

Summary

This example illustrated how the task served not only to illuminate the patient's maladaptive style but, in the process of finding the solution, enabled the patient to experiment and discover a more adaptive style which he could transfer to his daily life.

Clinical Example: Roy—Cowboy-and-Bull Problem

The Cowboy-and-Bull Problem is the second in the series of "Rider Problems" and demonstrates how the tasks are used sequentially to implement the therapeutic process. The Cowboy-and-Bull Problem, in drawing on analogous cognitive and affective processes, enables the therapist to follow up on and deepen exploration of important themes which were only touched on previously. For example, in the case of Roy, the Cowboy-and-Bull Problem brought into focus his central problems with activity-passivity and denial and isolation of feelings, and how they permeated his life. Most important, in the session following this sequential approach, we see how working through these problems with the task enabled him more effectively to deal with them in his daily relationships.

P: Didn't you give this to me once?
T: Does it look like it?
P: Well, I don't know, there was a similar problem. Oh, maybe it was horses. No matter how I put it, the riders are facing right and the bulls are facing left. *(Pause)* No matter how I turn those, the riders are facing the wrong way. *(Long pause)* You know what I'm doing now is playing, it's like a worn groove. I'm going through the same thing, making sure I've exhausted the very thing that I see doesn't work.

The patient perceives the new problem in the old way and inappropriately and repeatedly tries to carry over the old Horse-and-Rider solution.

T: What are you thinking of?
P: What does that remind me of? It's the feeling that I get when I do math sometimes. And where what I do is, once I learn some particular thing, it sticks in my mind very clearly and then I proceed to sort of play it out until it's exhausted. So here I have like an old idea that worked and I want it to fit this situation.

We see how the same rigid thought processes which interfere with his mastery of the task interferes with his functioning as a mathematician in his professional life.

T: Mmm-hmm.
P: And it's not fitting. I mean, the bulls aren't facing the right way. *(Pause)*
T: Yeah, so now what?
P: So now what? *(Pause)* I don't see what else to do. *(Pause)*
T: How do you feel?
P: (Pause) I feel . . . hmm. I guess I feel defeated by it.
T: What does that feel like?
P: (Pause) I just thought of, I'm going to get punished, but I don't believe I'm going to get punished for this.

The patient recalls a number of childhood events when he visited his permissive, seductive grandmother. When he stayed overnight, he slept in the same bed with her and was attracted to her large breasts. On one occasion, when he started to put his hand down the front of her nightgown, she said smilingly, "What are you doing that for?"

T: So that's why you don't take the initiative lots of times? *(Pause)*
P: I see everything as sort of mirroring this. Yeah, like if somebody says, "What are you doing," that's weird, you know. "What are you doing that for?"
T: Yeah, you're equating your grandmother with the whole world.
P: Yeah.

The patient equated "taking the initiative" and the taboo act with his grandmother with taking an active role in general. He no longer dared to do adventurous things for fear of punishment.

T: You're trying to . . . maybe you want the world to be like your grandmother, always giving all this stuff, she was overflowing, you said . . .
P: Overflowing with *nachas,* yeah.
T: Yeah. *(Pause)* And you wanted her [his girlfriend, Hannah] to be like that.
P: Well, that's the thing, once Hannah had done this, I guess I sort of was waiting for her to take an initiative and go ahead and grab my cock or something.

To avoid punishment, he has assumed a passive orientation. He waits for others to tell him what to do and to give him things.

T: That certainly provides a lot of impediment to your taking the initiative in looking for jobs, finding out where the real jobs are, even perhaps doing your dissertation.
P: Huh!
T: Maybe you're waiting for somebody to show the way for the method for your dissertation, so you're disappointed now that at the last minute, [the chairman of the department] points out what you have to do.
P: Huh!
T: Whereas all along, you have to take the initiative.
P: I don't know if it really matters, but I'm starting to look at some of the details of the pictures.

By focusing on the details of the task, the patient begins to demonstrate a more active perceptual mode.

Next Session

P: The cowboys aren't right. I don't understand it at all because no matter what, the cowboys are facing the opposite direction from the bulls.

T: Yeah, what does that mean?

P: It means that there's no way to put the cowboys on the bulls to make them come out like they're riding the bulls unless this is a lot deeper than I thought. I don't see any way of resolving either of those two problems. I mean I've almost put the cowboys in just about every possible position that they could be, or have I?

In the following interchange, we see how the patient's denial and isolation of feelings in relation to the task enabled him to become aware of how this fundamental defensive pattern plays a significant deleterious role in his daily life.

T: Yeah, what are you feeling?

P: (Pause) Well, I sort of feel like I don't want to do this problem.

T: How about the feeling, that's an idea. . . . What does it feel like that way?

P: I guess you sort of put me on the spot.

T: Yeah.

P: (Pause) As if you're going to laugh at me. It's very hard for me to describe. You know what I am doing is it's not like I'm feeling, it's like I'm trying to say, "Am I angry," no, I don't think I'm angry, am I this, am I that.

T: It's very hard for you to describe how you feel.

P: Yeah.

T: In other words, you hardly know how you feel.

P: That's what it seems like, yeah. That's what it seems like a lot, is that I hardly know what I feel. So it becomes very hard to make any decisions about things.

T: You have ideas, but they are not connected with feelings.

P: Well, yeah, that's what it's like. Yeah. I mean it's not always the case, but it's like now. Sometimes it's only way, way after that I recognize that there was feeling there. Some kind of a feeling. *(Pause)* So I feel on the spot and the only way I am going to get off the spot is by solving the problem. So, maybe I kind of am, I do feel angry. *(Pause)* I feel nervous now, the same thing when I came in.

T: And the nervousness is connected with what? *(Pause)* What's going through your mind? Does this feeling that you have, or the lack of feelings remind you or bring to mind a similar situation?

P: I don't think I've ever known, been aware, of how difficult it is for me to, I mean this distance from my feelings, so I think it reminds me of other times, like trying to decide whether to apply for a job [at the university] here, what schools to apply to, anywhere where I had to admit to myself what I really wanted, or with Hannah, anything like that. *(Pause)* I mean, partly I'm here because of that problem. I can't do that, or I haven't been able to.

T: As you look at this, what is your state? Your subjective world?

P: It's very hard. I mean, I'm frustrated, I'm impatient with it, I want it to fall together and it's not falling together. *(Pause)*

T: Are there any things, outrageous things that you would like to do with this puzzle?

Suggesting that the patient engage in *"outrageous things"* is a frequently used strategy to help patients to break out of their rigid patterns and adopt a new approach.

P: Outrageous? No, I mean my impulse at one point was I was going to fold it over. I don't know if that's outrageous, but . . .

T: Any other impulses? Folding is not allowed. But any other?

P: I guess somehow if I folded one this way and one this way, or something, they would fit, the way they are not fitting now.

T: Any other things?

P: (Long pause) Well, I mean, outrageous would be to just say this, it's not even outrageous, it's more ridiculous, but you know, find a way that the lines fit.

T: What if they are not facing in the right direction?

P: Yeah, clearly.

T: So how can you make them face the right direction?

P: This bull and this cowboy are looking this way, and this cowboy is looking that way. They're obviously the wrong orientation to each other and upside down from each other.

T: How can you . . .

P: How can I make them face the right direction?

T: What do you do if you want to go in another direction?

P: Turn them over? *(Pause)* But that's still. . . . *(Pause)* It suddenly works. It's pretty outrageous. If this is what it is, then it's pretty outrageous, because I didn't think of it at all, but they fit perfectly right now. It's got to be it.

T: What's going through your mind?

P: (Sighs) That I didn't think of it. I'm a little pissed because I don't feel like that was, somehow I feel like that, that was outside the ball park and I couldn't have possibly been expected to think of something like that. I mean, if folding it over isn't okay, that didn't seem okay either.

T: Had you thought of it before?

P: You know, I think I thought of it with the cowboys at one point, but I don't think I tried it.

T: What are you thinking?

P: Well, so you had to prompt me with the question.

T: What was the question?

P: How do you turn things around, how do you make things face the other way, something like that. So, I could certainly turn it over, that makes things face the other way.

T: I didn't ask anything great.

P: No, that's true.

T: You can't take the initiative and lead yourself to examine these new directions.

P: No, that's right. But once you told me, you didn't tell me, but you know, by asking me that . . .

T: I gave you permission.

P: You gave me permission!

T: So is that why you had to call up your parents right away, to get permission [to get married]?

P: (Pause) Boy . . . well, I mean, I didn't get it anyway, but I don't know.

T: Yeah, that's right and you're still trying, you still are looking for ways to get permission. Here, and with your parents.

P: (Pause) Sex. Huh!

T: How with sex?

P: Well, somehow I feel, I think I felt I don't have permission, something was not okay about just having it or wanting it. *(Pause)* This just kills me.

T: How does it kill you?

P: Now, it's so self-evident.

Next Session

In this session, we see how the insights derived from the previous session are translated to his daily life. He engages in a number of challenging pursuits in which he takes an active role, especially in relation to his Ph.D. dissertation. *"I have a little more balls,"* he said.

P: Now it's a funny thing. With this water skiing thing, the one thing that I noticed with that was I would never have dared, in fact, I remember one time that Veronica [his ex-wife] and I went with her brothers and friends or something and they were all flopping around trying it and I wouldn't try it. That's not long ago. I wouldn't even attempt it. I did all my flopping around the last time we went out. This time, I was up the first time and I stayed up. The feeling I had was, "Yeah, why shouldn't I be able to get on skis?" It's a very physical thing. I don't know if it's a masculine thing, that's what I was going to say, power, physical strength, agility, and a sportsman. It's not something I saw in myself, ever, and there I was, going ahead and doing it. Again, there were times when I felt like I couldn't quite sustain it, not that I fell or something like that, but even after I had done it, I had to get back up to do it again, to convince myself that I was still that person that was doing it before. While I was up, there was no question. I had a little more balls to get up and do it in the first place. That's changed. And making up this list of questions for the defense [of his dissertation], I have a little more balls.

Summary

This case illustrated the consecutive use of tasks which draw on similar cognitive and affective processes. Whereas tasks tapping divergent processes can broaden the therapeutic process by throwing light on different facets of the patient's problems, a sequential approach using tasks with analogous processes can provide continuity and deepen the exploration. It offers the therapist a potent therapeutic tool to counter the build up of the resistance and to increase the potential for working through and resolving problems.

Clinical Example: Sara—Jug Problem

The following case illustrates how interpretations of a patient's task behavior served as a critical turning point in her therapy. Sara was a twenty-two-year-old single woman who had severe problems in relating to men. She chose to have affairs with men who were the same age as her father (in one case the man, Philip, was her aunt's lover) and sado-masochistic relationships with men her own age who humiliated and treated her miserably. The roots of these conflictual involvements could be traced to an unresolved childhood relationship with her father. The emotional problems stemming from these early childhood conflicts not only affected her choice of men, but affected her thought processes and problem solving in a multitude of areas in her life, including the tasks of CET.

The tasks, therefore, served as an excellent arena to bring into focus the nature of her unresolved conflicts and how they interfered with her cognitive functioning. Most important, in the process of working on and surmounting the tasks, she began to resolve her personal conflicts and develop the cognitive operations necessary for mastery. The Jug Problem was particularly suitable for bringing to light many of these issues. The idiosyncratic way in which she interpreted the task revealed her basic problem of how her symbolic interpretation of things typically interfered with realistic appraisals and contending with them in an adaptive way.

P: *(The patient moves the jug around on the table.)* Hmm. Well, you can't tilt it. It's a straw. You put two fingers on here [the other two spigots] and suck on one of them. And the water will come up here. That's how you drink out of it.

There is no question that the patient is bright. She almost immediately grasps the possibility of using one of the spigots as a straw, and even realizes that two of the three spigots have to be closed off to allow for the siphoning action. However, she still has not discovered the hole hidden underneath the handle which also must be closed off to achieve total siphoning action.

T: How did that come to mind?
P: Because it looks so homey. I mean, it wasn't a threatening puzzle, I mean, there wasn't a piece of paper and a pencil where you had to sit down and answer the question which was typed out. This is handwriting.
T: Yeah.
P: And this is handmade, and I've worked in ceramics, and I know a little bit about glazes, and I know what kind of glaze that is. Stuff like that and, um, it felt like a friendly test.
T: Friendly because?

The therapist helps the patient to elaborate on her affective response to the task, keeping in mind that she still has not discovered the hidden hole or even tried to see if her solution works.

P: I felt reassured that there was a human at the other end of the test, someone who I could expect sympathy from, or I don't know what. When you first set it down here, I thought, oh, isn't that cute. It looks like it came out of a souvenir shop or something. Like a cutesy kind of toy that you'd buy when you went to Yosemite, for example. Gift shop kind of thing.

T: What is that now?

P: Well, it still looks like that, but I feel kind of like it doesn't matter.

T: What doesn't matter?

P: Because it's so unofficial. I feel *smug* about solving it. I think I've solved it, assuming that this thing is hollow. *(The patient moves the jug on the table.)*

T: Want to try it?

The therapist invites the patient to test reality.

P: No.

T: How do you know that you've solved it?

P: How? I don't want to. *(Laughs slightly)*

T: Why not?

P: 'Cause this is something physical. I don't know if that water is clean. I can assume it is, but we talk here. This isn't a place where you sit down and eat at, at a restaurant. This isn't, it's a different thing. And I'm not thirsty. I'm here to talk.

T: Yeah?

P: *(Pause)* So.

T: Then spit it out.

P: I'm not going to spit it out. I think that the answer is right. I'm satisfied with that.

T: Why don't you try it? It's just some water. You saw me put it in there.

P: It's too physical. It's too, I don't know, physical.

T: What do you mean by "physical?"

Because of the patient's idiosyncratic resistance to drinking the water, in this and the following response the therapist focuses on the patient's associations and the meaning that drinking has for her. He might also have inquired into the patient's feelings at the moment.

P: *(Pause)* Well, like I said, it's like sitting down and drinking.

T: What does drinking mean to you?

P: Relaxing. No inhibitions. That's what it means to me. *(The patient moves the jug around.)*

T: Do you think that would make you vulnerable?

P: Yeah. *(Moves jug)* And I'm afraid to do it, and I feel very strongly about it.

T: What will happen when you drink?

P: *(Sniffles, long pause, sighs)*

T: Yeah?

P: Well. *(Starts to sob) (Pause)* The image of Philip just flashed through my mind, that's what I'm afraid of. And this simple little thing is enough to, to bring that back. *(Sniffle, long pause)* [When Sara told her parents about the one-weekend affair she had with Philip, the whole family was thrown into an uproar in which they accused her of being a slut. Sara still suffered from tremendous guilt feelings over the incident, since she was vaguely aware that the feelings she acted out with Philip were similar to the incestuous feelings she held for her father to which she fears she could succumb.]

T: You mean, you feel so weak that you couldn't control yourself?

P: *(Sniffle)* Yes, that's true. Weak-little-me right now.

T: What does "weak-little-me" mean?

P: It means, I feel like going back to being a kid. *(Sniffle)* I feel threatened in my job, my job is where a lot of feelings of being competent and being adult and all that kind of thing come from. So I'm retreating a little bit. I know it's ridiculous, but . . .

T: What's ridiculous?

P: *(Sobs)* This thing I'm saying *(takes Kleenex from box)* is ridiculous. *(Blows nose)* Because it's not grounded in reality.

T: What isn't?

P: Those feelings I was just talking about.

T: But if a thing like this can trigger it just like that, that was a hairline trigger, that means it must be very close to the surface all the time.

P: My feelings came out as I did this.

T: Yeah. Well, I think you have to try to hold your feelings inside for a minute and solve the problem.

Although it may be tempting to pursue the content and etiology of the patient's incestuous feelings, the therapist temporarily holds this aside and focuses on her primary problem of control. He helps her to contain her primary-process thinking so that she can mobilize and use her rational secondary process to solve problems.

P: Okay. What, this puzzle?

T: Yeah.

P: It's solved. *(Sniffle)*

T: You'll never know. I think it's only in your mind that it's solved.

P: I know that's the way it works.

The patient is centered in her world of feelings and fantasies and does not test her inner mental events against the concrete world of reality.

T: I'll tell you, it *isn't* the way.

The therapist confronts the patient with reality to counter her private inner world.

P: It isn't?

T: No.

P: (Long pause) Well, then, one of the other holes must be the right one.

T: But you'll never know. I'm not going to tell you how to solve it.

P: Well, you usually don't tell me if it's wrong either.

T: Well, you didn't want to try it.

P: That's true. I still think the handle is a tube. *(Long pause)* I don't want to do it. *(The patient picks the jug up and looks at the bottom.)*

T: What are you looking for?

P: I wanted to see if there's a name on there.

T: What do you see?

P: Baron Barnstable, 198.

T: So what does that mean, do you think?

P: It's handmade

T: Yeah. What are you thinking?

P: I'm just arguing with myself about doing this. I don't want to do it.

T: What is the argument like?

P: It's like, just go ahead and do it, and then, well, no, it's too gross. Well, you know, one of these other ways must be it, you know that from the way clay is worked. And this part looks like one of those little handrolled tubes that you can do. I'm trying to think of another way to do it. I feel angry. I don't want to do it.

T: You're not willing to experiment with this, to find out what the solution is.

"Do it" provokes highly charged, angry feelings which prevent her from taking adaptive action. The therapist might have inquired into the idiosyncratic meanings of *"do it"* and *"too gross."*

P: That's right, I'm not. I'm angry.

T: Yeah, well, sometimes you have to contain your anger to reach some kind of creative solution to something.

Ultimately, the therapist could explore what makes the patient so angry, but now he focuses on how her anger is interfering with adaptive behavior. Again, by helping the patient to develop the ego controls to contain her anger and limit the intrusion of her irrational primary-process thinking into her cognitive processses, she is enabled to activate her secondary-process thinking to deal effectively with the task confronting her and her problems in general.

P: Yes, but this isn't the central issue, this isn't the important thing.

T: Who knows what's important? It's important right here and now. I'm not talking about big philosophical issues. Right here and now, solve this.

P: I guess I'd rather get mad *(moves jug on table)*.

T: Yeah, why is that?

P: 'Cause I want to blame somebody.

T: That's what I meant, that you have to contain your anger sometimes and move on, 'cause you could blame your parents for the rest of your life.

Because the patient is not in control of her primary-process thinking and her life in general, she "blames" people and does not take responsibility for her perceptions and actions. Helping the patient to gain control over herself goes hand-in-hand with assuming responsibility for her life and enables her to more effectively deal with her problems.

P: Yeah.

T: And you'll never move on. That's what you've been doing.

P: Blaming my parents?

T: Yes.

P: No, I'm blaming myself these days. *(Sniffle)*

T: Yeah?

P: *(Moves jug around on table.)* It's just too crude.

T: What?

P: I think that's what the main preventing thing is.

T: What's so crude about it? What's the crude part?

P: The crude part is touching my lips to this thing. It's like, some kind of a symbolic thing, and it bugs me. *(Sniffle)*

T: What is it symbolic of?

P: It's some kind of sexual thing. *(Sniffle)*
T: Like what?
P: Like oral sex. *(Sniffle)*
T: Well, that's in your mind.

This is the turning point in the session and critical in the whole therapeutic endeavor. The therapist tries to separate her inner world of symbolism from the outer world of reality. Only when the patient can keep her sexual symbolism and primary-process fantasy world from encroaching on her secondary-process problem-solving behavior will she be able to deal realistically and adaptively with problems and master them.

P: It sure is, and it's quite vivid, and it's strong.
T: The thing is, if you always think of symbolic things, then you're really tied because everything can have a symbolic thing. This is a jug with holes in the side and holes in the rim. It's *not* a penis!

In the most emphatic terms, the therapist confronts the patient with reality by distinguishing her distorting symbolism from the concrete realities of the jug.

P: Well, symbolically . . .
T: It is not symbolic. Symbolically is one thing. You've got to hold aside your symbolic ideas because it's still a jug. It's a jug with water in it. It has no symbolism at all. It is what it is. You have to hold aside all the symbolism, because if you think of the symbolism of everything, then everything can totally stop you in your tracks.

The therapist points out that containment and control of her primary-process symbolism is necessary for adaptive behavior.

P: That's the thing, that symbolism is really here.
T: Well, then if the symbolism is so strong, it's no wonder you can't move in life, because every time you see the symbolic significance of something, you say, "Oh, my God" and you're tied up.
P: That's right.
T: Then I think a big part of your problem is just to try to differentiate between the symbolism which is in your mind . . .
P: Uh-huh.
T: . . . and the concrete reality which is not in your mind, which is something you have to deal with.

P: Maybe I try to deal with things symbolically. Like all this defensiveness and stuff. This symbolism, that of Philip and my father. The age similarities and everything.

T: Symbolically doesn't help you contend with the realities of everyday life. It only interferes.

P: Well, I see it interfering here.

The patient takes a crucial step. She sees how her symbolism interferes with her adaptiveness in the sessions. The therapist can then bridge the gap between therapy and daily life by pointing out how this same process interferes with her problem solving in life.

T: It does in your life also. That's something that would be helpful for you to see.

Next Session

(The first few minutes of the session have been deleted.)

T: Let's work more on this jug.

P: Does it have water in it?

T: Mmm-hmm.

P: Stupid thing.

T: Stupid thing?

P: Yeah. I'm just really frustrated by it. *(The patient sucks on one of the spigots and obtains only a whistling sound.)* Must be another hole to plug up here. It's just air. Why is it just air? There must be another hole in here somewhere. *(The patient holds the jug up and explores it from all angles. She discovers the hole on the underside of the handle.)* Ah-ha! All right! *(She drinks from the spigot and smiles.)*

The insights obtained from the previous session are put into action and pay off. The patient contains her primary-process symbolism and activates her secondary-process thinking, which enables her to explore, experiment, obtain feedback from the consequences of her actions and solve the problem.

T: Yeah.

P: Okay, well, I've solved it. And I'm all wet, too. *(Laughs slightly)*

T: Why were you willing to do it today?

P: Because I decided I would. Since the last session.

By controlling her irrational, primary-process thinking, she gained the freedom and capacity to make decisions and to institute the necessary rational, secondary-process thinking to master the task.

T: Why did you decide that you would?

P: Because it seemed stupid, my reasons for not doing it last time.

T: Well, what was stupid about it?

P: It was very dumb, it wasn't reality, it wasn't rational. *(Pause)* I can't do that kind of thing and, you know, keep going.

T: How did you think about it?

P: How did I think about it? I thought, boy, are you acting dumb, with this stupid jug. Why are you letting your symbolism bother you? And I said, well, just do it and figure out if that's right. And don't worry about your symbolism. So, that was right.

Summary

Sara's central problems were clearly reflected in her approach to the jug. Thinking symbolically and in a drive-related way when the problem called for concrete and reality-relevant responses severely interfered with her problem solving. Dominated by primary-process thinking, she responded to the affective, symbolic significance of the spigot, which triggered idiosyncratic associations; i.e., spigot-penis-Philip-father-incestuous feelings-guilt-anger. (In subsequent sessions, she also related those feelings to her feelings toward the therapist.) These preoccupations interfered with her cognitive processes and distorted her perceptions. She was blocked from exploring relevant aspects of the jug which were essential for solution of the problem. The goal of these sessions was, therefore, to enable her to overcome her symbolism, distortion, denial, passivity and other facets of irrational, regressive behavior.

The jug thus served as a medium for reality testing and insight. The therapist used her behavior on the task to demonstrate how her symbolism blocked adaptive behavior. These reparative interactions with the therapist and the jug helped her to disengage her irrational primary processes, gain control over her symbolism and regressive and disruptive feelings derived from unresolved childhood events with her father and flexibly shift to the rational secondary process. She then was able to use her enhanced objectivity and cognitive differentiating capacity to control her symbolism and apprehend the concrete reality of the spigot. She could then perceive and react to the spigot as a spigot, not as a penis.

Shifting the balance from the primary-process to the secondary-process, adaptive pole was so central in Sara's life that this session was crucial in her whole therapy and, indeed, vital in her whole life's adaptation. When the same issues emerged repeatedly in subsequent sessions, the therapist referred back to the insights gained in the Jug sessions as a reference point to help her to separate her fantasies from reality. For example, when Sara commented anxiously that a new couch in the therapist's office could be used to seduce her, the therapist said, "Remember the Jug Problem? The same thing is happening. A couch is a couch. You have to realize that it is your fantasy that is intruding here. You have to keep them separate. Otherwise, you will have difficulty in acting realistically to things."

As a result of these insights, Sara gradually was able to contain her regressive, distorted, fantasy reactions from encroaching upon a multitude of areas in her daily life. She began to develop a more rational, de-aggressified, de-sexualized relationship to life and emerged from her fantasy world.

Starting from small, relatively insignificant areas of her life, Sara began to enlarge the sphere of her autonomous conflict-free functioning and to contend with her problems in a more effective way. Very gradually she also began to establish more gratifying, intimate relationships with both men and women.

3. STRENGTHENING SECONDARY-PROCESS THINKING AND EGO INTEGRATION

One of the obstacles impeding progress in life and in therapy derives from insufficient modulation of anger, distortion and other surges in irrational, primary-process, regressive behavior. Without being able to call forth the ego resources required to balance and control these regressive forces, a patient may be impelled to act out destructive actions which can obstruct therapy and destroy his life. To benefit from therapy, the patient needs to mobilize his ego resources to filter out and contain his primitive, impulse-ridden behavior.

CET provides a growth-inducing psychological framework for activating the patient's ego resources. Since the tasks are stable here-and-now reference points in the real world, the patient is given a concrete means of testing reality. For example, when the patient acts out his regressive mechanisms in relation to the tasks, he is made aware of his distortions, projections, denials, etc. He can see how his irrational primary-process functioning blocks mastery and interferes with achieving successful adaptive solutions. Deny and rationalize as much as he will with the therapist's interpretations, the patient cannot argue with reality. The tasks provide objective standards from which he can obtain corrective feedback from the consequences of his actions.

The tasks demand that the patient respond in a nonregressive manner. Engaging in the tasks is an ego-building and ego-integrative process which requires the patient to be analytical, logical, and organized. By strengthening and stabilizing his synthetic ego functioning and cognitive controls, the patient is not as readily overwhelmed by his unmitigated anger, distortions and regressive feelings.

Step by step the patient is led away from his autistic primary-process functioning and shifts to neutralized secondary-process thinking and improved contact with reality. Increased ego integration keeps disruptive conflict and affect from encroaching on adaptive functioning and provides the objectivity and clear-sightedness necessary for assimilating the therapist's interpretations. By restoring and improving secondary-process thinking and enlarging the sphere of his autonomous, conflict-free functioning, the patient can repair developmental arrests and begin to establish sublimated, aim-inhibited relationships in his daily life.

Clinical Example: Roy—Horse-and-Rider Problem

In the following excerpt, we see how the very doing of the task had a calming influence on the patient and helped him to contain his primary-process thinking. Although Roy was *"overwhelmed by everything,"* he was *"glad to have something* [the task] *to focus on. . . . That felt good."*

T: What did you think of this [Horse-and-Rider] puzzle?
P: You know, what I thought was I was glad to have something to focus on.
T: Yeah. Why is that?
P: Because I feel like, in a way, that's what I do when I study. I close off my problems and just think about what I'm doing. I put all my attention into that and try not to think about other stuff. It's necessary. I feel like there's so many things happening and I'm a bit overwhelmed by everything. And this [the task] is also a way of just kind of narrowing down my focus. It definitely had that calming influence. It was like now I can pay attention just to this and put everything else aside. That felt good.

Clinical Example: Anna—T-Problem

In the following excerpt, we see how a task serves to activate ego-adaptive processes. The task enables Anna to rise above herself by "energizing" and stretching her awareness. By engaging in the goal-directed actions required by the task, *"You wake up. You feel stronger."* By doing *"something playful . . . something visual . . . making something . . . improving something . . . accomplishing something . . . I felt really good, I felt really peaceful."*

(Following the solution to the T-Problem, the patient asked the therapist:)
P: Do you have any more puzzles? I don't seem to do very well anymore without puzzles.

This is a fairly typical response. Patients are highly motivated to engage in the tasks because they catalyze them to think and talk about important issues, and to behave in productive ways.

T: What do you mean?
P: I don't know. There were times when I would kind of ramble on about things and then ten minutes before the end of the sessions, you'd whip out a puzzle and then I would start talking and then the last few times, you've been giving them to me sooner. *(Pause)*
T: Has it been helpful that way?
P: Well, it's gotten me started talking sooner.
T: How does it get you started talking?
P: Well, it gives me things to talk about.
T: Like what?
P: I mean, usually negative, like what I'm doing that I don't like, or what I'm doing wrong, or what I'm doing that I do all the time to screw up my life.
T: Why negative things?
P: Well, that's usually what comes out.
T: Why do you think that comes out?
P: I don't know. Sometimes it seems like I'm all negative. I'm in a really lousy mood, in case you hadn't noticed.
T: Yeah, what's up?
P: I don't know, I'm tired. I feel like I'm coming down with something. My throat hurts, head hurts. But also I've been sort of stewing about a conversation I had with Nat [her boyfriend] last night. About cars, about the car. *(The patient rambles on and relates the conversation.)*
T: Maybe there is something that you need, a puzzle or problem. Just to help you think. *(Pause)*
P: Maybe I need something to do.

T: Yeah? How does it help, do you think? *(Pause)*

P: I don't know. Sometimes when I'm home I sort of energize myself by doing things.

T: Like what?

P: Working in the garden, hanging pictures. I don't know. Sunday night, I guess it was, I was really tired and I hung this, I have this kite with a twenty-foot train, and I hung the kite up on the wall and stuff, and I was wide awake. It was midnight and I was wide awake.

T: Energize?

P: Uh-huh.

T: How is that? *(Pause)*

P: Getting involved in something.

T: Mmm-hmm. So you have difficulty getting involved in things and then you feel kind of lazy and weak and lackadaisical, but you get involved, you wake up. You feel stronger.

P: And lots of times it's if I get involved in, I don't know if it's something physical, I think it's when I was working in the garden a lot, I thought it was going out and doing something physical. But, I think it's doing something visual. *(Pause)* Making something that I want to look at. When I went out in the garden, and I was through, I had improved something. And when I was hanging the kite, I had improved something. And that wasn't particularly physical. So if I can make something better, then I feel better. *(Pause)*

T: You mean like solving a problem is making something better?

P: I guess. Yeah. And I feel like I've accomplished something. *(Pause)* That's what I always felt when I came back in from the garden. I always felt, I felt really good, I felt really peaceful, like I had accomplished something. And it wakes me up.

T: Like what?

P: I wish I could find something to do every day that would make me feel like I accomplished something. *(Pause)* 'Cause my job always feels like I got something out of the way.

T: I wonder why you never brought up this idea that the puzzles may help you because they would energize you. You accomplish something if you solve it. Because the puzzles, as we said last session, always play a very distant role in here, in therapy. They're always in the background.

P: I didn't say they play a distant role. I just didn't talk about them that much when they weren't around. *(Pause)*

T: Even when they're around, you always said you didn't feel much about them. *(Pause)*

P: It's sort of like feeling something about your fork. It gets the food into your mouth, but it's not exactly something you spend much time staring at.

T: Well, is it like food then, these puzzles? It's giving you something? *(Long pause)*

P: No, it's like a fork.

T: Yeah? And what's the food then?

P: I'm the food. *(Pause)*

T: The puzzle is the fork and whom do you give the food to?

P: Part of me is the food and the other part gets the food. The part of me that I don't understand and recognize, that's the food. *(Long pause)* The food's not coming from the puzzle, the puzzle is taking it, pushing it around.

T: Where do I fit in that?

P: I don't know. The fork-maker? The table-setter?

T: Yeah. *(Pause)*

P: The mother. *(Long pause)*

T: Yeah? The mother who arranges things? The food?

P: Well, sets the table. Teaches you how to eat when you're little. Teaches you how to eat with a fork, I guess. *(Pause)* I guess that's why it's a fork and not a spoon.

T: Why is that?

P: Well, a spoon, when you're little, you get shoved in your mouth. But a fork, you get put in your hand and you have to figure out how to stick it in your mouth yourself. *(Long pause)* So, I guess I'm not an infant, I guess that makes me a two-year-old. *(Pause)*

T: What happens after two years old? What then? After a fork?

P: Well, I don't know if the analogy holds. You keep eating with forks. But you put them out yourself.

T: What happens if you put them out yourself? *(Pause)* You feed yourself?

P: Yeah. *(Pause)*

T: And what else do you feed yourself?

P: You choose what you're going to eat.

T: So then you don't need therapy? *(Long pause)*

P: I guess.

T: Yeah? *(Pause)*

P: I don't know, it depends on how much is there. Of my present food. I mean, I don't know if it's a can of baby food that I've got to eat and then it's over, or if it's a lifetime supply that I just have to figure out how to deal with. I haven't figured that out yet.

T: What does it seem like? *(Pause)*

P: It seems like, you ever look in the Putah Creek?

T: Yeah.

P: Looks like it's a hundred feet deep, and it's not. It's one foot deep, 'cause it's so murky. That's sort of what it's like. Could be anything 'cause it's just such a gloppy mess.

T: Yeah. *(Pause)*

P: So, I guess I won't know until I get some more out and see what's left.

T: Mmm-hmm. Until it clears up? *(Long pause)*

P: Yeah. That's true, it could clear up, couldn't it? *(Sniffle) (Pause)* And if it clears up, then I won't need therapy. It doesn't matter how deep it is if it's cleared up. Then I wouldn't need you. It's only 'cause it's all muddy.

Summary

We see how the task played a prominent ego-building role by mobilizing vital components of secondary-process thinking: awareness, control and decision making. For example, the patient experiences the task as an instrument which helps her to gain awareness and see clearly into the murky parts of her mind. Using the symbolic analogy of eating, with the task serving as a "fork," the task enables the patient to gain control and provides her with the ability to make choices. *"You figure out how to use them [the task]. You choose what you're going to eat."*

Clinical Example: Hal—Tangrams*

CET, with its emphasis on ego building, is particularly suitable for addressing states of regression which occur in varying degrees in all patients. In more serious pathology where there is an extreme shift from secondary-process thinking toward the primary-process, autistic pole, CET plays an especially vital role in the reintegration process.

In the following example, we will describe in detail the acute schizophrenic episode experienced by Hal (see p. 185–187). During his hospitalization, the therapist used Tangrams as an integral part of his treatment to help Hal to mobilize his ego-adaptive processes and make a speedy recovery.

Hal is a thirty-two-year-old married man who was the second of

---

*Portions of this section appeared in Weiner (1985) as part of a study on the treatment of schizophrenic episodes.

three sons from an upper-middle-class professional family. His father and brothers were physicians. The patient's first marriage had ended in divorce after a year and his present five-year marriage was full of bickering and conflict.

On two prior occasions, Hal had been hospitalized in psychiatric units of general hospitals for four to five months each time, the first occurring during late adolescence. A crippling illness of his mother precipitated his first hospitalization; divorce from his first wife the second. He had been treated with Thorazine, Mellaril, Stelazine, Navane, and Haldol, as well as with an orthomolecular approach. He also had been placed on a hypoglycemic diet, all with little positive results.

As noted in his case report, Hal had dropped out of his first year of medical school because of an acute exacerbation of schizophrenic symptoms during which he started to hallucinate, became delusional and suffered from a fragmentation in his thought processes.

Shortly after the patient started his current treatment, his wife also entered psychotherapy. As she improved, she was less and less willing to put up with the patient's unstable emotional states, his constant difficulties at work, and his lack of desire to start a family. Finally, after six months of therapy, she told the patient that she wanted a divorce and asked him to move out. Soon thereafter and unbeknownst to his wife, he cut his tongue in six places with a razor blade. Additionally, he took his wife's darning needle and perforated his penis in several places. Several hours later, the patient kept his regular twice-a-week appointment with the therapist. When questioned about the blood trickling from the corners of his mouth, he recounted his acts of self-mutilation and revealed his intense desire for "anatomical suicide." He also related vivid visual hallucinations involving rats defecating on his food, after which he stopped eating. He also expressed paranoid ideation, thoughts of telekinesis, and feelings that he could send and receive mental messages.

The therapist arranged for immediate, voluntary hospitalization in the psychiatric unit of a nearby general hospital. The patient's wife accompanied him to the hospital. On admission, since all patients routinely required neuroleptics as part of their hospitalization, the patient was given 4 mg. Haldol. The attending psychiatrist noted that since he knew that cognitive functioning was an integral part of the therapist's treatment, he would minimize cognitive side effects by prescribing a minimal dose.

When the therapist saw the patient in his private room on the first day of hospitalization, he was lying in bed, curled up in a fetal position, wearing only his shorts. The patient had entered a severely regressed state and was profoundly depressed and withdrawn. He looked utterly defeated and crushed. After pulling a chair up to his bedside, the therapist, saddened by the patient's condition, simply asked how he felt, whether he had eaten breakfast, and how he was being treated. Although he had carried on an articulate, intelligent, albeit paranoid, delusional conversation in the therapist's office the previous day, now in the hospital the patient talked in a slurred, vague and disconnected manner. Out of the morass of incoherence, the patient suddenly asked, "Dr. Weiner, do you have one of your puzzles with you?" The therapist inquired, "Why do you want a puzzle?" The patient replied, "Because it puts me in touch with that part of my mind which is rational."

The therapist had prepared for these sessions by selecting relatively simple tasks which focus on reality testing and perceptual organization (see Tangrams, p. 218, and the Embedded Figures Test, Witkin et al., 1954). The therapist drew the over-bed table to the bedside and started with one of the easier Tangrams, the skating figure. To emphasize the concrete perceptual aspects of the task, the seven geometrical pieces were made from bright red cardboard. The therapist laid the figure and the pieces on the table and said, "Yes, I do have something with me. Take a look at these, Hal."

The therapist first slowly named the geometrical shapes for each of the pieces and then asked the patient to name them and point them out. In this manner, the therapist related to the patient on a concrete perceptual level that was congruent with his regressed state. The therapist described the task to the patient, who slowly and gingerly leaned over and with one finger moved a triangle. After several seconds, however, he lapsed back into his fetal position and spoke of his wife and his sense of isolation and loneliness. With great effort, the patient then gradually raised himself on one arm and manipulated some of the other pieces with his finger. After twenty or thirty seconds, he fell back onto the bed and stared at the ceiling.

The patient worked for a minute or two on the task, then withdrew into fantasy and hallucinations, returned to the task, then talked about his wife, shifted to the task again, and then spoke of his feelings regarding hospitalization. As this alternating, point-counterpoint pattern continued, the patient eventually was able to prop himself up on one arm and, within the first half-hour, was able to sit with his legs over the edge of the bed.

The task, serving as a here-and-now reference point in the real world, gave the patient a concrete means of testing reality. Moreover, it required him to respond in a non-regressive manner. It called for cognitive organization and control, secondary-process thinking and synthetic ego functioning. Contending with the task was an ego-building process which served as a stabilizing anchoring point around which the patient could enlarge his sphere of autonomous, conflict-free functioning and be drawn back to reality.

The patient gradually began to dress himself, integrating this into the pattern: first one sock, then back to the task for a couple of minutes, then several more minutes of talking about his feelings, then the other sock. After about three-quarters of an hour, he was fully dressed and had almost completed the task. Intermittently he would get up and aimlessly walk about the room, then come back to the table and work on the task, then stand up and talk or lie on the bed and remain silent. After an hour, he walked to the mirror and combed his hair. He asked if he could open the windowblinds. After an hour and a quarter, he had successfully completed the task and talked with the therapist more coherently and forcefully. He still lapsed into fantasy and was distracted by his hallucinations, which the therapist asked him to draw.

Finally, after one-and-a-half hours, he said, "You know, maybe I'm ready to go out to talk to some of the other people out there. They might be nice to talk to." The therapist made another appointment to see him and walked the patient to the door. As he opened the door, the patient said he might eat something and walked into the common room on the ward.

The therapist saw the patient the following day and then every other day throughout the period of hospitalization. The same alternating pattern of working on another task and talking about present concerns, past experiences and feelings occurred. Although the patient continued to experience visual hallucinations, they were not as intrusive. After a week of hospitalization, the patient began to make plans about what he would do on the outside. Although he could not even think of divorce, he began to accept the inevitability of separation from his wife. With the help of his wife, he made plans to move to an apartment directly after being discharged from the hospital, which occurred on the eighth day of hospitalization.

Three days following discharge, the patient obtained a job managing an all-night grocery store. Although the patient had been maintained on 4 mg. per day Haldol while in the hospital, his psychiatrist placed him on Mellaril for two weeks following discharge. After discharge, the patient resumed his regular twice-a-week sessions with the therapist. During the following six months, hallucinations and paranoid ideation gradually subsided and finally disappeared. At this time, the patient and his wife were divorced. Although the patient suffered severe anxiety during the divorce proceedings, he maintained an amicable relationship with his wife. While working through the emotional loss, he began to date other women.

At termination of treatment at one year post-hospitalization, the schizophrenic process had stabilized. Although many of his characterological problems and disordered relationships still remained, he was free of hallucinations and suicidal ideation. He manifested increased competence in daily living skills, improved his relationship with his boss, and continued to work steadily. He also made important progress in developing a psychosocial support network.

Clinical Example: Hal—Tangrams

Further insight into how a task functions as an ego-building agent is derived from the following excerpt from Hal's therapy. After discharge from the hospital, Hal resumed outpatient CET with the therapist and was given another tangram to master. In discussing what he thought about the task, Hal clarifies how it strengthened his secondary-process thinking and ego integration.

T: Have you done this one? [Another tangram]

P: Not that I recall. But it is a problem to solve certainly. It's always beneficial to solve problems.

T: Why is that?

P: Because it puts your mind in a problem-solving framework. Which means that you reinforce problem solving. . . . The methods that you have activate, you know, my own internal problem-solving machinery. And internal resources. . . . I mean this is basically the model of reality, it *is* reality, it's no different really. *(Pause)* It's sort of what you do anyway. But it's a strengthening, it's a reinforcing process.

T: A model of reality?

P: Well, that's how I see what you do, in a way. That your therapy itself is a model of reality. In other words, in going through reality, physical reality certainly, you get confronted with decision making and problems that you have to deal with from moment to moment. And setting forth problems here is essentially modeling what you do anyway.

T: Which are the kinds of problems that are most helpful?

P: At different times, different types of problems are more helpful.

T: What do you think would be the most helpful at this time in your life, where you're having a problem with reality?

P: *(Sighs heavily)* I don't know whether, maybe manual problems are something I need to work on. Really, all of them, but in terms of physical reality, you're often manipulating and organizing objects, for example, in terms of my job.

Although the patient's reactions may sound like he is parroting the therapist's views, it is actually the other way around, or more precisely, since this patient was extremely insightful in articulating the therapeutic process, analysis of this raw clinical data was instrumental in the derivation of the theoretical concepts.

4. RESOLVING THE TRANSFERENCE

Transference is the most extraordinary of therapeutic phenomena, for in the transference the therapist need not hypothesize about the deepest layers of the patient's dynamics or reconstruct his early experiences and conflicts. As the transference relationship develops, all the components of the patient's unresolved childhood problems unfold and come into clear view as they are expressed in his behavior with the therapist. The transference is, in essence, a here-and-now experiential procedure which depends on the activation of the patient's unconscious past as it is mirrored in his present experiences with the therapist.

In a strikingly parallel way, the patient's cognitive and affective past is also activated and mirrored in his present experiences in contending with the tasks. Not only are dynamically unconscious meanings of interpersonal relationships reenacted in behavior toward the therapist, but the tasks provide the patient with a more definite field in which the unconscious can assert itself. As a consequence, the strength and effectiveness of the transference paradigm are enhanced.

Freud points out:

> We soon perceive that the transference is itself only a piece of repetition, and that the repetition is a transference of the forgotten past, not only onto the doctor, but also onto all the other aspects of the current situation. We . . . find . . . the compulsion to repeat, which now replaces the compulsion to remember, not only in his personal attitude to his doctor but also *in every other activity* and relationship which may occupy his life at the time. . . . We render the compulsion harmless, and indeed useful, by giving it the right to assert itself in a *definite field*. (1914, pp. 151 ff.; italics added)

CET is especially conducive to such repetitions, given the tasks which provide the patient with a broader and more definite field in which repetitions can assert themselves. Whereas the therapist may try to maintain an impersonality, implacability and opaqueness to capture uncontaminated transference reactions, the tasks have an actuality and neutrality of their own which highlights, in bold relief, the patient's transference of various infantile memories, wishes and perceptions. With certain more disturbed patients for whom the transference is based on delusional premises, simply interpreting is futile. Such unconscious schemes are inaccessible or resistant to rational examination or explanation of distorted beliefs and assumptions. It is precisely because the tasks have an objective reality of their own that confrontation and mastery of distortion can be engendered. (See, for example, the case of Hal with the Ping-Pong Problem, pp. 57–61.)

Within this broadened and objectified transferential field, the experiential-developmental laboratory contributes significantly to the resolution of the transference. It reconciles and balances two complementary bipolarities necessary for the development and analysis of the transference: it enables the patient to "regress in the service of the ego" while at the same time helping him to build the ego strength and ego integration to surmount the regression.

First, the patient needs to develop the ego strength to cope with the anxiety of the regression. In contending with the tasks, the patient strengthens his contact with reality so that he can then temporarily loosen controls and ease reality testing. He is enabled to "regress in the service of the ego" because he has developed the ego resources which provide him with the strength and resiliency to rebound and pull himself out of his regressive state. The patient is thus able to overcome his fear of sinking into the more regressive, primary process of the transference. He can dare to experience some transient aspect of the transference in regard to the therapist. Once the patient has safely experienced and "survived" this guilt- and anxiety-producing regression in regard to one area of the transference, he can risk future regressions, first in that same area, and then in new areas of the transference. The possibilities for leading the patient into the deeper layers of the transference are enlarged.

Second, the experiential-developmental laboratory also helps the patient to develop the essential secondary-process ego functioning and the cognitive integration and controls critical for resolving the transference. Even while being in the throes of a regressive transference reaction, an increase in the patient's ego resources provides him with the capacity to filter out his irrational primary process and hold in abeyance his regressive and disruptive feelings. The patient is enabled to shift flexibly from the primary process of the experiencing ego to the rational, secondary process of the observing ego. He can use his cognitive differentiating capacity to separate that part of his relationship to the therapist which is relatively non-neurotic and rational from his regressive, fantasy transference. He has developed the ego strength, clear-sightedness and objectivity necessary to test and overcome his distortions, assimilate interpretations and make adaptive accommodations to reality.

Clinical Example: Bob—Ping-Pong Problem

The case of Bob with the Ping-Pong Problem illustrates how the interaction of the patient with the therapist in dealing with the task acts as a springboard for exploring the transference. The patient's actions with the task and the therapist provide a tangible medium for bringing to life and reexperiencing the patient's unresolved childhood patterns where they may be more clearly seen and mastered.

(The patient has been working on the task for fifteen minutes.)
P: Do you have some water?
T: What were you thinking of?

Since the solution requires the patient to discover and effectively use water and not just to obtain the *idea* of floating the ball, the therapist does not answer the patient's question or provide the water, but asks him what he has in mind. In contrast, with more severely disturbed, borderline, psychotic or child and adolescent patients, a different approach would be more appropriate. The therapist would play a more active role as participant and ally in the therapeutic endeavor by more directly assisting the patient with the task and, without actually doing the task for him, providing more emotional support, clues and resources.

P: Well, I could pour water in here and it would float to the top.
T: Yeah.

Because the patient said "could" pour, and not "will" pour, the therapist's "Yeah" was noncommittal, and did not imply that he agrees or disagrees with this particular solution. As we will see below, this neutral stance is important because having the correct idea for the solution is one thing, while how the patient translates it into adaptive action is yet another and most revealing matter.

P: Do you have some water?
T: Well . . .

The therapist might have tried to find out why the patient needed to enlist the therapist's direct intervention in solving the problem. Is it because he wants to get the therapist to do something for him to gratify his passive needs, or is his question an overture to get closer to the therapist?

P: I could. You said, "Anything in the room."
T: Mmm-hmm. What are you looking for?
P: Well, do you have a jug with you or something? I might as well look.

Although the patient still wants the therapist to provide a jug with water, the patient finally, if grudgingly *("might as well"),* recognizes his need to take an active stance and seek out the materials necessary to master the task.

T: Mmm-hmm.
P: Is there any water in there [pointing to a vase]? I don't think I
      should put that [the water from the vase] in there [the cylinder].

The patient needed only to have looked into the vase to answer his own question.

T: Why not?
P: It looks like it's used for that dead flower. *(Laughs)*
T: Yeah.
P: It might get your tube dirty. I think that would work though, I
      mean, I'm going to have to try that. *(Coughs)*
T: Well, what's your reluctance in using it?
P: My reluctance?
T: Uh-huh.
P; I don't even know if that's yours. Maybe someone else's.
T: Yeah.
P: I guess my reluctance is it looks like it's been sitting there a long
      time. Probably just get the tube dirty.
T: Yeah.
P: And also, I know that it would work. I mean, I know that if I poured
      it in there. The other reluctance is that it might leak out the
      bottom and spill out all over the place.
T: Yeah.

P: But it's just sort of common sense that that would work. *(Pause)*

T: What are you thinking?

P: Well *(sighs)*, I figure that way would work. There must be, maybe there's another way too. Start thinking about a third way. . . . Let's see, water, air.

T: What about, that you needed permission to do these experiments?

P: Hmm.

T: Remember, you asked me.

P: Yeah. *(Laughs)* Well, it was just that I imagine you saying. . . . *(Long pause)* I don't know. I guess I imagine you saying, "Oh, no, don't do that, that'll work, but you don't need to do that."

T: Yes, but you said, "Is there any water in the room?" Well, if it's your problem, why should I, you know, help you along, give you assistance? Or hints? Like you almost needed permission from me to get up and to actually see if there was a jug around, to see if there's water around.

P: (Pause) Well, I don't know. That's, I guess, if you took that to it's logical conclusion, I could just, for example, go through all the drawers in there.

T: Yeah. Anything in the room without tearing it apart. It's similar to last week when you came in to use the phone. You asked me how to dial, how to make a collect call.

T: Mmm-hmm.

T: What do you think of that?

P: Well, there's a reason I did that. I was late and I didn't feel like using up any more of the session so I didn't feel like looking it up in the phone book.

T: Yeah.

P: I guess I could of, but it seemed the quicker and easier way to ask you how to do that.

T: Yeah, but what's another quick way and rely on your own resources?

P: Well, the other quick way would be either to look it up in the book or to call the operator.

T: Yeah. But still you wanted me to intervene. Just like now, you wanted me to intervene. In solving your problem.

P: (Pause) Hmm. . . .

T: Very similar.

P: Yeah, well, I guess so.

T: What does it mean? What does it feel like?

P: Well, it feels like I'm not so determined to do things all for myself anymore. It's like it's easier to ask for help or, I don't think I ever would have said that before. Generally, I would have just done it myself and not asked for any help.

T: So what does it mean when you ask me for help?

P: (Pause) What does it mean when I ask you for help? I guess it was something that I've tried out and knew that if you had refused to help me, for example, and said, "Well, that's your problem."

T: What do you mean?

P: Well, you could have said, "I don't know," you could have said, "No." Or you could have said, "There's a book there."

T: So you're trying, you think you're testing me to see whether you can depend on me?

P: No, I don't think I'm testing you. I think I'm not so concerned if you said, "No." I mean, it wouldn't make any difference to me.

T: Yeah, but, what does it mean that you want to ask me for help? You know, it could mean various things. Is that something that you like to have, a helping relationship with people? Or with me in particular? Is that something you want more of?

P: Gee, that's a hard one. I don't know. I don't think of that particularly in terms of a helping relationship. I guess I see it more as not being afraid to ask for things. Like I used to not ask and now I ask. I keep thinking about buying a car. If you don't ask, if you don't make an offer, then you can never expect to get it.

T: Oh, but how about in the problem solving here that you are very reluctant to just go on with it. You know, you wanted me to be a partner in your solving the problem.

P: Well, I don't think I wanted you to be a partner in it because I felt like I solved the problem. I mean, I solved it as far as what it took.

T: Yeah, but you needed my permission to look around. Anything in the room. Like you wanted me to give you the water. You said, "Well, water would do it. Do you have some water." Don't you think that's interesting?

P: (Pause) Yeah, well, I didn't know if there was water in the room.

T: How do you find out?

P: Ask.

T: Yeah, it's your problem. Like you want me to be the supplier of things that you need. It's your problem and all the other problems until you solve them. Why do you need me to help you? The supplier of water. I think it has a lot of implications in terms of how you may have related to your parents. And how you may see me as a parent figure.

P: Oh, maybe so. It's hard for me to see that. I mean, I think that's a natural question and people just . . .

T: There's no natural question. It's natural because it came natural to you. But that you wanted me to be the supplier of water. Or can you do this. There was no sign on there, "Verboten." It so happens I purposely put that broken flower in the thing to make it look like that way. Like a decoy, just like these were decoys [pointing to the various articles on the table].

P: I don't know. That's not something that you'd typically use. Going into people's offices and . . .

T: But this is not typical. The whole situation is not typical. I said "anything" in the room. Yes, it's atypical for therapy that you have to get up. But so is problem solving atypical for therapy.

P: (Pause) Well, I don't know. I guess you could make a case with that, but to me it just seems like it was kind of stretching it.

T: I think you don't want to look into some of your feelings about needing to ask my help, wanting my help. Maybe even the dependency that you feel here. Maybe that's threatening to you or something that you don't want to look at. Makes you anxious to feel that you depend on me. You want to be, but, on the other hand, you don't want to really admit and see where it leads.

P: And yet it would seem that you're saying just the opposite. That, you know, why should I have to ask for help. I mean, I should be able to do it myself.

T: I'm not saying whether you should or shouldn't. Your way of solving a frustrating problem is to look to me for help. What does that mean? We don't know. And asking permission whether you can do certain things, so you can take assertive action. Like you needed my permission. "Okay," you know, encouragement, support. "Yes, go ahead, sure, look around, go ahead, take a look and see if." *(Long pause)* Maybe that's it. In certain situations, you feel better if you have encouragement from people rather than a kind of neutral, aloof attitude where everything's in your hands and you have to decide that. Because there's a lot that's going to be in your hands within, you know, days, if not tonight. [The patient is a psychiatry resident who was "on call" in the emergency service that very evening.]

P: Hmm.

T: I think you were looking for guidelines here and you're not comfortable in making your own guidelines. You being the director.

P: Hmm.

T: It may be a part of yourself that you don't feel comfortable about, comfortable looking at.

P: (Pause) Well, I don't know. That whole idea is kind of new to me. I can't . . . I don't know, it just seems, it just seems confusing to me.

T: Well, it's confusing because it's different from the way you would ordinarily consider yourself. But maybe this is worth exploring because it will open up some part of yourself that's new. Therefore, in being a physician and psychiatrist, you have a lot of control over things. And you may have covered over a lot of your needs. You have all of the professional acceptance that gives you this control, but it could be that underneath it are certain needs that are different from the control you got from being a doctor. *(Long pause)* What are you thinking?

P: Well, I'm trying to put that together. *(Long pause)* I mean, I think, in fact, that I'm the type of person that doesn't ask for help.

T: It could be. But here you did. And here you were reluctant to take control of the situation in solving your problem. I mean, this is a living example, you can't deny what we've experienced. That's why these things are helpful 'cause they, it's the here-and-now, not the there-and-then. What you remember or what you think about yourself. 'Cause what you think about yourself may be somewhat distorted. But here's the here-and-now. We have to look at this like, this is one thing experienced. It's not something that you remember. This is the spontaneous stuff.

P: But if that's true, why wouldn't you encourage that?

T: Why wouldn't I encourage what?

P: Trying out something new.

T: So you could see how you are spontaneously, without encouragement or discouragement. Okay, we'll have time to explore it next time.

Next Session

(The therapist draws the patient back to the previous session to explore the issues raised at that time.)

T: Have you thought more about that task that we worked on last time?

P: Yeah.

T: What did you think about it?

P: About the task itself?

T: The task or how you approached it.

P: I thought there was quite a paradox in there. There was a strange kind of irony in that. I felt criticized. I don't know, I guess I felt proud of myself that I got up and checked things out rather than . . .

T: Rather than what?

P: Rather than sitting here thinking about it. And yet I felt like that wasn't really acknowledged. I felt like you were nit-picking.

T: Yeah.

P: Rather than focusing on what I did and expanding on that, you focused on what I didn't do. That's what it felt like.

T: Yeah.

The patient seems to be conflicted about his longing to be close to a parent-figure and the vulnerability that ensues from this dependency. Contending with the task brings this conflict to the surface because, on the one hand, the patient wants acknowledgment for his independence (*"I got up and checked things out"*) and, on the other, he wants acknowledgment of his vulnerability in daring to ask for help. The therapist could have provided more explicit support in both areas; i.e., he could have recognized the patient's real accomplishments in taking independent, assertive action, and acknowledged how hard it must have been for him to make himself vulnerable to rejection by asking for help. This conflict is explored later in the session where the therapist asks the patient, *"What happened with your mother if you asked for help?"*

P: *(Long pause)* I don't know, it just seemed arbitrary to me that you picked that particular theme, you know, that I did ask.

T: Well, actually it's not arbitrary because that same theme came up in another task, the Ruler task. The exact same phrase you used.

P: Yeah?

T: Yeah. And we discussed that and I didn't pursue it then until I was more certain that it was a real theme. But, remember with the Ruler task, what was wrong with the ruler?

P: Uh-huh.

T: There you asked whether I had another ruler and whether you could get up and measure another piece of paper, if I had another piece of paper you could use for measuring it as a standard against, and whether it was a standard piece of paper, and you asked many things even to the point of whether you could get up and measure that piece of paper.

P: Yeah. Well, there are different ways of looking at that. I mean, I could see that as using all the available resources I've got, including you.

T: Yes, of course, I'm a resource. But it's interesting that you want to use me as a resource. In solving a problem-solving task.

P: *(Long pause)* Yeah, I do want to use you. I mean, I do want to, if I can get the help, you know, I'll ask for it.

T: Yeah, but in all the other problem-solving tasks where you're able to work on your own, you don't ask for help. It's when you have difficulty and you feel frustrated, then you look for outside help.

P: Yeah. I mean, that's, I mean, I think there were some things that were happening around that time too when I was feeling over-whelmed about a case where this woman was, the family was having problems and I had to make some decisions and I made some decisions and felt uncomfortable about that and wondering whether there was other things that I could. And I wasn't really certain. And that's when I was getting ready to go home, and I was going to brood about it and I figured well, damn, you know, Jane Scott [the head of the training program] was right there.

T: Mmm-hmm.

P: And she's offered to help out with this case. Why don't I go talk to her. So I went and talked to her, and I came out feeling a lot better, realizing that, you know, there were some things that I could do. And that, yeah, that's what supervisors are for. It's not something to. . . .

T: Fine. That's what a supervisor is for. But I'm not a supervisor. That's different. You want to use me as a supervisor.

P: (Long pause) I want to use you as a supervisor.

T: As you would use a supervisor, but that's not my role here. I'm not a supervisor.

P: Well, what is your role?

T: Well, what do you think?

P: (Long pause) I guess, I don't know. I mean, I think your role is help me to figure out how I can be more effective. Or figure things out better. *(Pause)*

T: Yeah. What else?

P: (Long pause) To point out to me, you know, how I operate.

T: Yeah, to help you become more aware of how you tick. What makes you tick. What makes you tick is how you approach things. What makes you tick is not my becoming a resource person. Unless you see a resource person as somebody who helps you become more aware of yourself. But it's not to actually provide concrete clues in helping you solve tasks in these particular situations that I provide. *(Long pause)* I can provide clues. I can provide encour-agement. But that's not my primary role. That you look for these things in me means that that's the kind of relationship that you want to develop with me. You've always said you want a more helping relationship with me. For me to be more supportive. And you are frustrated when I'm not that way. And you become angry.

P: (Pause) To me what I was asking for was not help so much as . . . *(pause)* permission doesn't sound like the right word, but I think it's probably the only word that you can use in this situation.

T: There's nothing wrong with asking for help or permission, but maybe this will give you some clues to what's really important in your life in relation to me as I may represent other figures in your life. From these tasks. Maybe these are the kinds of things that you would have liked more of in relation to your parents, for example. Or never felt comfortable in asking for with your parents. Asking for guidance or help. Maybe you felt that, well, with your mother. What happened with your mother if you asked for help?

P: *(Laughs)* You got to be kidding!

T: What happened?

P: She couldn't help herself, how could she help me?

T: So, could that be that it made you very reluctant to ask for help because you're afraid you'll be very disappointed and let down? That it's difficult for you to develop that aspect, to have a helping relationship, that is, when you need the help, because you're afraid that you'll reenact all the pain that you suffered when you wanted to get help from your mother.

P: Yeah. I mean, I do tend to do things on my own. I mean, that's the way I see myself.

T: Uh-huh. *(Pause)* So this is an area in which you feel uncomfortable with. Because, as you said, you tended to do things on your own and asking for help is only letting yourself in for some more disappointment and pain.

P: Well, I guess that was the irony of it. I mean, it's kind of incongruous that I would ask for help.

T: You mean, that you'd finally ask that of me and I turn you down. Or analyze it.

P: Yeah.

T: I don't give it willingly.

P: Yeah.

T: Yeah. But we'd never find out any of these things if I would just give the help and not analyze it. The idea is not to act out these things, but to understand them.

P: *(Sighs)*

T: Sure, there's always frustration in the therapeutic process because that's what it is. It isn't acted out, but understood.

The technical issue is that these conflicts over dependency and vulnerability might not have been revealed so clearly if the therapist had gratified the patient's longings.

P: But can't you, can't you act it out somewhat and then analyze it? I mean, it seems like, you can't really analyze it until it's somewhat, I mean, until it's gone its route. It seems like it nips it in the bud right there. That you can't really explore it if you can't experience it.

T: Yeah. So from that point of view, if a female patient wanted to be seductive, wanted to sit in the therapist's lap, let her act it out and let her see and experience it, and while she's acting it out in life, then you analyze it.

Since the patient is a psychiatry resident, the therapist uses this example to illustrate his point.

P: (Laughs) Well, that's a bit of an extreme.

T: No, it's very similar. There's a whole school of thought that goes into that approach.

P: Well, depending upon the patient. *(Laughs)*

T: (Laughs) Yeah, what kind of patients would you say that to?

P: Well, it depends on what she looks like. *(Laughs)* Well, yeah, that's something that I can't really . . . I don't know. I can't put all that together. I can only say what it feels like. That it would be much clearer to me if I had that experience.

T: Well, because you want that, otherwise you feel frustrated. This is a longing of yours. That you never got enough of helping relationships from parents. It was never fulfilled, that wish. And that need. A legitimate need for a growing kid. And we don't know all what happened because it was frustrated, and you never really felt comfortable with your mother and not only that, you got just the opposite from her. How it affected your life. We're not that clear on that yet. *(Long pause)* And one way we know it's affected your life is that it's inhibited your spontaneity. Which is something that you find very disagreeable. You want to really develop more of. So what you want me to be is to be the mother that you never had. To encourage you and let it develop.

P: (Long pause) That's not a bad idea.

T: It appeals to you.

P: Yeah.

T: Why not?

P: That sounds like, well, just as an aside, I mean, to me that would be sort of a Kohut approach that you let that develop. You let that grow. I mean, you let that, you don't nip it in the bud.

T: Yes. But from a technical point of view, you do it with the person with severe rents in ego functioning, who is so stifled by early attempts at ego development that you have to treat them very much like you would treat this woman [borderline] patient of yours. But you're not in the same category.

P: (Laughs) I'm not so sure sometimes.

This statement is an important revelation, a moment of truth for both the patient and the therapist that significantly affected the course of the patient's therapy. The patient's professional demeanor and good adaptive front had obscured the severity of his regression. Although the therapist took into account that the patient's transference may have contributed to his regression, after this interchange the therapist perceived the patient in a different light, as a more severely disturbed and needy individual. From this perspective, the patient's need for closeness, help and direct intervention made more sense, and was not considered merely as a transference reaction. In subsequent interactions, therefore, even though the therapist did not encourage the patient to act out and gratify his needs in the session, the therapist did become more supportive and focused on ego-building and reintegrative strategies, although not to the exclusion of uncovering interventions or transference interpretations.

P: When I left here last time, what I was asking was not so much help, as it was asking, to let me into your space because I was raised to be polite. It's like I got this courtesy award in high school. And I always thought it was sort of a bunch of shit because like a brown-noser or something. I was real popular with the teachers and I did all the right things and so I got awarded for being a nice, courteous student.

T: Mmm-hmm.

P: And yet in some ways I felt like I was kind of ripped off because, I didn't really get to experience some things that other kids did. It was like a real trade-off. I was really the company man and it . . .

T: A goody-goody, you mean?

P: Yeah.

T: So what you're saying is that here you want to experience some of the things that you never had the freedom to experience when you were growing up.

P: Well, I keep thinking about kids playing with finger paints and I know I used to play with finger paints, and I know I used to love it. But I don't remember doing that. All I keep imagining is I was probably the kind of kid that would stick my finger in the finger paints and would want to wash it off, you know, my mother would kind of discourage that. And it would really be fun to, you know, smear it and *(laughs)*. I had a patient, that, I had this little girl *(laughs)* and she wanted to play with Play-Doh. She wanted to combine it and make colors. And I got real interested in it myself because these are real bright colors, and so I took the primary colors and I was showing her how you mix yellow with blue to make green. And I was wondering how you make brown. So I started to mix it together and I made this brown, out of yellow and green and red. Or yellow and blue and red. And I was telling Phil Stein [his supervisor] about it and I said, boy, I made this beautiful brown, you know, with this Play-Doh. *(Laughs)* And it was so sensuous, it was great. And he said, "Brown, interesting color for Play-Doh," and it suddenly occurred to me what I was doing. And I cracked up. And it was so funny. But it felt so good. I mean, it was like I could do what kids do and would enjoy doing that. It was like a real chance to play with shit that you'd never, you know, never had a chance to play with as a kid.

T: Yeah.

P: I guess in that sense I was always kind of restricted. And I see it in this little girl, too. Because her mother has never bought her Play-Doh. Her mother buys her books and sends her to music lessons.

T: Mmm-hmm.

P: So she just goes berserk when she gets around Play-Doh. She loves to play in it. So that was one of the things that I suggested to the mother.

T: How old is she?

P: She's seven.

T: Mmm-hmm.

P: I suggested to the mother that she, you know, get her that. And the mother said, "Oh, yes, yes, I wanted to get her that but I've never gotten around to it," or something like that. But this little girl is just so socialized, over-socialized that, she's never had a chance to be a kid. I guess in some ways that's the way I felt. It's like, I always had to live up to other people's expectations.

T: Mmm-hmm.

P: Otherwise I'd embarrass the family or embarrass my mother. I had to be quiet and act like I was supposed to act. Follow the rules. It is just a bunch of shit. *(Long pause)* When I see kids that, whose mothers really care about them, it's like that's a whole gap in my life. I don't think my mother ever really, really cared. It was like she did the basics.

T: Mmm-hmm.

P: She did enough to get me by. But never really enough to fill me up or to make me feel good about it or something. And I think my father helped in some ways, but *(sighs)*, you know, he had problems of his own too.

T: Mmm-hmm.

P: So. *(Long pause)* I mean it would have been so nice to grow up in a family where, you know, you could see my parents really love each other. But I remember, you know, that the last time I really saw them kiss was when I was just a little kid. I was maybe five or six.

T: Mmm-hmm.

P: And I can remember that feeling. I mean it was just, it was just a good feeling. I mean, I could feel it in my chest. It was just a feeling of warmth. To see them loving each other. And in some way that all disappeared.

T: Mmm-hmm. *(Pause)* Okay. Let's talk about this some more.

Summary

In this case, we noted how transference issues were addressed effectively in the context of the patient's task behavior. In fact, the task appeared to help bring to light aspects of the transference and of the patient's pathology not previously revealed. With the new perspective thus obtained, the therapist modified his therapeutic strategy and more vigorously engaged in supportive and ego-integrative procedures. The use of the tasks in the context of an ego-building approach did not, however, dilute the development and resolution of the transference. Rather, it appeared to help the patient to deal more readily with transferential issues and to contend more effectively with his problems of dependency, intimacy and self-esteem. The case report follow-up presented on pp. 180–182 discusses how these issues were resolved.

An analysis of the transference and the experiential-developmental laboratory in terms of ego processes clarifies how and why they are vital components in the therapeutic process and helps us to identify the essential ingredients in therapeutic change.

In establishing the transference, the patient reanimates unresolved childhood patterns and acts them out with the therapist. When the therapist, for example, does not give the patient unlimited time or treat him without charge—which would symbolize the patient's desire to obtain unconditional love from his mother or father—the patient may become enraged at the therapist. His childhood anxieties may also revive a fear of retaliatory anger.

When the therapist acts out neither of these fantasies, but says, "You want me to give you special consideration to make up for the lack of closeness and love in your relationship with your mother," the patient is confronted not only with an awareness of his childhood patterns, but with an experience of how this repetition distorts his perceptions and expectations of the therapist. Faced with the discrepancy between his maladaptive schemes (i.e., the inappropriateness and nonveridicality of his perceptions, feelings and unreasonable demands) and the reality presented by the therapist, the patient is provided with an opportunity to test his schemes with the therapist. From the feedback obtained, the patient can transform his schemes and accommodate them to reality. As the patient's schemes change, his capacity for assimilation improves; transference interpretations are increasingly understood and assimilated, the patient experiences less distortion, and the growth cycle repeats again and again until the transference neurosis is resolved.

An analysis of the experiential-developmental laboratory in terms of ego processes indicates that it functions in a structurally parallel manner. CET tasks reanimate unresolved childhood schemes. In attempting to master the tasks, the patient is confronted with the inadequacy of these schemes. Faced with the discrepancy between these maladaptive schemes and those required for effective solution of the tasks, the patient is provided with the opportunity to test his schemes. From the feedback obtained, the patient can transform his schemes and accommodate them to reality. As his schemes change, his capacity for assimilation improves. Relevant features of the problem needed for its solution and clues from the therapist are increasingly assimilated. The patient develops the capacity to act upon the task in a slightly altered, improved way, making new accommodations and new transformations in his schemes possible. The growth cycle repeats again and again until the problem is solved.

Both the transference and the experiential-developmental laboratory permit and even encourage the playing out of the patient's unconscious conflicts in nonveridical and nonaccommodative ways. In both, however, the repetition is not simply a passive reviving of the repressed patterns which mirror unconscious functioning and which lead to distortion. The goal is to help the patient to rise above and overcome his conflicts and distortions. Through acting upon and obtaining corrective feedback from the tasks and/or the therapist, the experiential-developmental laboratory and the transference both promote reconstructive processes which implement veridical and accommodative, adaptive contact with reality and therapeutic change.

Viewing the transference and the experiential-developmental laboratory in terms of their inherent ego processes enables us to see that the therapeutic processes in each are not isolated psychological events having little to do with other psychological events, but that they function in the context of a larger framework of growth-inducing processes essential for therapeutic success. Moreover, as we noted in the case of Bob, since the experiential-developmental laboratory and the transference mutually complement and synergize each other, their effective synthesis in CET provides for an integrated analysis and resolution of cognitive and affective problems, and points the way toward an integrative ego psychotherapy.

5. PROMOTING MASTERY AND COMPETENCE

CET helps the patient to change the image of himself from a person who is the victim of and overwhelmed by his symptoms and problems to one who can master them. People who are burdened with a sense of being unable to master the difficulties facing them not only suffer from feelings of low self-esteem and inadequacy, but from an inability to use their resources. They have learned only too well how *not* to learn from experience and, consequently, their failures are self-perpetuating.

Paradoxically, a person fails by not risking more surely than if he risks and fails, because he may be called upon to make decisions and initiate actions when he is least prepared to take chances and learn from his errors. CET induces the patient to try something new, take risks, struggle with challenges and learn how to learn from experience.

It is, however, important for the therapist to insure that the patient eventually succeeds at a task. With a vast history of defeat, it is essential that the patient does not relive failure in the session; otherwise he will experience yet another blow to his already weakened ego. Consequently, by using tasks of graded difficulty and appropriately introducing graded clues, the therapist insures that the patient, regardless of his problems, can achieve some measure of success. Realistic successes in the sessions provide the patient with multiple opportunities to work through his feelings of unworthiness and inadequacy. The patient with a long history of failure can discover that he has more ability in mastering tasks than he has ever known.

Moreover, when a patient reaches an impasse while grappling with a task, he is neither given the solution, which would undermine his feelings of competency, nor allowed to flounder in maladaptive attempts. Rather, the therapist and the patient together can explore why and how it is difficult, and how the patient's defenses (e.g., denial, avoidance, or projection) may be obstructing effective apprehension and mastery of the problem.

The patient discovers that difficulty in finding a solution and even outright failure are not to be disdained or avoided because they can provide important learning experiences. They can even be more helpful than success if the patient can learn the reasons for his failure and develop new strategies for achieving success. Success demonstrates the patient's potential for mastery, is gratifying and ego-building, and adds to or confirms the patient's sense of competence. But it does not really increase his ability to master the challenging, anxiety-provoking tasks of life. If, on the other hand, the patient comes to understand under what conditions he fails and why, he can develop more adaptive strategies, which help him to overcome failure and more effectively master the challenges in his life. He is helped not merely to master the tasks, but to comprehend how one achieves mastery. He gains a real sense of his adaptiveness and power. He is no longer the victim. He can take control of his life. There is hope.

6. COORDINATING THE PAST WITH THE PRESENT

A central factor contributing to a patient's problems is that he does not live in the present, the here-and-now. He is preoccupied with and absorbed in the past and holds onto "unfinished business," i.e., with events that the patient for various reasons feels are incompleted or unresolved because of his dissatisfaction with the outcome. Holding on to the past can develop into an entrenched pattern which can destroy a person's current interpersonal relations and decision-making processes.

CET leads to a better understanding of the past. It reveals the ways in which the past is vividly alive and interconnected with the present. The patient sees from his task behavior how the past is not safely tucked away, but is deleteriously influencing and limiting his life. The therapy sessions become the very stage of life as the patient unveils monuments from the past and revives their covert messages through his actions on the tasks.

We recognize, of course, that relating the past to the present is not something new, but something that is surely done by all psychodynamically oriented therapists, especially in the analysis of the transference. However, CET broadens and deepens the possibilities for exploring the relationships of the past to the present. Past events are reconstructed and understood not only through flashbacks randomly scattered through a patient's associations but, as with the transference, by demonstrating how they shape the patient's actions in the sessions. The patient does not simply remember things, like selections from an old film library; rather, past events are revealed in their relationship to his current actions with the tasks. The past assumes a here-and-now, relevant and real quality that makes it more accessible to understanding and more meaningfully related to the "why" of his current dilemmas. The patient can start to gain control over the lingering effects of the past, make more free choices and live more fully in the present.

(1) Early Memories and Core Relationship Themes

What is known about early memories is that we do not have many memories and that we do not have nearly as many as we should have. Why are early childhood memories so elusive and why do we have so much trouble remembering early childhood?

The memory process holds a strategic place in psychological theory. It is one of the main bases of learning and development. Memory is crucial to growth because it influences the patient's readiness to learn from the past and to assimilate new behaviors. Failures in memory and acts of repression can severely restrict the patient's cognitive and emotional repertoire, and limit the range of his intellectual achievements and interpersonal relationships. A whole school of thought, psychoanalysis, started from observations of failures of memory. Repression is central in the theory of unconscious determinism, and is considered the basic psychic defense mechanism. The retrieval of "lost" memories and the lifting of repression are the cornerstones of psychoanalytic therapy.

The pioneers of psychoanalysis attached much significance to early memories. One early analyst, Alfred Adler, raised these recollections to a place of prime importance in understanding human nature. "The first memory," Adler wrote, "will show the individual's fundamental view of life, his first satisfactory crystallization of his attitude." He continued, "I would never investigate a personality without asking for the first memory" (1931, p. 75).

Research into the memory process and especially early memories can, therefore, make a distinct contribution to the clinical enterprise. For example, we have been struck by the connection between retrieval of a patient's early memories as revealed through associations to the tasks and his adult approach to life. (See Luborsky, 1984, for further discussion of the role of core themes in the therapeutic process.)

Clinical Example: Frank—Triangles Problem

For example, while grappling with the Triangles Problem, Frank recalled his first memory, which crystallized what he was all about: When he was about two or three years old, he tried to climb out of his crib.

P: I don't know where it came from, but I have this image of being in my crib. I'm trying to feel what it is like. I must be about two years old, because I can't walk that well. I'm leaning against the railing and it looks like it will be nice to get out and crawl around outside. So I put my leg over the railing. *(The patient shows how he lifted his leg.)* But, I think if I get out, my mother will see that I'm growing up and she won't do things for me anymore. So I fake it. I put my leg back inside and make like I need her. I cry for my mommy to get her to come to me instead of getting out and going to her. I'm just wailing and wailing, until finally she comes to take care of me. *(He returns to the task.)* I just can't figure these bloody things out. I'm stumped. *(He puts down the sticks and looks at the therapist.)*
T: Does that mean you would like to get me to help you, like your mother came to help you?
P: Do you think that's what I'm doing, the same thing, like I'm setting you up?

Both the patient and the therapist were struck by the intimate connection between this early memory and his fundamental view of life: Frank still sought, even demanded, that the therapist and other significant figures in his life do things for him.

P: I recall the struggles I had when I was an infant and how I battled with them then, how I coped with them then. Because I'm probably still coping with them in the same way. And if it's not a successful way, then the defeat is still there, just as it was thirty years ago, or forty years ago, whatever the hell. *(Pause)* They show me that I'm still tackling things in the same manner.

(2) Recovering Early Memories

Even though CET focuses on the current realities in the patient's experiences, one of our surprising findings is that working on the therapeutic tasks actually stimulates recall of early memories. When a patient associates while engaging in the real-world events, these associations not only bring his current feelings to life, but strikingly enough, they reanimate the feelings and emotion-laden events which played a key role in the formation of these current feelings and difficulties in daily life. Feelings, images, and events, sometimes from as far back as the second or third year of life, such as the crib scene with Frank, are recaptured and vividly reexperienced and related to the patient's struggles with the tasks and current dilemmas. These early memories can cut through the patient's defenses and provide clues to the developmental roots of his problems. The following example illustrates how the tasks served to reveal the patient's early memories and helped heal the wounds and alter the defensive forces which caused them to be repressed in the first place.

Clinical Example: Bob—Code Problem

In this example, we see how the task helped the patient to get in touch with his past so he could function more effectively in the present. One of Bob's central problems was that he did not live in the here-and-now. He felt he did not respond spontaneously and did not "think on his feet." During interpersonal interchange, he was not "all there." He ruminated on what he should have done or should have said. As a consequence, he frequently felt on the spot. When other people reacted spontaneously, he became anxious and was flooded with feelings of loss of control.

The Code Problem was particularly suitable for addressing these problems. To effectively master the task, the patient has to maintain a focus on the present while relating to it the immediate past. Bob *"got lost . . . I can't hold all the possibilities at one time."* The feelings evoked by his difficulties with the task elicited memories of critical events from his past which played a significant role in his current problems. Strikingly, after Bob recalled and worked through some of these feelings of being abandoned, he returned to the task and readily mastered it.

(The patient had been working on the Code Problem for fifteen minutes.)
P: Oh, gee! Oh, this is just getting too frustrating.
T: How do you feel?
P: It feels like what I'm doing is just kind of a back way and like I, I get lost in the maze of trying to follow the logic. It's like I can't hold all the possibilities at one time.

T: Does it remind you of some feelings that you've had?

P: Well. *(Pause)*

T: Is that how it felt, getting up [to speak] for this presentation?

P: Yeah, yeah. That's what I was going to say. It feels like that at work, but, ah, you know. I can start with the basics and follow some simple reasoning, but then when it gets into the complexities, I can't get the big picture or hold it all in my mind at one time while I'm . . .

T: But I mean the feeling. That's the thinking, but the feeling of being, what is the feeling like?

The therapist is trying to uncover the feelings related to and intruding upon the patient's thought processes.

P: The feeling is one of grasping, kind of, feeling like I'm groping around trying to grab something tangible. It's like in a calculator you have a memory, you can stash it away in the memory and then recall it. But the feeling is like . . . I'm a calculator without a memory.

T: You feel on the spot, is that it?

P: Not so much on the spot right now, it's just that there's the feeling of just kind of being lost.

T: Mmm-hmm.

P: And it's more on the spot when I'm, yeah, in a group of people.

T: Mmm-hmm.

P: The idea of being lost in a group of people. . . . I just remember when I was real small, I was in a theatre one time and I was just, I was holding onto this man's pant's leg and, you know, I thought it was my father, I was just happy. And it was a crowded lobby of the theatre. And I looked up and it was somebody else. *(Laughs)* It was like I was shocked and I couldn't find my mother anywhere, I panicked, I ran around.

T: You mean, you were just holding on, following this pant's leg?

P: Yeah. And I was just walking around. *(Laughs)* And I looked up and this man started talking to me and it just scared the shit out of me. I didn't know who he was and I didn't know where my mother was, and it was like the lobby was crowded and I just started screaming and crying and she finally found me. The theatre also had a bathroom that was just down, I mean you had to go down the stairs, it was like in the basement. It always gave me the creeps, especially when I had to go down there by myself. 'Cause, I never knew what kind of characters would turn up down there. *(Pause)* But I noticed it with, I mean I think even Nadine's [his three-month-old daughter] starting to pick up, I don't know how much of that is genetic or hereditary, but she, she just loves to be held and I was the same way. I just loved to be held. I just wanted somebody close. And when somebody wasn't close, when my mother wasn't close, I just, I panicked. Especially in a crowded place like that. I still have a fear of crowds. That must have . . . I mean crowds don't bother me so much except when the attention focuses on me and then that sense of security kind of leaves. It's like there's nobody, there's nobody there. I'm all alone. *(Pause)*

These associations help us to understand the developmental roots of the patient's current problems. First, we see how the anxiety and frustration of the task affect his thought processes. He "gets lost" and "can't hold onto all the possibilities at one time." Although different in content, he reacts to frustrating events at work in a similar way. "I can't get the big picture and hold it in my mind." The feeling evoked is "one of grasping, trying to grab something tangible." This leads him to recall a traumatic event from his early childhood when he actually got lost, panicked, and grabbed onto the nearest leg, which he hoped would be his lost parent's leg. We see how his childhood reaction of panic and disorganization became his typical reaction in adulthood. In dealing with his current problems, anxiety triggers the same panic reaction and problems in thought organization *as if* he were abandoned as a child.

T: So that's why it seems, why it's a point to have things under control because when things are not under control, you feel lost and lost means abandoned, not having your mother around and panicked. The ways to try to save some panic is to have things in order and in control.

P: (Pause) Yeah. Yeah. I mean, it's a nice feeling to be able to, to order it. It makes a lot more sense. I don't like that feeling of being lost. It's funny because I have sort of a preoccupation with maps. I love maps. I love to look at maps and I bought an atlas, it's a National Geographic atlas and, um . . . I never was very good at geography. I never could remember where the states all went. And I still can't. I mean, I still have to look at a map to figure out where Ohio is in relation to Illinois. It's like I can't form . . . I can't keep a mental picture there. It just seems real elusive. I have to refer to something, I have to refer to something concrete to reorient me. I mean it's the same thing, I was talking to Jerry White [a colleague] the other day. It's like the feeling that I need something tangible. At least putting it on paper. Doing these things where I organize things, it approaches being tangible. I mean I can sit there and look at it. Make it objective and put it out there. But when I try to synthesize it in my mind without it being on the paper, I feel lost and I feel like . . . I can't keep the picture in mind. I just can't . . . I don't guess object permanence is the word, but that's the closest thing I can think of. It's like something that is not permanent, it just doesn't stay there.

T: Mmm-hmm.

P: I don't know. I was a hanger-on when I was a kid. I remember, you know, holding onto that guy's pant's leg and that was the same way I would hold onto my mother's skirt. I would just follow her around. And, um . . . I just wanted to be close. Like if I let go, she really might step away. She might, she might go somewhere else and leave me all alone. *(Pause)* Hmm.

T: What are you thinking?

P: Oh, I just had a . . . *(The patient grimaces and leans his head all the way back and to the sides.)*

T: A twinge?

The somatic manifestations of his anxiety are revealed.

P: No, my neck is just kind of stiff. Just from the stress, have to stretch it out. No, I was just thinking that, ah, when I was, when I was back in Portland, we had the baby there. . . . And my mother and father were telling stories about me when I was, when I was a kid. But they said that I had an uncanny ability to track my father down. And there was even one time when my father had been to some kind of meeting and ah . . . he had gone to Eugene for a meeting and drove in late and got in like two o'clock in the morning and we were staying at my grandparents' house. And I was about three years old at the time. And, and he stayed, he was sleeping up in an attic room at my grandparents' house and he said that I managed to find him, at three o'clock in the morning. Here was this little three-year-old kid and he couldn't figure it out. He said he could never get away from me. Because, because I always wanted to be close to him. I always wanted to . . . you know, if it wasn't climbing in his lap and sitting in the rocking chair, wanting to, you know, climb in bed and just get close to him. *(Pause)* And I'm still like that. That's still my favorite time with Ellen [his wife], is to just, is just climbing into the bed and feeling that warmth, feeling close. I think there's something about it that's very tangible and real and comforting. I just sort of feel distant or removed before. Like *(pause)* kind of lost. Like, I don't know. Just lost *(softly)*.

T: Mmm-hmm.

P: (Long pause) Let's see. I have to figure this thing out.

T: Isn't it interesting that this triggered all these thoughts?

P: Yeah. Well, there's something to it that sort of, it's almost visual. I mean, you can see that there's a line of logic and I guess I see the line of logic and it's getting gradually more complicated. And that's sort of the way I feel at work. With some of the simple basic stuff, it's okay. But as the logic gets more complex, then I get more lost. *(Pause)* But that's funny. I used to hate to be alone. I find a great deal of pleasure in being alone now. But I feel really pressured at work. I mean, I feel pressured to perform. It's like you got to solve the puzzle, but I need time to think it out. *(The therapist provides feedback as to the correctness of the patient's code. Very long pause while the patient continues to work on the problem.)* Well, I'm getting closer.

T: Mmm-hmm.

P: Let's see. Two of these were right. Right here. The blue and green. *(Long pause)* No. It's the green and the blue. *(Long pause)* *(The patient solves the code.)* Whew!

T: What do you think?

P: Well, I think that's not bad. Seems like it was easier when I went back to it the second time.

T: When you went back to it when?

P: After I had been talking.

T: Why do you think that was easier?

P: I think I got blocked the first time. It stirred up some feeling that I just couldn't do it and I was going to be trapped and I couldn't finish it.

T: Just sort of overwhelmed with panic and you were just disorganized.

P: Yeah.

T: And then talking about it, what did that do?

P: Well, it kind of surprised me that it brought all that stuff up, but it made a lot more sense and I didn't feel as anxious about it. I was able to get a different perspective on it when I went back to it. Like it sort of cleared the decks. I was able to get a fresh look at it.

Summary

These sessions with the Code Problem played a significant role in facilitating Bob's therapy. He experienced how traumatic events from his childhood were not just experiences to be pushed out of awareness and forgotten, but were meaningfully related to his present maladaptive way of responding to stress. He reacted to the present stress of the task with the same kinds of feelings of panic and disorganization that he had experienced when he got lost as child. As a child, he panicked and grabbed onto the closest pant's leg. In an uncanny parallel, under current stress, he felt he was "groping around trying to grab onto something tangible."

Working through these fears of "being lost and abandoned" as a child enabled him to gain control over his panic reaction and to see that he was no longer as vulnerable as he had perceived himself to be as a child. The immediate positive result was that he was capable of mobilizing his rational and ordered thinking processes: he returned to the task and very quickly solved the code. He was able to "clear the decks" and let go of the past. Subsequently, he was increasingly able to respond to his present professional and personal relationships less anxiously and more spontaneously—one of his main goals of therapy.

(3) The Dynamics of Remembering

Cases such as Frank's and Bob's enable us to study both why and how the past intrudes into and influences adaptive behavior. We can reveal the ways in which childhood themes as recovered from early memories continue to reemerge and are refashioned and expressed throughout a person's life.

Since the tasks appear to facilitate the recall of early memories, CET offers special opportunities to investigate a number of variables relevant to repression and early memories. Do early memories reflect a deeply rooted, early developed core theme that has influenced the course of a patient's life, or do patients select those elements of childhood memories that accord with their present needs and perceptions of themselves? Do our memories make us, or do we make our memories, or are memories in our lives expressions of a different underlying, pervasive process influencing both? What is the relationship between the degree of repression, the depth and kinds of pathology, the return of the repressed and amenability to therapeutic progress?

We may offer three interrelated hypotheses to explain why the CET tasks may be effective in helping to reveal early memories. First, the tasks serve to modulate the disruptive effects of the patient's anxiety, anger or guilt. When the patient cannot contain these emotions and they persist in unmitigated form, they promote a regressive momentum and exert a disorganizing effect on the patient's cognitive functioning. Under these conditions, the patient's thinking and memory are impaired, resulting in selective forgetting or repression.

The tasks serve to reverse this impairment in ego function by promoting the secondary process. The act of contending with the tasks mobilizes islands of neutralized, secondary-process thinking. The tasks are stable, tangible, here-and-now reference points, objects in the real world. The sights and sounds and touch act as a lure, drawing the patient out of his rumination and breaking the cycle of regressive and limiting ego processes. By lending structure, coherence and focus to the patient's functioning, the tasks help to control disturbing sexual and aggressive impulses and keep them from intruding into his thinking. He is not as completely or as deeply overwhelmed by his anxiety or anger.

When his emotions are thereby contained and temporarily held in abeyance, the patient can think and remember more effectively. He can reach those painful or shameful events and feelings that have been walled off and blocked from consciousness. The tasks thus help neutralize or, as one patient put it, "defuse" the disruptive effects of his emotions. Since memory is a function of a particular state of consciousness and the motivational states impinging on it, as the patient's mental structure is altered and is less dominated by the primary process, ego function and recall of "forgotten" events are optimized, and repression is lifted.

The second reason why tasks may facilitate recall of early memories is that the tasks can help the patient enter into a state of consciousness which is similar to past states. The past experiences we had as children and the ways in which we reacted to stress and frustration often leave residues which shape the ways in which we react as adults. We are, therefore, heir to similar emotions and cognitive reactions when an event similar to an early event grabs us. When a patient is confronted with a task that evokes these early emotional and cognitive reactions, he is enabled to recall the original event associated with them. Most important, by bringing the original event and his associated feelings to awareness, the patient has a new opportunity to resolve them and free himself from their deleterious influence.

For example, while Bob grappled with the Code Problem, he had an experience of *déjà vu* in which the emotional tone evoked by his present experience with the task, that of "being lost and groping," called forth a parallel state in his early childhood where he was lost and actually groping for his father's pant's leg. The patient was struck with a feeling of fittingness. The remembered past event and associated feelings fit in explicit detail the patient's current emotional and cognitive state, and provided clues to understanding his current problems with the task as well as his daily problems involving similar emotional and cognitive components. Moreover, after capturing the early memory and reliving its emotional contents, the patient was able to work through some of the early trauma, and his cognitive functioning improved. He then returned to the Code Problem and solved it.

These clinical findings, observed repeatedly with our patients, indicate that associations to the tasks not only facilitate recall of early memories, but help the patient to master the task. Since associations to the task are anchored to the objective frame of reference of the task, they do not simply loosen controls or lead to explorations of feelings. Rather, by promoting recall of early memories and working through of conflicts related to them, these associations enable the patient to assume an attitude of decreased intrapsychic defensiveness. The patient can then come back to contending with the task and approach it in a conflict-free way—that is, freed of the disorganizing effects of unresolved anxiety, anger or guilt. He can progress to a higher level of functioning and address the task in a more effective and creative problem-solving mode, and master it.

A third factor contributing to CET's facility in recovering early memories may be that since the tasks stimulate nonverbal and sensorimotor action, they invite the patient to enter into the nonverbal mode. Because adults tend to think and remember things in words, words we did not have as young children, it may be more difficult to remember early experiences where there are no words attached. The nonverbal mode of the tasks enables the patient to reach the distant past where the nonverbal mode predominated, and to capture those early experiences which have been encapsulated by virtue of their roots lying in that era in life where the nonverbal, sensorimotor mode was primary.

Observing these relationships between the tasks and recovery of early childhood memories has developmental implications which can facilitate the therapeutic process. Although recalling an event does not necessarily undo repression, and although undoing a repression is more than recalling a "lost" memory, recovery of memories can provide the therapist and the patient with a new avenue for revealing the *meaning* and *significance* of early events, such as in the cases of Frank and Bob. This new level of comprehension can help the patient to develop new perceptions of causal links in his early relationships to which he had been impervious. Awareness of a previously uncomprehended relationship can help the patient to perceive, code and assimilate early relationships more correctly which can help him to resolve their deleterious and inhibitory effects. The patient can thereby become more responsive to feedback from present events and can start to grow again.

CHAPTER V

Treatment Manual

It is important to emphasize that no matter how useful a clinical tool CET might be, the decisive factor guiding its application is the *total* therapeutic equation—the art of therapeutic technique derived from the therapist's empathy and skill in relating to a human being. The therapist, therefore, applies the same fundamental principles of sound psychotherapeutic technique with CET as he does with any of the other aspects of therapeutic procedure.

Although we offer therapists guidelines for applying the technique, we stress that CET is not etched in stone. It is not intended as the "last word" on technique, suggesting rules for slavish imitation.

1. THE INITIAL SESSIONS

Freud's comments on the initial therapy session are still relevant:

What the material is with which one starts treatment is on the whole a matter of indifference—whether it is the patient's life history or the history of the illness or his recollections of childhood. But in any case the patient must be left to do the talking and must be free to choose at what point he shall begin. (1913, p. 134)

When are we to begin making CET interventions with the patient? Almost from the beginning. We do not wish to intrude into or block the patient's account of his difficulties; nevertheless, as the patient relates his life story and the problems disturbing him, the therapist follows the patient's line of thought and associations as far as they lead and, at a point of resistance, weaves one of the tasks into the therapist-patient interaction.

The first and second sessions are, therefore, scheduled for two hours to accommodate the greater time needed to incorporate a task without impeding or interrupting the flow of the patient's critical initial presentation. Although a flexible approach is maintained, especially under emergency treatment conditions, all other sessions are 50 minutes and are scheduled on a twice-weekly basis.

The main consideration of technical importance is that the therapist pays attention to the effects that introducing tasks may have on the patient's experience of the therapist and the therapeutic relationship. The therapist can ascertain this by asking the patient what he thinks and feels about these interventions and the kinds of fantasies and expectations of the therapeutic interaction which they evoke.

2. INTERVENTIONS

(1) Timing: When to Introduce a Task

Tasks are introduced to address the patient's resistances. For example, the therapist should be sensitive to when the flow of associations is obstructed and when confusion, contradiction and inconsistencies appear in the patient's account. Similarly, when the patient is obviously evading exploration of his feelings and seems doggedly intent on escaping the here-and-now into the seemingly intimate details of past experiences or is ruminating on trivia, the therapist can introduce a task by saying, "I think a task will help us to understand what you're feeling and thinking at the moment. Let's work on this task."

However, a task should not be introduced mechanically during any temporary impasse and misused as a crutch to avoid analyzing the resistances and perplexities that are always natural parts of any intensive therapeutic endeavor.

The therapist must adopt a flexible approach in planning to incorporate a task. He should not rigidly follow a routine of administering a task in a particular session or of introducing tasks in a predetermined sequence. Although the tasks themselves, especially those involving reality testing, can play an integrative role during crises and disruptive anxiety states, the therapist will not want to unduly press the patient with tasks or demand continued effort when supportive interaction is indicated. The exigencies of the patient's life are always primary.

(2) Task Selection: Which Task to Introduce

In order to determine which task would be most suitable for use with a particular patient, the therapist reviews the major psychological processes which are interfering with the patient's functioning. For example, although all patients can gain from improvement in reality testing as a means to overcome their narcissistic preoccupations and distortions, some patients are blocked from any substantive psychological development by their pervasive problems in reality testing. Narcissistic personality disorders and borderline and schizophrenic disturbances are especially prone to failures in reality testing, as are, in lesser degree, severe hysterical and obsessive-compulsive neurotics.

For example, schizophrenic patients like Hal have a particular need to develop their capacities to test reality and relate to the world in consensually validated terms. When Hal showed signs of fragmented contact with reality and loss of control during his acute psychotic episode, the therapist selected from his armamentarium of tasks the particular ones which focused on reality testing. The commentary accompanying the tasks (see *Resource Materials,* pp. 199–219) elucidates the processes which each task addresses. Thus, during Hal's hospitalization, the therapist first selected Tangrams. By emphasizing concrete perceptual contact and cognitive organization, Tangrams helped Hal to get in touch with reality and counteract his withdrawal and disorganization. After his discharge from the hospital, the Ping-Pong Problem and the Ruler Problem were introduced to help Hal to discover how clinging to his denials and projections interfered with adaptive behavior, and how testing reality could help him move out of his private world and more reasonably communicate and relate to people.

In addition to addressing different psychological dimensions, the tasks also vary in difficulty, ranging from very easy to extremely demanding. All of the tasks were pretested with normal subjects to obtain an idea of the general level of a task's complexity and difficulty as well as the range of the cognitive and affective dimensions which it taps. However, patients manifesting extreme pathology may exhibit unique talents and strengths in various areas of ego functioning. For example, a task involving syllogistic reasoning was quite challenging, but was readily mastered by a patient like Hal, who exhibited a high degree of abstract thinking. In contrast, since this same patient suffered from serious blind spots in ego functioning, those problems requiring reality testing were experienced as extremely stressful.

Therefore, task selection must be guided by the therapist's knowledge of the patient's idiosyncratic ego strengths and weaknesses. To be most effective, a task must be challenging and almost solvable, but not completely so, in order to stretch the patient's capacities just beyond his current repertoire. If the challenge is too far out of the patient's adaptive range, he will become so anxious and frustrated that he will continue with the task only with great difficulty or will ignore or avoid the problem altogether. On the other hand, if a task is too easy, the patient will become bored and lose interest and may even feel humiliated that the therapist has such a low expectation of him.

For example, during Hal's state of acute regression, the task selected in the hospital, Tangrams, was one of the easier ones which focus on reality testing, and the particular Tangram used was one of the simplest. In contrast, after Hal was discharged from the hospital, he was presented with the Ping-Pong Problem, which is a more demanding task for testing reality. Moreover, since it can be solved on two levels of difficulty, Hal could step up to it and master it first on an easy level and still achieve a sense of success before tackling the more complicated solution on a higher level. Six months later, when Hal showed signs of increased reintegration, the Ruler Problem, which consists of even greater challenge and difficulty, was then presented.

(3) Strategy for Intervention

When the patient encounters difficulty with a task and seems to be reaching an impasse, it is tempting for the therapist to step in and ease the patient's tension and frustration by showing him the solution. The therapist must resist this temptation because not allowing the patient ample freedom to grapple with the task can undermine his self-esteem and rob him of a precious opportunity for growth.

The therapist should urge the patient to express his mounting frustration and anxiety so as to uncover his characteristic response to difficulty. The critical element is to encourage the patient to experience his feelings fully and to capture the associations and fleeting images that are connected with them at the time. At this strategic juncture, a patient often can more precisely identify and describe the kinds of situations that make him depressed and anxious and the feelings and events that promote his passivity and inertia and undermine his cognitive capacities.

When, for example, the therapist introduces tasks requiring the patient to use new adaptive modalities or to contend with themes which depart from his preferential and safe choices, the patient is helped to interact with the world in ways that, although initially adverse or strange, help him to develop new adaptive modes. The patient is encouraged to break out of the habitual, stereotyped automaticity of his repertoire and to experiment with alternative ways of interacting with the world. He is helped to discern that there are parts of the world which, although at first appearing strange and foreign and even inducing anxiety, can be grasped through explorations into new avenues of perceiving, reasoning, remembering, feeling, and acting. In short, the patient is to be challenged, not threatened.

The therapist should not require a solution to a task by the end of the hour. The patient may be allowed to come back to a task in the following session or even continue working on the task on his own at home, although working on and finding the solution in the session are to be encouraged to allow both the patient and the therapist to see the process of solution and the patient's response to it *as* it occurs.

On the other hand, the therapist should not continue hour after hour waiting dumbly and stubbornly for the patient to solve a problem in the vain hope that in the third or fourth hour he will finally arrive at the solution. Some patients, if left to their own devices, will run on seemingly endlessly, but secretly may be building up considerable suppressed or obliquely expressed resentment and anxiety while continuing to be a "cooperative" patient by complying and not complaining. To burden the patient with unlimited time to master a task may represent hostile demands on the therapist's part and may express the therapist's resentment of the patient's problems.

The problem often becomes one of an unrealistic, inhibiting fear on the part of the therapist that he will hurt, depress, anger or otherwise disturb the patient by interrupting the process of solution. A *laissez faire,* nonresponsive attitude without limits or demands may well stimulate rather than assuage or avoid increased anxiety and distress in the patient. The therapist must participate. He must assert his authority, assume responsibility, and take control by setting realistic limits and, when appropriate, provide helpful, graded clues to assist the patient. The technique for providing clues is discussed in the following section.

The therapist should always feel free to interrupt the patient's problem solving with open discussion not only of his difficulties and strategies with the task, but of his emotional reaction to the task and the therapist. These discussions encourage the patient to express his feelings on any subject and demonstrate the value of keeping up-to-date and in touch with his feelings. Exploring the patient's feelings at the time when they are being acutely experienced is potentially of great benefit because it may reveal his inner state before his defenses close off and obscure those aspects of his self which may be silently and secretly undermining his behavior.

In fact, allowing the patient to go on and on with seemingly cooperative behavior and verbalizations and not interrupting him to find
out the thoughts and feelings behind his actions may allow some valuable material to be lost, particularly material that clarifies the inner
cognitive processes behind the observable responses and the patient's
attitudes and feelings towards these responses. The loss of such material may even impede therapeutic progress because insight into these
processes may not only implement mastery of the task, but facilitate
understanding of these processes when they intrude into his daily life.
In addition, not knowing what is going on in the patient's mind may
deleteriously affect the working atmosphere because the therapist may
feel that he is being excluded from the patient's world.

On the other hand, one does not want to handle the patient's silences
and difficulties through excessively intervening, which can be experienced as intrusiveness and which can disrupt the natural flow of
associations and problem-solving processes. Neither is prematurely
terminating the patient's attempts a satisfactory approach. Persistent
interruptions and a demanding and provocative inquiry into the patient's feelings and responses can increase the patient's tension, build
up his resentment and be misinterpreted as a form of psychological
rape. If the therapist does not allow the patient to struggle with a task,
he may undermine the patient's self-confidence and belief in his ability
to solve the problem on his own. Another defensive and unproductive
approach to ward off the therapist's anxiety over the patient's silences
and difficulties involves resorting, mechanically and without a specific
rationale or therapeutic plan, to pushing additional tasks on the patient as if just working on puzzles will assuage the patient's anxiety
or contend with his possible ambivalence toward his relationship with
the therapist.

It is wisest for the therapist to steer a middle course between interrupting the patient's attempts at solution with open discussion of the
personal issues which the task elicits and allowing the patient free
rein to grapple and experiment with the task. When the therapist
focuses, in point-counterpoint manner, on the task, then on conflicts,
then on memories and past experiences, and returns to the task, he is
not necessarily dodging the patient's task anxiety or allowing him to
avoid confrontation with personal issues or the transference. Rather,
it should be indicative of a lively, collaborative exploration which en-
hances the potential for therapeutic success.

(4) Interpreting Task Behavior

How the patient approaches the task, his emotional reactions to it
and to the therapist during his attempt and even his response to ob-

taining the solution may be more significant than the solution itself. Granted that the therapist has been supportive, the patient's approach may offer a vital assessment both to the patient and the therapist of the depth and rigidity of the patient's problem-solving strategies and emotional reactions to stress. The therapist, therefore, must not allow the patient's mounting anxiety or depression to have a contagious effect. The patient's insecurity should not deter the therapist but can, by providing a better understanding of the patient, offer him improved feedback.

The therapist's message throughout is, "I can't tell you how to solve this task, just as I can't tell you how to solve your problems in life. But I can help you to discover inner blocks to problems and to learn how to approach solving problems." The therapist affirms that there is no one right way to solve problems, only more effective approaches. It may be helpful, he notes, not to try so hard to discover the solution, but to examine one's inner feelings and thoughts for a new way of viewing the problem itself. The therapist can help the patient to see that sometimes a problem is a problem only because it is looked at from only one angle; looked at from another, the solution becomes so obvious that the problem no longer exists.

The therapist may point out how defining a problem too narrowly can inhibit finding a solution. Patients who persist doggedly in the same direction, even after the problem does not yield to their efforts, may be shown how they are blocked from considering new directions by stubborn commitment to the old.

Some patients may need to adopt a less impulsive, more analytical attitude. Here, the therapist should encourage the patient to slow down: "You don't have to panic. Begin at the beginning and take your time. All is not lost because you can't get it right out. Try to isolate what the problem is and where you're going before you jump right in."

The therapist constantly is alert to how the patient's approach to the task is a metaphor of how he approaches problems in his life. He may help crystallize the patient's problems by asking, "Is this the way you get into difficulty with other things in your life? Does the way you are doing things or feeling now with the task remind you of the way you do things and feel in general?"

The therapist is ever ready to shift ground, balancing interpretations of the cognitive and emotional dynamics of the task with interpretations of the patient's intrapsychic dynamics. He may move away from the task per se, only to relate it to the transference; the therapist may then emphasize the developmental roots of the patient's conflict and finally focus on how the transference and these developmental aspects bear on the task.

Above all, the therapist takes the patient and his resources seriously. This involves helping the patient to grapple with the here-and-now, with areas that were put aside because they involved far too much anxiety and humiliation or because the patient's depression, negative self-image and low self-esteem inhibited his even attempting to contend with problems. The patient can learn to see that all problem-solving attempts are preparatory in the sense that one never can predict where they will lead, whether to success or failure. Every end is a beginning. The patient's behavior can spotlight the as yet unrealized problem-solving potentialities within his existence. After each attempt, both the patient and the therapist can ask questions and see new possibilities that could not even have been formulated before the attempt was made.

The patient becomes aware of and learns to use his full emotional and intellectual resources by opening his eyes to new approaches to problems. He begins to entertain fresh conceptualizations that stem from asking daring and fundamental questions about himself and how he approaches the world.

(5) Providing Clues

At appropriate times, the therapist may assist the patient by providing various clues to implement mastery of the task. These clues are not intended to tell the patient how to solve the problem or to do it for him. Rather, they may help the patient to use his capacities more effectively and to enlarge his cognitive repertoire. The therapist can provide *cognitive clues,* or hints which sensitize the patient to the relevant aspects of the problem and focus on enhancing his perceptual, thought or memory operations that afford him a new way of viewing the problem, or *psychodynamic clues,* which take the form of interpreting and resolving the patient's defenses and conflicts that are blocking his problem-solving processes.

Before intervening with clues, the therapist should assess the kinds of interventions that would be most helpful. In formulating a therapeutic plan, he should determine the patient's readiness for clues and the kinds of clues that would be most effective by addressing the following issues:

—If the patient says, "I can't do it," or "It can't be done," or "It's impossible," the therapist should clarify the patient's reasons for withdrawing from the problem.

—Does the patient ask for clues or ask the therapist to complete the task for him, or does he steadfastly redouble his efforts in the face of frustration and failure?

—What are the patient's feelings and thoughts as he proceeds from one unsuccessful solution to another?

—Does he give up easily or persevere, and how and why?

—Does he become anxious, hostile, and verbally attack the therapist, or does he become depressed and withdrawn?

—Does he feel that he is being tricked or that the therapist is angry with him?   .

—Does he insist that the task is insoluble, or does he belittle the task?

—What are his fantasies?

—Does he hope the therapist will intervene and rescue him from this seemingly hopeless predicament?

—Does he sexualize the situation or in other ways attempt to manipulate the therapist to get him to give clues or solve the problem for him, or divert attention from his inability to solve it?

—Does he playfully and creatively make a game out of it, which may help him in reaching the solution?

—Does encouraging the patient actually increase productivity? If it does not, is it in spite of real effort on the patient's part? Do clues elicit only a token compliance?

—If nothing else seems to work, instead of looking for new solutions from within himself, does he externalize the problem and attempt to alter the task to suit his needs by changing the instructions or altering the constraints placed on the task?

Exploration of these issues not only is important in determining when and how to provide clues, but is vital for understanding the patient's emotions and perceptions of the task as well as his relationship to the therapist.

(a) Cognitive clues

Clues are provided not merely to help the patient solve the problem, but to expand his awareness of how to approach problems in general. Therefore, the therapist offers clues so the patient can gradually learn how to learn and to approach problems more adaptively. To this end, the patient is helped increasingly to focus on the relevant dimensions of the problem and thus to extend the range of his problem-solving capacities.

When the patient reaches an impasse with a task, the therapist can gradually introduce clues graded in order of increasing potency. In the beginning, the clues offer only the slightest hint so as not to give away the solution too soon, which could undermine the patient's self-esteem and rob him of the opportunity to mobilize and develop his ego-adaptive resources. The early clues simply try to nudge the patient out of his repetitive position by encouraging him to adopt a different perspective. For example, clues initially are general and abstract in nature and simply direct the patient toward perceiving the problem in a new way. The therapist might say:

"Take a new perspective."
"You've tried that way many times. Start fresh and try to approach it from a new angle."
"Try to see the problem in a different framework."

These abstract clues are usually effective with patients who are already functioning at a highly abstract level of development and where the problem is almost assimilable, requiring only the slightest nudge. Less cognitively developed individuals require clues of a more concrete nature. Such patients typically are sensitive to and perceive the world in sensory, functional, concrete and pragmatic ways. For example, with the Triangles Problem, the therapist might say:

"Think of constructing a house with the sticks."
"If you were traveling in Egypt, what building comes to mind?"
"How do you pitch a tent?"

By embedding clues in concrete, subjective experience, like pitching a tent, the therapist reaches toward the patient's developmental level and frames the problem in a way in which less developed individuals comprehend the world.

Table 2 illustrates the gradient of cognitive clues that has been found useful in implementing the problem-solving process with the Triangles Problem.

These guidelines for providing clues in terms of developmental level are, of course, parallel to the guidelines which a developmentally oriented therapist uses in all of his communications with his patients. For example, the therapist always tries to organize his interpretations and strategies in terms of the developmental level of his patients so that they will be assimilated and effectively used.

Some issues to consider while formulating clues are:

—What kinds of clues are most helpful?

TABLE 2
Gradient of Clues for the Triangles Problem

1. Try something different.

2. Look at the problem in a really different way.

3. Look at the sticks from a different perspective.

4. Touch, hold, and feel each of the sticks.

5. What could you do with these sticks if they were not being used for this problem?

6. What would be a really far-out way of using the sticks?

7. Instead of doing it on the table, think of doing it on the floor.

8. Instead of little sticks, think of them as longer pieces of wood. What if they were large, one-foot long rulers? What if they were large pieces of lumber?

9. Think of building something with the sticks.

10. Think of constructing something with the sticks.

11. Think of constructing a house with the sticks.

12. What kinds of things do you do with your hands?

13. Have you ever built things with Legos, Lincoln Logs, or Erector sets?

14. Think of the sticks as if they were part of an Erector set.

15. Would pieces of styrofoam help in building something with the sticks?

16. When you go over the Bay Bridge to San Francisco, what's the outstanding thing you see?

17. Is there a building that stands out?

18. If you were traveling in Egypt, what comes to mind?

19. What are the special buildings which you would see in Egypt?

20. If you were to camp out, what special experiences would you have?

21. How do you pitch a tent?

—Do the clues supplied encourage or discourage the patient?

—Are they appreciated or resented?

—Do clues lead to self-disparagement or childish responses, like direct pleas to be told that this or that approach is "right" or "acceptable," or do they mobilize the patient's ego resources and lead to new cognitive integrations?

—Is the patient grasping the general principles of the clues by applying them in a general way to help him to contend more effectively with succeeding tasks and problems in his life, or are the clues seen only in a narrow context, limited to the specific task?

Remember that our goal is not merely to facilitate mastery of the tasks, but to gain insight into how the patient approaches problems in general and how he can surmount them. By viewing the patient's problem-solving processes as they occur and seeing how he assimilates clues, organizes information and interacts with the therapist, we obtain a first-hand view of the patient in action, and can develop a more productive therapeutic plan to implement the therapeutic process.

It is helpful, therefore, for the therapist and the patient to become aware of the ways in which the patient uses clues as well as the degree to which he needs clue support to solve the problem. How the patient integrates clues and the extent to which he needs clues are also valuable prognostic indicators. Difficulty in assimilating clues and a constant need for clues may indicate limited cognitive capacities or pervasive emotional problems. With these patients, a more active and supportive approach, stressing concrete interpretations, may be helpful.

However, extensive "cluing" and providing ever simpler clues poses a dilemma, for it risks undermining the patient's feelings of independence and self-worth and depriving him of the therapeutic value obtained from self-discovery and mastery. On the other hand, withholding clues risks confronting the patient with an impasse and outright failure and increases the possibility that excessive anxiety or regression will disrupt the therapeutic process.

Even with its potential drawbacks, in the early stages of therapy we find it useful to provide more emotional and clue support, especially with the more serious disturbances. The therapist can establish a therapeutic alliance and demonstrate that he is not merely a detached observer who is clinically scrutinizing and evaluating the patient, but is entering into a helping relationship in a mutual quest to find solutions to the patient's problems.

Where extensive clue support is perceived as demeaning or as an affront to the patient's self-esteem, the therapist can focus on the patient's hurt feelings and how he perceives his limitations and relationships in which he needs help. Difficulty in mastery and even the humiliation of potential failure can be turned into an opportunity to explore the emotional and cognitive reasons for that difficulty.

With patients suffering from severe anxiety and rents in ego functioning, rather than unduly stressing the patient and testing the limits and possibly exacerbating the symptoms, the therapist can temporarily suspend work on a task and shift to less threatening issues. The therapist can say, "Let's put the task aside for a while. Perhaps later on you will gain more perspective on it." When there are signs of improved ego integration, it may be possible for the therapist to draw the patient back to the task. In cases of severe ego disorganization or fragmentation, the therapist may not be able to return to a task until months or even years later, when the patient has achieved a higher level of integration. (See, for example, the case of Sara with the Golf Ball Problem discussed later in this chapter.)

The therapist need not, however, invariably avoid using a task simply because it arouses anxiety. As we have seen in the case of Hal, contending with tasks during his schizophrenic episode was itself ego-building and mobilized his secondary-process thinking. Moreover, as in the case of Bob with the Code Problem, a task can also help the patient to explore, identify and resolve the affective factors and developmental arrests which may have contributed to impaired cognitive functioning.

At the end of a session, it is important to reassure the patient that nonsolution of the problem should not be considered a failure because the patient has another chance to overcome the difficulty and successfully master it in the following session. Moreover, the therapist can point out that it is the "bottom line," the end result that counts. Hanging in there and struggling with a problem over an extended period of time is an important strategy for solving problems.

With some tasks, it may also be possible to suggest that the patient work on the problem on his own at home. While this approach diminishes our view of the patient in action, this kind of "outside homework" with a task can be helpful to maintain continuity between the sessions, to provide a bridge between the sessions and the patient's daily life and to enable him to work through and integrate issues addressed in the sessions.

If, even with the help of cognitive clues, the patient reaches an impasse, the therapist can approach the problem from another direction. He can introduce psychodynamic clues (to be discussed in the next section) which can assist the patient in resolving the underlying conflicts that impair cognitive functioning and interfere with mastery of the task.

Clinical Example: Sara—Clown-and-Donkey Problem

The therapist does not always provide clues or answer the patient's inquiries, especially when the instructions have previously spelled out the answer to the patient's questions. The therapist tries to clarify what the patient is really asking and what underlying emotional purpose is served by his questions.

For example, in the following case with the Clown-and-Donkey Problem, rather than answering Sara's questions and allowing the patient to reenact unresolved childhood issues of passivity and dependency, the therapist is able to show her how she uses her "stupidity" and helplessness as a way to manipulate people to be like a parent to her and tell her what to do. This opens up the whole area of how she is "not sure of her ears" because fantasies intrude into her realistic perception of the world. Exploration of the patient's reaction to or withholding of clues, therefore, brings into focus the important issues of the patient's distortions and the transference.

P: They're both riding the donkeys upside down. (*Long pause*) Do they have to be sitting right side up?

T: What do you mean?

P: Do they have to be sitting straddling the donkey's back, or can they be lying like this or something like that?

T: What were the original instructions?

P: You just said sitting on the donkey. Well, sitting on the donkey's back, I guess, is normally the way they do it. (*Pause*) This is pretty strange. Sitting on the donkey, sitting on the donkey. On the donkey's back? (*Sighs*) (*Pause*) Question: Is this part here part of the donkey? (*Sniffle*) (*Pause*)

T: What part?

P: The part that the little clown is sitting on. (*Sniffle*)

T: What do you think it is?

P: It can't be 'cause otherwise you'd have to overlap it. But it looks like it's supposed to be. (*Pause*)

T: Well, I think you have to work with that yourself. I can't tell you how to solve it.

P: Hmm. I guess that's a hint. If you were to answer that, then that would be a hint.

T: What you do is that you try to ask this question and in this subtle way try to manipulate me to give you a hint. And maybe you do that a lot in life. I mean, you always said that you were a manipulator.

P: Mmm-hmm.

T: Maybe this is how you do it. You kind of act helpless, or what about this or that, and in kind of indirect ways, you're always trying to get hints on how to live your life.

The therapist confronts the patient with how she uses her helplessness to manipulate others to get them to do things for her.

P: I get hints. And then I get frustrated because I don't get ground rules. Just hints.

T: Ground rules? What do you mean? Somebody to take over your life and tell you to do it this way?

P: Uh-huh. Like a policy manual or something. "This is what you do when this happens," like Amy Vanderbilt or whatever that etiquette book is.

T: Uh-huh, like a parent would tell a child: "This is what you should do."

P: Mmm-hmm. (*Pause*) Apparently I'm back in that old rut again. I thought I'd managed to break away somewhat. (*Pause*) Well, you're right, I ask for lots of hints, I am not sure of my own ears, I guess, and hearing something, I keep thinking there's more inferences or something like that associated. Like a simple statement might have all kinds of meanings. And so I keep asking questions that might help clear that up.

Clinical Example: Sara—Golf Ball Problem

Up to now, we have discussed a number of alternative strategies for dealing with a patient's difficulties with a task, such as providing emotional and clue support. In this case, we shall focus on a strategy that may be feasible when the task seems so far beyond the patient's current cognitive repertoire that even with clue support, it is unreasonable to expect her to master it at that time.

There may be a tendency for the therapist to try to rescue the patient from the humiliation of failure and show her how to master the task, which may fit in with her rescue fantasies. This may be what her parents did when she was growing up and may be just the kind of experience that originally prevented her from growing up cognitively and emotionally. The alternative of allowing the patient to struggle futilely hour after hour is, of course, to be avoided. Under these circumstances, it is better to defer the task to a later date and return to it when the patient has shown signs of improvement in cognitive and emotional organization.

For example, in this case, Sara had worked on the Golf Ball Problem for the better part of two sessions and continued to perseverate on the same ineffective solutions. Finally she said, "I have this feeling that I'm never going to solve it, no matter what." Because of the severity of the patient's problems at this time, the therapist was inclined to agree with her and, therefore, did not pursue the task. Two years later, however, after the patient had made considerable therapeutic progress, the therapist returned to the task for the third time. This time, the patient readily mastered it.

(The patient talked about her problems with her job for several minutes. Then, the therapist presented the task.)

P: I think it has to do with visualizing the ball sitting in the bag, imagining it in a different way. (*Pause*) Maybe he could get another golf ball or something. Maybe he can pick up the bag and carry it over to the hole. (*Long pause*) Well, he seems to have eliminated both of the possibilities. He can either take it from the bag and it costs him a penalty stroke.

T: Right.

P: Or if he hits the ball and the bag together, he loses control of the shot.

T: Right.

P: So you've got to get the ball from the bag without him taking it. Oh! Well, he could set a match to the bag! He's removing it, but he's not moving the ball. It's not going to burn the lawn of the fareway, I don't think. (*Pause*) He's got to eliminate it somehow. He can get it wet. I kind of like the idea of the match. That's sort of neat and clean.

T: How did that come to mind?

P: Well, trying to get rid of the bag. I've got to think about the bag as just paper and it, you know, what are you going to do to just instantly make it disappear? You're going to burn it or dissolve it or you're going to do something to it. Tearing it is going to move the ball.

T: Mmm-hmm.

P: I kind of think that's the answer.

T: It's kind of interesting that you struggled with this for two or three sessions previously and you never came across this match idea. You thought of letting it soak in water until the paper disintegrated.

P: Well, I was on the right track, I just didn't, you know, water and then fire.

T: Why do you think you were able to do it now?

P: (*Sighs*) I don't know. I'm concentrating on other things. The same old problems aren't bothering me. Now these are new problems.

T: Yeah, what made you more able now?

P: Changed. These are changing. That's all. Thinking about different things.

T: But how does that help you solve the problem?

P: I'm not stuck in a rut. I can think of a different way to approach it. My life isn't quite so ordered and, well, it's ordered . . . not stagnant, I guess, is the right word.

Summary

This case illustrated how tasks can play a dual role as a producer and product of therapeutic change. While the main purpose of the tasks is to implement therapeutic progress, subsequent progress implements the development of the cognitive and affective mechanisms which enhance the patient's ability to master previously unmastered tasks. Tasks, therefore, serve as an agent and a barometer of change, and provide tangible evidence to both the therapist and the patient of improvement during the course of therapy.

(b) Psychodynamic clues

It is fascinating to note that even with all of these cognitive clues, some patients still encounter extreme difficulty with or are unable to master a task. In these instances, it becomes glaringly obvious that deep-seated intrapsychic emotional conflicts and developmental deficits are blinding the person and blocking mastery of the task. Impediments to mastery and impairments in cognitive functioning which show up on a task provide a unique opportunity for the therapist to demonstrate to the patient how his inner problems contribute to his difficulties, both with the tasks and in life. Specifically, the therapist provides psychodynamic clues by pointing out and clarifying how the patient's problems and conflicts interfere with adaptive behavior. Psychodynamic clues can implement important cognitive reorganizations which facilitate productive thinking and improve problem solving.

These clues not only help the patient to master the task, but are a powerful means to clarify how the patient's emotional problems contribute to his difficulties in life.

For example, after reaching an impasse with the Triangles Problem, Frank was severely self-reproachful and recounted how miserable he was at work and in his personal life. The therapist pointed out how the patient's self-castigating and masochistic orientation contributed to his failures.

P: You mean I have to be punished in order to enjoy success?
T: Yeah. Either somebody will punish you and that will satisfy you or you'll do it yourself, by avoiding success.
P: By not letting my mind think straight.
T: Right.

Almost immediately, Frank thought of the three-dimensional solution. The psychodynamic interpretation not only shed light on his central emotional problem, but appeared to free him to think in a more productive way and master the task.

Similarly, Sara's idiosyncratic symbolism interfered with her mastery of the Jug Problem (see pp. 102–111). Interpreting and demonstrating the deleterious role of her symbolism on the task helped her to contend with the task as well as with her problems in daily life.

3. INTERPERSONAL DYNAMICS

A CET session has a complex psychological structure. It is not merely a getting-together of two people in order that one, the patient, works on "puzzles" or listens to audiotapes while the other, the therapist, observes and objectively evaluates that person's perceptions and problem-solving abilities. Because the patient approaches the task as he does other tasks in life and he is in some acute or chronic life crisis, he cannot but bring his many hopes, fears, assumptions, demands and expectations into the situation. As with his relationship to the therapist, the patient responds intensely to certain real as well as fantasy attributes of the task situation. He may perceive the task situation as a test which will reveal not only his personal conflicts, but his intrinsic intellectual capacities as well. He may fear and resent being exposed and seen as dumb, open to ridicule and disapproval. Therefore, the patient's responses assume interpersonal and symbolic, transferential meanings which pervade the simple task responses. This is not an evil to be avoided. On the contrary, the patient's actions and accompanying interaction with the therapist are a possible gold mine for exploration, observation and interpretation. It is particularly important, therefore, that the therapist maintain an empathic and involved but neutral attitude during the task so that the patient can respond without being burdened by the therapist's personal contribution.

The question of how much a therapist should tell a patient of what he sees in his task behavior is a complex one. To "tell all" is to throw tact to the wind. The patient may interpret these revelations as a hostile means of exposing the patient, as if one were to give a patient a Rorschach and interpret the unconscious meanings of the patient's responses. The patient may interpret these intellectualizations as an intrusion and an assault on his defenses. By having to confront rejected, perhaps repressed, aspects of himself, the patient may respond with anxiety and, in the least, may be forced into an acutely ambivalent position. He may react defensively and self-protectively, and assume a negativistic and withdrawn attitude.

Moreover, since an impatient glance, a sharp word, or a curt gesture on the therapist's part can make a great difference in the patient's definition of the relationship and his attempts at resolution of the problems presented to him, the therapist must be on the alert for a significant degree of anxiety, affective disorganization and primary-process thinking that may be stimulated. These signals must be readily identified, taken seriously and effectively dealt with by the therapist as he would any other therapeutic material.

What should distinguish contending with a task in CET therapy sessions and contending with a task in an ordinary test situation is that, instead of the information being used evaluatively by the therapist, the information is available to both the therapist and the patient for their mutual enlightenment. The therapist's role, therefore, is significantly different from that of tester or interviewer in a psychological test or diagnostic situation where they find out but tell nothing. The therapist cannot take a crisp and detached attitude toward the patient, as if to maintain that the patient is only of research or theoretical interest and that the ultimate fate of the patient is really of no concern to him. The therapist must always be ready to interrupt the patient's task performance to contend with the urgent demands of his life. The patient's welfare is primary.

4. COUNTERTRANSFERENCE ISSUES

Applying the tasks or audiotapes as "tests" or assessment procedures in which they extend and articulate the *therapist's* understanding of the patient's problems represents a misuse of the approach and may be therapeutically futile. This approach might even backfire as a kind of psychological rape, seriously disturbing the course of therapy. Especially with severely disturbed and paranoid patients, where the therapeutic relationship is so fragile, a diagnostically oriented approach carries too much of an air of finding out things about the patient, which may make the patient feel too vulnerable to emotional abuse. In such cases, the patient may respond with a disruptive increase in anxiety and more guardedness in the therapeutic relationship. Helpful though our method may be, the therapist should, therefore, be sensitive to the repercussions that the task may have on the patient-therapist relationship. "What are the patient's feelings and fantasies concerning the task?" and "How does he experience the tasks and conceive of their role in the therapeutic process?" are important issues that the therapist can focus on.

Against the background of trying to understand the patient's adaptive and maladaptive style, the therapist should not allow the tasks to become too much of a detached, logical, verbalistic, puzzle-solving affair. The intellectualizing therapist may inappropriately use the task situations mainly to see how the patient solves puzzles. He may go blithely on and gather data and interpret everything in sight without the least twitch of personal anxiety and with absolutely no feel for the emotional context of the task situation. This kind of detached and omniscient pose abuses the task and uses it to gather data against the patient to expose him rather than as a means for helping him. Something of this intellectualization will certainly be communicated to the patient, who will understand it—in part correctly so—as cold and narcissistic self-absorption and a need to maintain strict control over the patient. There is no easier way to alienate a patient than to convey to him the feeling that the therapist views him only as an "interesting case."

On the other hand, the therapist need not be faint-hearted. He can more readily call a spade a spade. The patient's performance on the task allows the therapist, without rancor, criticism or condescension, to be freer to show the patient just how he is mismanaging his life. With a concrete example in front of him, it will be easier for the patient to see and handle the destructiveness in his masochistic maneuvers and the mockery in his pseudo-conscientiousness or compliance. The therapist will not be too eager to be taken in and manipulated by tears, smiles, and groans. Because he is willing to perceive and acknowledge the signs of strength and adaptability in the patient, he will not have to undo every true-to-the-mark interpretation with a benign, supportive one. The therapist can be bold and daring lest his anxiety and guilt over broaching sensitive areas communicate to the patient that these areas are indeed taboo and to be avoided. And he certainly will not have to avoid the aggressive, sadistic and vicious aspects of the patient because they will be apparent to both therapist and patient in the here-and-now actions and emotional responses of the patient *in* the session. Because they are expressed openly, the therapist will not be blind to the pathological implications of the patient's task behavior or lead him to minimize them or undo them by weak qualifications.

The therapist ordinarily need not return comments or interpretations in exchange for the patient's task behavior or self-exposures, as if the patient's responses are but a means to manipulate or make demands on the therapist. Rather, the therapist may note that this is the patient's characteristic interpersonal style. One can speculate with him whether he uses this method with other people as a means of avoiding anxiety and obtaining control in a relationship.

It is important that the therapist not allow increases in the patient's anxiety to stimulate his own anxiety and induce him to change his therapeutic plan. He must see this anxiety as a useful response just as any other response in the therapeutic situation would be. There is a tendency to try to save the patient from discomfort and to assuage his anxiety by "jumping in" and prematurely providing the solution to the task. This countertransference reaction only undermines the patient's feeling that he can contend with frustration and the problems facing him and deprives him of real gratification when he discovers the solution.

It is more therapeutic to support the patient in his attempts and to help him face his anxiety and frustration. The therapist can reassure the patient that the task is indeed difficult but that, given time and perseverance, he can and will be able to come to an adequate solution.

There are other countertransference reactions which the therapist should be alert to. He may become irritable, anxious or impatient, possibly even bored and sleepy. His helpfulness may become condescending or his friendliness, eagerness, and exaggerated supportiveness may humiliate the patient and undermine his efforts. Also, excessive concern or inquiry into the patient's difficulty in grasping the solution may instill even further anxiety or confusion. These affective, countertransference reactions to the patient are avenues for the therapist's self-exploration which can play a vital role in deepening the therapeutic process. By discovering what in the patient triggers these reactions, the therapist can better understand himself and the patient, refine his strategy and develop a more comprehensive therapeutic plan.

CHAPTER VI

The Effectiveness of CET

A novel approach can be justified if it improves the outcome of therapy and extends the range of patients who can be effectively treated. Therefore, effectiveness is the prime criterion to apply to any new therapeutic approach.

After extensive use of CET from 1967 to 1979 on an experimental basis with a wide range of diagnostic categories and patient populations, intensive clinical trials were conducted between 1979 and 1983 on a random population of ten patients (Weiner, 1984). Because of the highly promising results obtained in this pilot study, research is continuing to more thoroughly evaluate CET with a larger and broader sample tested in different institutional settings.

1. HOW THE CLINICAL TRIALS WERE ORGANIZED

(1) The Patient Population

In 1979, referral sources in the community were notified that clinical trials for CET were being conducted. To put the method to a rigorous test, we explained that we hoped to treat the most difficult cases they could find, those considered resistant and recalcitrant and who had failed in previous therapeutic attempts. In order to test the limits and usefulness of CET as a short- and long-term therapeutic intervention, for the clinical trials we accepted the first ten patients who applied for treatment or consultation and provided CET for lengths of time ranging from one session (for consultation) to a maximum of four years. Although the one patient who was seen for a one-hour consultation could not be included in the quantitative pre- and post-therapy assessments, she was qualitatively evaluated in terms of the usefulness of the CET consultation in her overall treatment. All of the CET sessions were recorded and transcribed with the patient's written permission, resulting in 15,000 pages of verbatim transcript.

The sample thus obtained could fairly be described as "difficult": nine of the ten cases had previously undergone psychotherapy and/or pharmacotherapy. Three patients had been previously hospitalized; two of these were still psychotic when first seen by the CET therapist. Three of the ten patients had previously attempted suicide, two seriously enough to be hospitalized. Two of the patients made a serious suicide attempt just prior to being admitted for treatment and two others were contemplating suicide. The one patient who had not received previous psychotherapeutic treatment was in a state of life crisis. She was trapped in a horrible marriage and was severely depressed.

(2) Safety

There were no adverse reactions or side effects due to CET. No extended or emergency sessions were necessary to contend with a patient's reaction to the CET methods. On the contrary, all of the patients not only expressed satisfaction after being engaged in a CET intervention, but looked forward to and requested additional therapeutic tasks. Also, as we will presently demonstrate when discussing the method used to assess therapeutic change, there were no cases in which the patient was worse off after a CET method was introduced. Further, only in one case, a paranoid schizophrenic who had been twice previously hospitalized, did a patient require hospitalization during the course of his treatment. In this case, he was discharged as greatly improved after eight days of intensive CET.

Lastly, there were no drop-outs or abrupt terminations. Only one patient, this same paranoid schizophrenic, terminated "prematurely"; i.e., although he was making progress, he decided, "I want to try things on my own now."

(3) Therapeutic Compliance

None of the patients rejected a therapeutic task or refused to continue after it was introduced. The patients looked forward to the tasks and, when none had been introduced for one or more sessions, asked the therapist if he had "any more tasks" for them to do. An outstanding example is provided by the schizophrenic patient who had been hospitalized. While lying half-naked and curled up in a fetal position in bed, out of the morass of incoherence and withdrawal he asked the therapist, "Do you have any of your puzzles with you? They put me in touch with that part of myself which is rational."

2. THERAPEUTIC OUTCOME

(1) Assessment Instruments

The Health-Sickness Rating Scale of Luborsky (1975) was used to assess each patient's mental health. The assessments were made by the therapist, who scored each patient in seven key areas based on evaluation of audiorecordings of the patients' first and last four therapy sessions. While it was possible to randomize the order in which the pre- and post-therapy tapes were presented for scoring, the ratings could not effectively be "blinded" because of references within the sessions. The rater, however, attempted to score the patients solely on the basis of the recordings and not to be unduly influenced by whether the sessions were pre- or post-treatment. The patients were evaluated on the following seven dimensions:

1. Need to be *protected and/or supported* by their therapist or hospital versus ability to function *autonomously.*
2. The *seriousness* of the symptoms.
3. The patient's *subjective discomfort and distress.*
4. The *effect* of the patient on his environment. Is he dangerous? Does he make others uncomfortable?
5. The effectiveness of the patient in *utilizing his abilities*, especially in work.
6. The quality of the patient's *interpersonal relationships* (warmth, intimacy, sincerity, closeness, degree of distortion in his perception of relationships, impulse control).
7. The *breadth and depth of the patient's interests.*

The scale points are defined in Table 3.

(2) Ratings at Intake

The overall score for each patient represents the average of the scores in the above seven areas. The ratings, pre and post, are presented in Table 4.

TABLE 3
Definition of Scale Points for Health-Sickness Ratings

Definition	Scale Point 100	Examples
At 100: An ideal state of complete functioning integration, of resiliency in the face of stress, of happiness and social effectiveness. From 99 to 76: Degrees of "everyday" adjustment. Few individuals in this range seek treatment.		Some patients who complete treatment, and some who come for and need only "situational" counseling.
At 75: Inhibitions, symptoms, character problems become severe enough to cause more than "everyday" discomfort. These individuals may occasionally seek treatment.	75	Patients with very mild neuroses or mild addictions and behavior disorders *begin* here and go on down, depending on severity.
At 65: Generally functioning pretty well but has *focalized* problem or more generalized lack of effectiveness without specific symptoms.	65	Clearly neurotic conditions (most phobias, anxiety neuroses, neurotic characters).
At 50: Definitely needs treatment to continue to work satisfactorily and has increasing difficulty in maintaining himself autonomously (even without expressed or recognized need for formal treatment). Patient may either be in a stable unsatisfactory adjustment (where most energy is bound in the conflicts) or an unstable adjustment from which he will likely regress.	50	Severe neuroses such as severe obsessive-compulsive may be rated at 50 or lower, rarely below 35. Some *compensated* psychoses, many character disorders, neurotic depressions.

TABLE 3 *(continued)*

Definition	Scale Point	Examples
	35	*Most* borderline schizophrenics; severe character problems. Psychotic depressions may be this high or go all the way to 0.
At 25: Obviously unable to function autonomously. Needs hospital protection or would need it if it were not for the support of the therapist. The fact that the patient is in the hospital does not mean he must be rated at this point—he may have changed since admission or be hospitalized for any of a variety of reasons.	25	Most clear-cut, overt psychoses, psychotic characters, severe addictions (which require hospital care).
From 24 to 1: Increased loss of contact with reality; need for protection of patient or others from the patient; high degree of regression.		
At 10: Extremely difficult to make any contact with patient. Needs closed ward care. Not much chance of continued existence without care.	10	"Closed ward" patients, such as chronic schizophrenics, excited manics, profound suicidal depressions.
At 0: Any condition which, if unattended, would quickly result in the patient's death, but not necessarily by his own hand.	0	Completely regressed schizophrenics (incontinent, out-of-contact) who require complete nursing care, tube feedings.

The pre-treatment scores (the bottoms of the vertical bars) indicate that all ten of the patients were moderately to severely disturbed. All of the patients initially scored below 65; the highest score was 62 where one finds, according to Luborsky's guidelines (1975) based on eighteen reliability and validity studies carried out over the course of twelve years, "clearly neurotic conditions." Nine of the patients scored 55 or below, which signifies "definitely needs treatment" with "severe neuroses, psychoses, character disorders or neurotic depressions." The two lowest scoring patients were psychotic. Their scores, 15 and 22, represent "most clear-cut overt psychoses, obviously unable to·function autonomously, increased loss of contact with reality, and high degree of regression."

(3) Length of Treatment

As noted in Table 4, the quickest effective response to CET was demonstrated with acute outpatient neurotic depression (Marj) after four weeks. Only one case (Sara) continued in CET treatment for the maximum four-year clinical trial period. But even here, major improvements were achieved during the clinical trial. This patient continued in treatment for an additional nine months before successfully terminating.

(4) Quantitative Change

The lengths of the bars connecting the pre- and post-ratings represent the degree of improvement in each case. An analysis of pre- and post-therapy change scores demonstrates that CET had a clinically significant impact on all of the patients. There were no cases of deterioration; all patients improved 29 or more points. After treatment, eight of the nine therapy patients scored in the 76–94 range where, according to Luborsky's criteria, few individuals seek treatment. Six of these patients scored 85 or above, which represents "everyday adjustment and good health." Although one of the psychotic patients still needed treatment, he had made notable improvements, reaching almost into the 55 range. The other psychotic patient was seen only once in consultation and was not, therefore, evaluated quantitatively.

(5) Qualitative Change

The main clinical finding was that eight of the nine therapy patients had been able to "make good" and "get ahead." In addition to relief of

TABLE 4
Pre and Post Health-Sickness Ratings

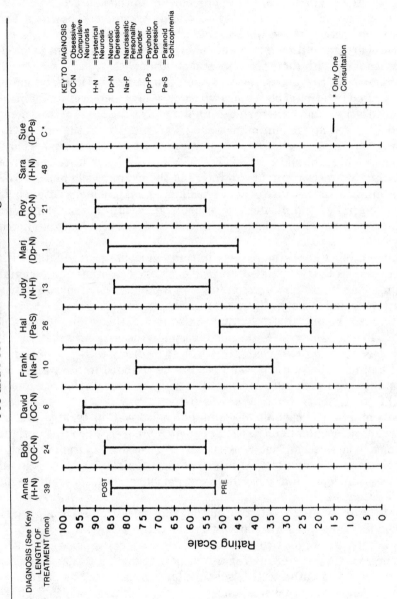

symptoms and enhanced ability to deal effectively with stressful situations, they showed marked improvements in their interpersonal relationships and in their ability to work. As will be shown in the following section where we present their case reports, they were capable of greater intimacy and were able to establish and maintain close relationships with their partners and children.

Progress in the work area was the most striking. Dramatic gains were noted in terms of better jobs with impressive increases in financial compensation. One patient, for example, had at the onset of treatment worked part-time at minimum wage as a waitress. At the end of the clinical trial, she was city-wide manager of two stores, supervising fifteen employees and earning $40,000 a year. In another case, the patient at onset was unable to work and the business she had started was falling apart because of her severe emotional problems. After therapy, she pulled the business together and, within a year, had four skilled workers in her employ and more than doubled her take-home pay.

Individuals whose studies were initially in jeopardy graduated with Ph.D.'s or M.D.'s, completed medical residency or other professional training and obtained outstanding, high-paying positions. In other cases, new and more gratifying career choices were noted.

Because the initial pre-therapy adjustment of the psychotic patient in CET was so low, it could not reasonably be expected that in his treatment lasting two years, a withdrawn, disorganized, delusional and hallucinating patient could readily be changed into a well-functioning person with intimate, satisfying interpersonal relations and a well-paying job. Nevertheless, this patient showed notable improvements and is now capable of leading, if not a well-integrated life, at least an independent and reasonable one. Moreover, since this patient seemed to be suffering not from psychotic regression but from an early-developmental arrest and a lifetime of disorganization—the so-called "process schizophrenia"—psychotherapy of longer duration would seem to be essential.

Furthermore, it is likely that not all that needs to be accomplished in the treatment of schizophrenia can be achieved by individual psychotherapy alone, particularly with those patients who are closer to the process than the acute, regressive pole of these disorders. By this we mean that a multifaceted, multimodal approach may be more critical for these process disturbances, one that includes not only pharmacotherapy, but community support networks and especially family involvement in an integrated treatment program.

For example, consider the case of Hal, the schizophrenic patient.

After his wife divorced him, he suffered from an acute schizophrenic episode from which, with the help of CET, he made a remarkable recovery and reintegration. Although he continued to gain post-hospitalization, without the emotional and financial support from his wife and relatives who, in essence, gave up and abandoned him, the forward thrust that he had experienced with CET prior to their loss was slowed.

3. CASE REPORTS

We now turn to the case reports for each patient where we summarize their problems and the impact of CET on their resolution.

Anna
Age: 31   *Score* **Pre:** 52
Married, no children   **Post:** 85
Diagnosis: Hysterical neurosis
Length of treatment: 3 years, 3 months

At the onset of treatment, Anna was severely depressed. Her first marriage had been a disaster. She obtained a divorce after slashing her wrists. Now in her second marriage, to a schizophrenic man, she felt paralyzed with anger and depression and spent most of her time in bed. Her entire life was crumbling. Although she had completed the coursework for her Ph.D., Anna had taken a leave of absence and was doing nothing to start work on her dissertation. She disdainfully looked back on her previous therapy experiences as a waste of time. She felt trapped. Her life had come to a lonely dead end.

After three years of CET, Anna reported that she surely would have killed herself had it not been for her treatment. During the course of CET, a broad transformation in her life was noted. Not only was she free of all depressive symptomatology, but she made marked progress in working out her very strong narcissistic tendencies. She also resumed her doctoral work and obtained a well-paying, gratifying job. At the same time, she met a very loving professional man. After living with him for a year, they married. Very soon, she became pregnant and then gave birth to a healthy child. "I was beginning to doubt whether I'd ever have children. It's been my dream ever since I was a child."

At a follow-up interview after one-and-a-half years, she brought her one-year-old son, a robust, cheerful, active and curious toddler, with her. She was happily married and planning to have another child. In thinking about her life, she reflected upon how she was more in control.

"I know there are a lot of times now when I don't do things that I know I would have done before, like get too excited about things or get hyperemotional, and get too angry about things without knowing why. I guess it's almost like while I'm being different, I'm seeing that I'm different. And I don't pick on people as much."

Bob

Age: 29　　　　　　　　　　　　　　　　　　　*Score* Pre: 55
Married, no children　　　　　　　　　　　　　　　　Post: 87
Diagnosis: Obsessive-compulsive neurosis
Length of treatment: 2 years

Bob was a second-year psychiatry resident who had been previously involved in group psychotherapy for severe depression due to the breakup of his relationship with a girlfriend prior to marriage. He feared that he could suffer another serious depression.

During the initial sessions, Bob's attitude was, "There's really nothing much wrong. I'll give it a few months. Maybe six months. I would like, however, to become more spontaneous. I feel dead inside. Sometimes I'm so bored with my work, I feel like quitting the program and getting out of the medical field altogether. Just do woodworking or listen to my shortwave radio upstairs in the room." Despite his tendency to deny the seriousness of his problems, Bob did admit to severe arguments with his wife's two children from a prior marriage who were visiting: "I can't wait for them to go back where they came from." Also, the patient frequented "adult" bookstores to watch X-rated movies and buy porno magazines to which he masturbated, sometimes while "on call" at the hospital.

At termination of treatment, Bob said that he felt more free and spontaneous. His relationship with his wife grew more intimate and they engaged in more frequent sexual relations. He no longer masturbated or frequented adult bookstores. He now had a four-month-old daughter whom he loved dearly. At the same time, he greatly improved his relationship with his wife's children and planned to move closer to them so that he and his wife could see them more frequently and play a greater role in their upbringing. Professionally, he became much more committed to his career, entered a fellowship program and began private practice.

One year post-therapy, a one-hour follow-up interview was conducted. After inquiring about Bob's life, the therapist asked what stood out in his therapy.

P: One of the main things I remember about therapy is that you pointed out one time that my mother wasn't going to change. It was like that was such a surprise to me at the time. I think that was the crucial part [of therapy]. It was really a shock to me. I had never considered that she wouldn't. I always assumed.

T: Hoped.

P: Yeah, I guess I always hoped that she would. It's funny, I ended up telling my little sister about that. I mean, I said the same thing to my sister. She was just as shocked. 'Cause I guess I've always kept this fantasy that somehow if I did something different or that I could do something different to make her change. And I think once that kind of sunk in, it affected my relationship with other people too. Like the faculty. I don't get caught up in arguments or I don't get as worked up anymore about things the faculty do. I just go there and put in time. And the thing is, I don't care as much if they like me anymore. That used to be real important. And now I feel like, as long as I get my work done, if they're satisfied, then I'm satisfied.

We see how giving up his childhood fantasies with his mother was central to working out his relationships at work and with authority figures.

T: Any other memorable things from therapy?

P: Well, I think that was the main thing. I felt like I kept trying to get you to change and now that I look back, I realize that I was angry a lot. And I was trying to get you to be different. (*Long pause*) I guess if I did it [therapy] again, I wouldn't spend so much time trying to make you behave different, or trying to make you act like you were somebody else.

Here we see how working out his childhood relationship with his mother is related to resolving the transference relationship with the therapist. Just as he gave up the infantile hope that his mother would change, so also did he give up the longing that the therapist would change.

(*Five minutes later, Bob returns to the process of therapy.*)

P: The process of therapy kept going even after I left the therapy. Because I kept thinking about things that we had talked about in here. (*Long pause*) Come to think of it, the other thing that changed was, I guess my whole body image in relation to you in therapy. I actually felt small during the therapy. I just felt like

I was just a little kid. I felt bigger near the end. It's like, I don't know, I guess I regressed or something, but I felt like physically I was much smaller and that you were much bigger than you really were. And that's changed.

During therapy while the patient was in the throes of the transference regression, he literally felt small "like I was just a little kid." As he resolved the transference, his body image changed and he felt bigger.

From a psychodynamic view, a critical criterion of growth in therapy is the resolution of the transference. Three manifestations of mastery of the transference were noted with this patient: (1) dissolution of his Oedipal attachment to his mother; (2) reorganization of his expectations and perception of the therapist; and (3) development of a more realistic image of self and others.

David

Age: 26   *Scores* Pre: 62
Married, no children   Post: 94
Diagnosis: Obsessive-compulsive neurosis
Length of treatment: 6½ months

David was a fourth-year medical student who was initially seen for several months by the medical school psychiatrist. He was referred for CET because "we hate to lose a student in the last year. He's very bright, but I fear he may not get through. His obsessional thoughts interfere with his work. He needs CET's problem-solving approach to help him learn how to contend with all the decisions a physician has to make."

During the initial CET sessions, David was overwhelmed by guilt feelings. He was tearful and depressed. He felt guilty about being molested by an older boy when he was four or five years old. Also, when he was four years of age, his mother died a slow death of stomach cancer and David still harbored enormous guilt feelings over his not being able to prevent her death.

David displayed the same obsessional thoughts in dealing with the CET tasks as he did in his work at medical school and at home. During the course of treatment, these tasks became the arena in which he was able to work through his guilt feelings.

At termination, David graduated from medical school with very high recommendations from his preceptors. He was no longer plagued by his obsessional thoughts which had intruded into his work and "really got in the way of getting a good history and the right diagnosis." He also clarified his career goals and obtained a first-rate internship in a leading training program. The patient's overall therapeutic progress was also reflected in his improved relationship with his wife.

Frank
Age: 42
Single
Diagnosis: Narcissistic personality disorder
Length of treatment: 10 months

Scores Pre: 34
Post: 77

Frank was referred because of severe career problems and acute depression. Even though he held a Ph.D. in biochemistry, he could not find work. After he had received his doctorate, he pursued his career in applied research but, after two years, he quit his job and found work abroad in basic research. Upon his return to this country, however, he could not find a job and lived like a "fourth-class citizen." He resigned himself to volunteering as a non-salaried lab assistant with the hope of finding a job by collaborating with a well-known scientist.

Leading a friendless, isolated existence, Frank spent most of his time in his shabby apartment without even a telephone to the outside world. He had never married, but slept with one woman after another and actually kept a log detailing his 560 liaisons. He was still searching for the "perfect" body type—very hairy and "whory looking." His life revolved around "singles" groups and attempts to seduce woman after woman. He received very little gratification from these contacts because he did not dare to pursue the women he was really attracted to and, at most, had to be content with viewing them from across the dance floor and then going home, fantasizing and masturbating.

When he started therapy, Frank was desperate. He was a depressed, isolated, angry and arrogant man. Thoughts of killing himself with his .22 caliber pistol filled his fantasies. Overwhelmed with feelings of failure, he feared he would fail even at suicide and planned to purchase a .38 caliber revolver to do a proper job of blowing his brains out.

At termination, he had made a complete change in his career goals. He realized that he never liked biochemistry, but had chosen that field to try to please his father. Now he had entered and was successfully completing a graduate program in engineering. "Working with concrete things is really what I wanted all along." In the personal sphere, he met a divorced woman who really "turned me on." At termination, Frank was no longer depressed nor did he evidence any suicidal ideation. His feelings of self-worth and confidence were greatly enhanced, bolstered by his feelings of hopefulness and improvement in both work and personal spheres.

An intensive five-year follow-up interview with Frank revealed that the choices he had embarked on while in therapy had been a turning point in his life. Brief excerpts are presented.

P: I got a master's degree in engineering and got the hell out of biochem. That was the whole problem. I got a good position. I'm making good bucks. This is where the action is in life. It isn't back in biochemistry. It's an entirely different world.

T: How about socially? How did things work out there?

P: That little gal I was running around with, she was a bit of a nut, and I suppose the age difference and all. I met another lady after her, about a couple of months later. Although I haven't married her, I've been palling around with her for the last four-and-one-half years.

T: What was noteworthy about your therapy with me? What were the good things and what were the bad things?

P: I told myself, if you don't take care of yourself, nobody is going to take care of you, and that's what I did. I started taking care of myself. I started treating myself better.

T: How did you get the knack to do that?

P: I decided to take the bull by the horns. Why don't you go out and identify where the action is and try to get a piece of it? More efficient, less sabotage. I'm more efficient.

T: Do you think therapy helped? Do you think those tasks were helpful?

P: There were probably one or two statements that were outstanding. "You can't look for an easy way. You got to pay the price. You have to struggle with it. You have to get in and fight it through." I couldn't let old convictions, like "you can't do mathematics," that bullshit I got from [name of university deleted] when I took that whole series of tests, and that led me to believe that I didn't have the ability. That's bullshit! Whatever you don't have in I.Q., you can make up by sheer fight. When I went through calculus, I wasn't a great student in calculus, but man, I got through, I got C's, but I got through. On the tasks, that was a big issue, to struggle with it, to keep at it, don't cave in. That's the attitude I took in the [master's] program. If anything, that was the issue that I did not take seriously, the issue of struggle. It was in the back of my mind, but I tried to discount it and write it off, that you needed some special I.Q. In other words, you needed to be born with certain gifts.

T: Like a bright, quick solution, like getting insight without having to sweat.

P: Exactly. That was the way I operated and when I got into this new area, I figured, the hell with it, man, I don't give a damn how sharp some guy is in the first round. In the end, I'll catch up with him.

T: Did you ever think of getting into any kind of counseling or therapy in these past five years?

P: No, not really.

T: Did you ever find that special kind of hairy woman that you found really sexy?

P: I never have been able to couple up with that.

T: This woman now?

P: No, she's not that way, but she's got other, let's say, there's certain spiritual aspects to her. There's compassion or empathy that draws me to her.

In addition to significant improvement in Frank's career achievements and gratifications, we note a remarkable change in his relationship to women. As is typical of narcissistic personality disorders, Frank had related to women mainly as sexual objects to be exploited, with special emphasis on their physical attributes. He slept with one woman after another; his longest relationship was six months. Presently, he has maintained a monogamous relationship with a woman for four-and-one-half years, with an appreciation for, and attraction toward, her emotional characteristics, such as compassion and empathy.

Hal
Age: 31   *Scores* Pre: 22
Married, no children   Post: 51
Diagnosis: Paranoid schizophrenia, chronic (two hospitalizations)
Length of treatment: 2 years, 2 months

Hal was very articulate, intelligent, witty and good-natured. He had chosen medicine in large part to try to please his father and two brothers—all physicians—and his wife, who wanted "the better things in life"—a house and a family. (For further discussion of Hal's background, see his clinical presentation on pp. 116–120.)

When the stress of his first year at medical school mounted, Hal showed signs of severe pathology. Florid hallucinations interfered with his concentrating at school because they intruded into his viewing slides and listening to lectures. His delusional preoccupations also made it all but impossible for him to read. He could not get through one page without being distracted. He isolated himself from most social activities. Clashes with his wife mounted. She became depressed, withdrew, sulked and was sullen most of the time. At other times, she left Hal while she sought relief by visiting relatives or friends in other cities for weekends or a week at a time. On one of these occasions when Hal was alone, he panicked and, in a state of disorientation, wandered away from their apartment and could not find his way back home.

Hal dropped out of medical school at the end of his first year and was referred for outpatient psychotherapy by the school psychiatrist. Although Hal had been hospitalized twice previously for schizophrenic breaks, he made impressive progress during CET treatment. His relationship with his wife improved. Previously, his best and longest job was as a security guard at a construction site, which lasted for six months. Now, although he was not ready to return to medical school, he was able to obtain a position teaching junior high school, the most responsible job he had ever held. Several months into treatment, his hallucinations also disappeared. He began to read again, and to compose and play music—he was a very talented musician—with his wife. At the same time, he took better care of himself physically and, on his own initiative, stopped following a very limiting "hypoglycemic" diet. He and his wife celebrated by flushing hundreds of megavitamin pills down the toilet. Hal said he had never felt better and his functioning in every area of his life showed improvement.

At the same time, however, his wife had entered psychotherapy. She became more assertive and made plans to further her career. She obtained an excellent job and, at the same time, started to work on completing her Ph.D. dissertation. When she made increasing demands on Hal to be the kind of husband she dreamed of—a man with a good and stable career and father to her children—he found these expectations too much, too soon. His wife began to resent him and again reacted by taking off alone to visit friends, which was just the kind of stress with which Hal was least able to cope.

Signs of disorganization soon began to appear. Finally, after a series of bitter clashes in which his wife told him to move out and that she wanted a divorce, Hal experienced another acute schizophrenic episode during which he suffered blatant hallucinations and self-inflicted bodily mutilations. (His eight-day hospitalization was discussed in detail on pp. 116–120.)

Hal showed a remarkable recovery during and after this hospitalization. He was able to move into an apartment by himself and maintain an independent life. He lost his teaching position when he was hospitalized, but was able to find another job as the manager of an allnight grocery store three days after being discharged.

Post-hospitalization treatment focused on working through the feelings which were brought to the surface by the divorce concerning abandonment and the loss of a symbiotic relationship and the consequent intolerable feeling of emptiness. Therapeutic efforts dealt with helping him to reintegrate ego functions, develop cognitive and problem-solving skills necessary for everyday living, improve social relations (he started to date other women again), sort out problems and possible ways of coping with them, clarify current real dilemmas and find a workable way of life. Although much work still needed to be done, Hal terminated treatment one year after hospitalization because he wanted to test his strength and feelings of self-worthiness.

Follow-up evaluations during a two-year period revealed that the gains Hal had made were maintained. He had required no further hospitalization and did not seek psychotherapy or pharmacotherapy. He had reestablished a stabilized relationship by obtaining a job caring for a woman suffering from cerebral palsy.

Judy
Age: 23   *Scores* Pre: 54
Married, no children   Post: 84
Diagnosis: Hysterical neurosis
Length of treatment: 1 year, 1 month

Judy was unhappily married. She felt emotionally starved. Her husband, while a good provider, was detached and unfeeling. To precipitate her divorce, she moved out and had an affair. Because her lover was a co-worker, she lost her job. In addition, although she had managed to complete the course work for her master's degree in nutrition, she panicked when she even thought of tackling the thesis.

After thirteen months of CET, her life had turned around. She obtained a divorce and began to date men who were much more giving and attuned to her needs and feelings. She successfully completed her master's degree and was offered a much-coveted position as a nutritionist in a prestigious hospital. Because this meant moving to a distant city, she accepted the job with some misgivings because she would have to terminate therapy. However, because she had married young and went directly from her parents' house to setting up a home with her first husband, she took this opportunity to strike out on her own and pursue her career.

Marj
Age: 42   *Scores* Pre: 45

Divorced, one child   Post: 86
Diagnosis: Neurotic depression, acute
Length of treatment: 1 month

Overwrought by a sense of disappointment, failure and despair when
her boyfriend left her, Marj had attempted suicide with an overdose
of barbiturates. The fortuitous intervention of a neighbor aborted the
attempt. Several years earlier, she had been hospitalized for a week
for another suicide attempt.

During her depressed state prior to this second attempt, Marj had
stopped working, withdrawn into her misery and no longer took care
of her thirteen-year-old daughter. She allowed her daughter to fend for
herself, neither looking after her needs, shopping for food, nor cleaning
the house.

After one month of CET, the patient was free of all depressive symptomatology and suicidal ideation. She began to care for her daughter
and renewed her social life, dating and seeing friends again and even
giving a large dinner party. She returned to work and, having recently
started her own business, picked up the loose ends and put into action
many of the productive ideas that she had thought about but never
carried through.

Because of the seriousness of her presenting symptoms and the brev-
ity of her treatment, extensive follow-up was conducted. These evaluations revealed that Marj had continued to improve. For example, at
a six-month follow-up, she noted, "Things have been on a gradually
progressive road of getting my act together. I hit the skids a few times
during the summer, but something finally clicked and I started to take
a more active role in my life for a change. Business is booming. I have
an assistant who works afternoons. I am enjoying things and not feeling
guilty about it.

"I guess the main difference I have noticed is that instead of sitting
back and waiting for things to happen to me, I'm getting in there with
both feet and hands and at least attempting to control my destiny
somewhat.

"Haven't felt even mild depression (let alone suicidal depression) for
over three months now, which is almost a record for me. Possibly this
is because I have become less neurotic. Possibly this is because I don't
have time to be depressed."

At a one-year follow-up, the patient wrote, "A series of crises have
occurred over the past couple of months which kind of 'tested' my state
of being, or whether the changes I felt had been internalized actually
had. [The patient described several legal problems she had encountered

in her business.] A year ago I would have been totally intimidated by this, but this time I found it hilarious and so, instead of sitting and waiting to see what 'they would do to me,' I wrote some of my wittier letters to [deleted] and totally boggled his mind and he dropped the whole thing. It has not made me suicidal either in thinking or acting. I'm just kind of enjoying sitting back and thinking up new ways to agitate.

"The main thing where I feel I have done some more active things than simply sitting back and being passive is with the business. During the slow month of January, instead of sitting here chewing my nails to the quick and getting ulcers and worrying about impending starvation, I made up letters to small businesses and have started to advertise. Gradually, the business is building up rather than withering down.

"In short, what I am trying to say is that instead of sitting passively back and waiting for things to happen to me, I'm taking a more positive and active stance in controlling (or attempting to control) my environment and what happens."

Roy

Age: 33   *Scores* Pre: 55
Divorced   Post: 90
Diagnosis: Obsessive-compulsive neurosis
Length of treatment: 1 year, 9 months

Roy, a twice-divorced graduate student, had been in therapy twice previously. He had spent nine years working unsuccessfully on his doctorate, during which he switched graduate schools and fields two times. Presently, he was encountering considerable difficulty with his dissertation and with his responsibilities as a teaching assistant. His relationship with his new girlfriend was also full of conflict. He was very depressed and considered himself a loser at both love and work.

During the course of his twenty-one months of CET, Roy completed his dissertation and earned his Ph.D., obtained a tenure-track assistant professorship at a leading university and worked out his problems with his girlfriend. This was the best relationship he had ever had with a woman. They married and, soon after, his wife became pregnant. The healthy baby, a son, was born soon after termination of treatment.

A follow-up interview after one year revealed that his relationship with his wife had continued to improve. He loved his son and enjoyed the trials and tribulations of fatherhood. In spite of his hectic home life, he pursued his career with vigor. In contrast to his previous conflictful relationships with his colleagues, in his new position he developed cordial relations with members of his department and, again in contrast to his inability to generate and complete fruitful research, completed several important research projects which he presented at national conferences.

When asked what stood out in his therapy, he said, "What I really remember most is the need to take charge of my life. Things were often sort of rolling out of control. Very often it was something that I knew. It was in my power to do something. It was easier to complain about it or to feel just helpless."

Sara

Age: 21
Single
Diagnosis: Hysterical neurosis
Length of treatment: 4 years

Scores Pre: 40
Post: 80

Sara was the oldest of three children from an upper-middle-class family. She had previously undertaken psychotherapy three times, with only minimal gains. She had flunked out of college twice and worked as a part-time waitress at minimum wage in a short-order restaurant. She had recently broken off with her boyfriend, the last of a string of ungratifying sado-masochistic relationships in which she was abused and humiliated. Severely depressed, she muddled along day after listless day, without friends or goals and withdrew into a fantasy world stimulated by reading one novel after another in her broken-down two-room apartment. She considered returning to live with her parents, who wanted her to "come home."

After four years of treatment, she resumed her university education and established herself in the business world. Starting out as a clerk in a word processing company, she worked her way up, became city-wide manager of two stores, and was earning of $40,000 a year. She became active in civic affairs and started to engage in a wide variety of social events, hostessing biweekly dinner parties. She began to establish more mutually satisfying interpersonal relationships and has developed a close relationship with a man. Although she visited her family about once a year, she was far more capable of living an independent and well-organized life on her own. Although these evaluations were made at the end of the four-year clinical trial, Sara continued in treatment and successfully terminated nine months afterwards.

Sue

Age: 19   *Scores* Pre: 15

Single

Diagnosis: Psychotic depression, nonbipolar

Length of treatment: One-hour consultation

This last patient is included in our sample mainly to indicate the usefulness of CET as a consultation instrument. In this case, CET enabled the therapist to reach the patient and to demonstrate her potential for therapy when she had continued to deteriorate and all other approaches had failed.

Sue had made several serious attempts at suicide prior to her second hospitalization. Throughout her hospital treatment, the whole gamut of antidepressants and antipsychotic medications, including Lithium, Tofranil and Haldol, had been used with minimal change in her affect or behavior. She had also been inaccessible to psychotherapeutic treatment, including a strong behavior modification program. As a last resort, the author was asked to see Sue in consultation.

As a result of the contact made with the patient during this one CET session, her psychiatry resident, who had attended a number of the author's CET seminars, developed renewed interest in the case. The resident noted, "I had practically given up any possibility or hope of establishing a working alliance with her. She remained remote and sullen. I decided CET might be a way of engaging her in therapy." This encounter with CET enabled the patient to break out of her hard-core, resistant stance and to enter into and gain from a continuing therapeutic relationship with her therapist.

In conclusion, we are fully aware that the results of our clinical trials require verification with a broader sample of patients. However, experience with CET suggests that it holds promise for effectively treating a wide variety of emotional disturbances. Resolution of the question of CET's efficacy when compared to or used in conjunction with other treatment approaches, including drug therapy, will depend on the results of controlled evaluation studies, which are underway.

We are not suggesting, moreover, that CET, as it is currently practiced, represents our complete and final words on technique, or that it is *the* experiential method. Research is continuing to improve the effectiveness of experiential methods and to expand the repertoire of experiential techniques, to which we now turn in the concluding chapter, *The Future of CET*.

CHAPTER VII

The Future of CET

In the early days, new directions in psychotherapy consisted of courageous efforts to bestow unconditional love to undo and repair the hypothesized parental rejection in the manner of Ferenczi (see Jones, 1957, pp. 147, 163-165) or Sechehaye (1951), to provide "corrective emotional experiences" after Alexander (1946) or respond symbolically with "deep" interpretations in the style of Rosen (1947). These approaches depended very much on the style and force of the therapist's personality rather than, as with CET, on a systematic, readily teachable method based on the nature of empirically derived developmental processes and strategies of therapeutic change.

We owe a great deal to the research of behavioral and cognitive therapists, such as Beck (1976, 1979) and Meichenbaum (1977), for helping to systematize the therapeutic process. Their emphasis on operationalizing the principles and techniques of therapy has facilitated communication between therapists and researchers and helped in the development of objective methods for evaluating therapeutic effectiveness.

Using these advances as a point of departure, CET has focused on systematic interventions which, though dependent on the therapist's skill and knowledge of the ways in which individuals function and change, escape the vagaries of subjectivism.

CET transforms psychotherapy. The therapy session becomes the stage of life on which the patient's integrity can be restored. In the context of mastering the real-world events, the patient gains a new perspective on himself: his self-worth, power, and ability to control his destiny. He can see that challenge, risk and frustration are not threats or signals for panic, retreat and hopelessness, but guides to survival. He can adopt a creative view of his life and dare to plan and dream.

The implications for the therapist in CET are also far-reaching. The method opens up a new dimension of professional intervention. CET elicits the therapist's creative potential. It restores his curiosity, sense of challenge and confidence—all of which may have been strong motivations for his choosing to be a therapist in the first place.

CET invites the therapist to become a more active participant in the therapy. The therapist's work with each of his patients can become truly creative. In addition to assuming a more active role in planning and choosing from an array of experiential interventions, the therapist can go beyond purely technical application of the method by participating in the development of new experiential interventions.

1. NEW CET TASKS

A CET therapist can break new ground by developing new therapeutic tasks. To be most effective, new tasks should be designed to explore, help develop, and resolve particular areas of ego function or intrapsychic conflict. The best tasks are ones that are difficult to do, yet have only a few pieces or movements, something that is simple and elegant, involving multiple sensory modalities and manipulation of objects. A task must catch the patient's attention and hold it with a solution sufficiently complex that the patient can gauge his progress as well as learn from his mistakes and derive a feeling of accomplishment from having successfully completed it. A task that is too easy or too difficult is of little use to the patient or the therapist and may even be a hindrance to the course of therapy. Some tasks, like Rubik's Cube, require so many steps or movements that the problem solver would need too many hours to master them. Such tasks have not been found useful.

2. NEW EXPERIENTIAL CONTEXTS

CET is being extended to other areas of psychotherapy as well. For example, we have made favorable beginnings in applying CET tasks to adolescent and child therapy with children as young as eight. Work is also moving forward with couples, family, and group therapy. By asking couples, families or groups to master a task "ensemble," one captures their vital give-and-take decision-making and problem-solving processes *in vivo*, and their dominance-submission, active-passive, constructive-destructive roles in social relations. By seeing the truth about themselves through their participation in goal-directed interpersonal interactions, patients can learn more effective, mutual and collaborative decision-making strategies—a critical aspect of harmonious interpersonal functioning.

CET shows especial promise with inpatient groups. The safe framework provided by the tasks enables patients to mobilize their conflict-free, secondary-process functioning so that they can reach out and begin to interact with other members of the group. While relating to the tasks, patients can overcome their isolation and unreality. They can test reality and discover the inappropriateness of their interpersonal behavior. With the aid of corrective feedback and consensual validation from the other members and from the therapist, they can learn to see themselves as others see them, see how their behavior makes others feel and influences others' opinions of them, and learn more appropriate social skills.

3. THE AUDIOTAPE TECHNIQUE

The audiotape technique is an experiential method with untapped potential. The prime advantage of recordings is that they provide interpersonal feedback which is not mediated through a second person. Profound self-confrontations occur; one cannot hide from oneself. The tapes bring the patient's interpersonal patterns home to him with undeniable force. He can discover for himself aspects of his behavior that challenge long-cherished images and fantasies. For example, one can be told, but without impact, that one is destructive, but the recordings can capture just what a person does that is destructive.

The scope of the audiotape technique has been broadened to encompass a variety of contexts, such as couples therapy, group therapy, family therapy, and special parent groups. For example, we have conducted with therapeutic effect "parenting seminars" where up to ten parents have been asked to tape their interactions with their children at home and then bring these recordings into the group for playback. Parents can examine, reflect upon and gain a new perspective on their child's and their own relationships with the clarity and insight rarely obtainable when they are caught up in the interactions of the moment.

What is important in this as well as in other group contexts is not merely that the patients' interactions are relived, but that they are experienced correctively. The group feedback enables the patient to discover and assimilate ways of viewing and changing his behavior that may be more acceptable than when provided by the authority-transferential figure of the therapist. It is not unusual for the patient then to recall previous comments made by the therapist. Often with dramatic impact, he understands that the therapist has been honest and, if anything, overprotective in previous confrontations. The therapist may then be experienced less as a critical or punitive transferential figure. The patient may subsequently be more amenable to the therapist's clarifications, confrontations and interpretations. This combination of feedback obtained from the group, the therapist and from one's own discoveries while experiencing the tape playbacks provides powerful self-observatory experiences that make important contributions to the therapeutic process.

4. THE CET PRACTITIONER-SCIENTIST

Although the primary goal of CET is to help improve the patient's life, it also enables the therapist to be a practitioner-scientist. In addition to providing a method of treatment, CET procedures offer the therapist an investigative tool and method for research to help deepen our understanding of patients' problems and the therapeutic process. During the course of a patient's task performance, the therapist can illuminate in detail not only the "why" of the patient's problem-solving behavior—its ontogenesis and psychodynamics—but the "how"—the intricate mechanisms of how solutions are arrived at and explication of the cognitive and affective processes which interfere with mastery. We are not referring here only to the defense mechanisms. By "mechanisms" we mean the preconscious processes or underlying psychological apparatuses which determine the way a person feels, perceives, remembers, reasons, learns, uses language, etc. As thus defined, it is a description of the *modus operandi* shaping and directing a patient's behavior, rather than a focus on the content, motivation, or symbolic meaning of that behavior.

Many therapists certainly consider a patient's perceptual, thought and language patterns, and analyze and clarify the defensive aspects of the patient's cognitive mechanisms. In some cases, especially those involving severe pathology or certain forms of schizophrenic disorders, it is therapeutically advisable or even necessary to consider how the patient's deviant cognitive processes interfere with his adaptive attempts. For the most part, however, the details of the cognitive patterns under analysis are not likely to be systematically and thoroughly mapped out and understood. The CET tasks enable the therapist and the patient to identify more precisely and understand more explicitly how his way of thinking, perceiving, and remembering contributes to his problems as well as how the patient's problems play a role in producing distortions and deficits in his cognitive and affective functioning.

For example, if a patient's problems in thinking and writing clearly and coherently prevent him from completing his Ph.D. dissertation, the therapist can focus on the motives, symbolic meanings, and past events which are related to his difficulty. On the other hand, the therapist can concentrate on helping the patient become aware of how he perceives, reasons, remembers, and uses language, and how these mechanisms contribute to his difficulty. A unified "why" and "how" analysis combines these two approaches. Even though the developmental crises—the "why"—may have been instrumental in the formation of the patient's impaired cognitive style, his cognitive style may have contributed to his developmental crises. Since they are interrelated developments in the patient's ontogenesis and pathology, an approach integrating both the "how" and "why" may be necessary to resolve the patient's problems. (A case study illustrating this integrative approach is presented in Weiner, 1975, pp. 87-113.)

A systematic exploration of these two aspects of behavior can play an important role in helping to produce a more coherent, unified theory of psychopathology and ego psychotherapy. While the patient is contending with the tasks, CET provides a multitude of *in vivo* opportunities to gain a deep understanding of the relationship between the "how" and "why" of behavior. These kinds of insights cannot but help us to develop a more incisive, decisive and productive treatment. Not only can the patient be helped to understand why and how his problems are related to his cognitive and emotional functioning and to improve his adaptation, but the therapist is provided with a viable medium to explore some of the many unanswered questions concerning human behavior and the therapeutic process.

For example, observing various relationships between the "why" and "how" of behavior offers the clinician-researcher multiple opportunities to isolate and develop testable hypotheses concerning the dynamics of the significant cognitive and affective variables in the evolution of a patient's life and his course in therapy. The CET therapy session becomes a naturalistic, controlled environment amenable to systematic study of a wide variety of psychological and therapeutic phenomena which are not readily discernible in the traditional therapeutic situation or easily discovered in the laboratory. One can ask questions about phenomena which may not have been thought of before, and explore and bring to light *researchable* new dimensions of a problem. Furthermore, one may devise analogue studies in which certain procedures identical to or analogous to those used in therapy with the tasks are systematically applied to experimental subjects under highly controlled conditions.

When one looks at life as a problem-solving venture, a continual interplay between primary- and secondary-process thinking, then one might want to explore how anger, conflict and defensive processes can produce transitory altered states of consciousness which result in a momentary weakening of synthetic ego functioning, and how resolution of conflict can strengthen ego integration and adaptive behavior. Why and how do challenging tasks engender regression in the service of the ego and creative problem solving? What are the cognitive and dynamic factors which influence repression? What are the processes which facilitate the lifting of repression and recovery of early memories? What is the role of free association and expression of affect in altering ego functioning (e.g., memory, problem solving, etc.)? How do various cognitive factors (e.g., the perception of causality and symbolization) affect the patient's ability to overcome resistance, assimilate interpretations and change his behavior?

Every practicing therapist is, therefore, offered not only an effective treatment modality, but a research tool and a unique researchable context. In the process of treating his patients, he can stand at the leading edge of clinical science and participate in the excitement and gratification of contributing to an emerging science of ego psychotherapy.

APPENDIX

Tasks and Resource Materials

Without the benefit of actually experiencing Cognitive-Experiential Therapy first-hand, the reader can best understand the method by working on these tasks before reading the solution. By reflecting on his or her cognitive style and emotional reactions while contending with the tasks, the reader can better understand what the patient experiences during therapy.

Tasks

Clinical Examples Illustrating the Tasks

1. Brook Problem — Marj, p. 70
2. Code Problem — Bob, p. 141
3. Golf Ball Problem — Sara, p. 164
4. Horseshoe-and-Ring Problem — Anna, p. 53; Judy, p. 91
5. Jug Problem — Erik, p. 21; Sue, p. 85; Sara, p. 102
6. Ping-Pong Problem — Hal, p. 57; Bob, p. 123
7. Horse-and-Rider Problem — Roy, p. 93, 112
8. Cowboy-and-Bull Problem — Roy, p. 96
9. Clown-and-Donkey Problem — Sara, p. 163
10. Ruler Problem — Hal, p. 61
11. T-Problem — Anna, p. 113
12. Tangrams — Hal, p. 116, 120
13. Triangles Problem — Frank, p. 140, 167

1. BROOK PROBLEM

Materials

A line drawing of a brook, 8″ × 10″.
Two flat wooden sticks, each 2 ¾″ × ¼″.

Task

At a bend in a brook there are two solid boards lying ready, but each is a little too short to span the brook. How would you get to the other side without getting wet, jumping, or in any way tying or nailing the boards together?

Commentary

Instead of trying to elongate the sticks by combining them in various ways, the solution requires a change of perspective in which one shortens the width of the brook. This can be accomplished by apprehending the special characteristics of this brook. The unusual angularity in the bend in the near shoreline permits that segment of the brook to be spanned by one of the sticks. This bridge extends the shoreline so that the distance necessary to span the entire brook is shortened. The solution readily follows: one can perpendicularly connect the second stick to the first and construct a bridge across the brook.

The patient can be helped by focusing on what is unusual about this brook and what makes it different from other brooks.

Brook Problem

2. CODE PROBLEM

Materials

"Master Mind" game (Invicta Plastics, Ltd.) is composed of a De-Coding Board of ten rows of large holes (Code Peg holes) and ten groups of small holes (Key Peg holes), and four shielded holes (for the hidden code). It also contains a shield to hide the hidden code. There are seventy-two round-headed, colored Code Pegs, consisting of twelve each of six colors. There are also forty thin flat-headed Key Pegs, consisting of twenty each of black and white.

Task

The therapist sets up a line of four of the colored Code Pegs behind his shield. The patient has up to ten opportunities to try to duplicate the color and exact position of the hidden Code Pegs without ever seeing them. After each row of guesses is completed by the patient, the therapist provides feedback as to the correctness of the patient's guesses by placing a black Key Peg in a hole alongside the row for every Code Peg placed by the patient which is the same color and in exactly the same position as one of the Code Pegs behind the shield, and a white Key Peg in a hole alongside the row for every Code Peg

Code Problem

placed by the patient which is correct in color only, but not in position. Vacant Key Peg holes are left by the therapist to indicate that the patient was incorrect for color. The code is solved when the patient duplicates the code for both color and position.

Commentary

This task challenges the patient's ability to use deductive logic and sequential reasoning. Because the therapist sets up the code and provides feedback as to its correctness, the task throws light on the patient's cognitive functioning in the context of an interpersonal relationship. The task, therefore, provides an excellent opportunity to explore how affective mechanisms intrude into and shape the patient's cognitive functioning. As a consequence, the therapist should be alert to the broader interpersonal aspects of the task and be ready to shift from focusing on apparently humdrum cognitive processes to exploring the roots of the patient's anxiety and its transferential implications.

3. GOLF BALL PROBLEM

Materials

The patient is handed a sheet of paper with instructions for the task printed on it. A golf ball and paper bag are provided as clues only after the patient has encountered considerable difficulty with the task.

Task

It was the sixteenth hole in the annual golf tournament play. A newcomer had an excellent chance of winning. His iron shot had fallen short of the green, and he had a good chance of making a birdie. He bounded down the fairway, then stopped in dismay. His ball had rolled into a small paper bag carelessly tossed there by someone in the gallery. If he removed the ball from the bag, it would cost him a penalty stroke. If he tried to hit the ball and the bag, he would lose control over the shot. For a moment, he stood there pondering the problem. Then, he solved it. How did he solve it?

Commentary

The solution to this problem does not depend on any knowledge of golf. Rather, it requires a change of perspective. If the patient focuses on various ways of removing the ball from the bag, the solution is impossible because any method for extracting the ball from the bag moves the ball and results in a penalty. Reversing perspective by removing the bag from the ball is important but only the first step toward the solution since one still has to explore ways of removing the bag without moving the ball. Tearing the bag away from the ball, for example, inevitably moves the ball. The solution to the problem has to be approached from the entirely different angle of not moving either the ball *or* the bag, but *doing away* with the bag, such as burning it.

When a patient encounters considerable difficulty with the task and reaches an impasse, the therapist assists the patient by actually producing a golf ball in a small paper bag. By concretizing the problem and facilitating reality testing, the patient is helped to adopt a new perspective. The problem is transformed from the purely abstract to one in which perceptual awareness and manipulation of real materials are emphasized. It is easier for the patient to "reverse" the problem and adopt a new perspective with real objects in front of him. Rather than limiting the patient to mentally manipulating the various alternatives, actual materials concretize the problem and provide the patient with an effective means to test reality and experiment with various options.

4. HORSESHOE-AND-RING PROBLEM

Materials

Two metal horseshoes connected by four metal links. A circular metal ring which is narrower in diameter than the widest part of the horseshoes is placed along the links between the two horseshoes.

Task

Remove the circular ring from the two connected horseshoes.

Commentary

The solution to this topological task is exceedingly difficult to comprehend without handling and experiencing the objects themselves. To solve the problem, the patient needs to change his perspective. At first, when viewed in two dimensions, the task looks impossible because the horseshoes are wider than the ring. However, when one folds the horseshoes over against one another, one can see that, although one cannot pass the ring *over* the wider parts of the horseshoes, one can slide the ring along the *sides* of the horseshoes, where their width makes no difference at all, and free the ring.

What is required for the solution, therefore, is actually to move the ring and horseshoes around in unexpected, novel ways to reveal that the ring can be moved not only back and forth across the linking chain, but along the sides of the horseshoes after the horseshoes are folded together.

Horseshoe-and-Ring Problem

5. JUG PROBLEM

Materials

A specially designed 4″ jug with twenty-one holes equally spaced around its sides. The jug is made with a hollow handle connecting the inside bottom of the jug with the hollow rim which contains three small spigots. There is also a hole on the underside of the handle which is visible only if the jug is raised above eye level. The jug is filled with water to just below the level of the holes in the sides.

Task

The task is written on the side of the jug: "This jug was made to try your skill, drink if you can, but do not spill" (or in any way become wet while drinking from it).

Commentary

One cannot effectively close up the holes on the sides of the jug with one's hands and drink from the rim or one of the side holes without spilling the water or wetting one's hands. The solution depends, therefore, on discovering, through a series of explorations and tests by the patient, how the spigots, hollow rim, and hollow handle can function together as a straw to siphon up the water from inside the jug.

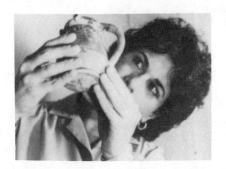 

Jug Problem

When one sucks on one of the spigots while covering the remaining two spigots, one would think that one could create a siphoning action and obtain the water. One obtains, however, only air. The lack of siphoning action is confirmed by blowing into one of the spigots while covering the remaining two. Where one would expect to produce bubbles in the jug, one feels only air escaping somewhere and hears a hissing sound.

To solve the problem, one must conclude that there is a leak somewhere in the route between the water and the spigot which is breaking the siphoning action. One must then engage in extensive visual and tactual exploration of the jug to discover the hole hidden on the underside of the handle. This is the key to the solution, for in covering this hole in combination with two of the spigot holes, one closes all leaks and completes the siphoning action.

The patient can be assisted by encouraging him to adopt an exploratory attitude whereby he can more effectively test reality and discover the hidden hole and the causal relationships necessary to solve the problem.

6. PING-PONG PROBLEM

Materials

A glass cylinder (9″ long, 1⅞″ diameter) closed at one end and containing a ping-pong ball. Various tools, including 5″ plastic forceps, metal pliers, 6″ chopsticks, a variety of string, paper clips, and a large clip from a clipboard are laid out near the cylinder in a random way on the same table on which the cylinder is placed. A vase filled with flowers and water is placed on a bookcase on the opposite side of the room.

Task

Remove the ping-pong ball from the cylinder in the quickest and easiest way without breaking, moving or tilting the cylinder. Without opening any drawers or tearing the room apart, you may use anything in the room to help you.

Commentary

The task can be solved in a variety of ways. It is extremely difficult and cumbersome to solve the problem with the tools provided. Their

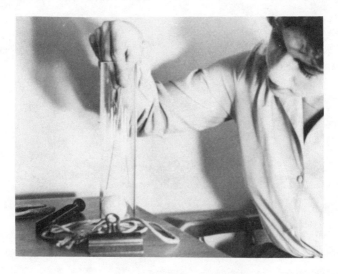

Ping-Pong Problem

main purpose is to serve as decoys and divert attention from considering a more effective way in which the tools play no part. For example, it takes little ingenuity but considerable dexterity to solve the problem by using the "grabbing," "lifting," or "scooping" tools provided, such as the forceps or chopsticks. With these methods, one approaches the problem concretely and considers the ping-pong ball merely as an object without special characteristics. It could just as well be a golf ball.

The preferred method is to approach the problem in a more differentiated way where one appreciates the unique characteristics of the ping-pong ball. This method requires a three-step process: first, after sizing up the situation and seeing that the chopsticks are really too short to grab the ball, the patient has to free himself from the restrictions imposed by the tools and consider the problem from a broader perspective; second, he must apprehend the special, floatable attributes of the ping-pong ball; third, he must implement this insight by exploring the broader context of the office and searching for a liquid to float the ball. This is a problem in itself because the only water available is functionally embedded in a vase of flowers placed on another table in the office. Finally, the patient needs to take action. The solution requires not only thought and perceptual discrimination, but movement and action in the broader office environment.

One way to help the patient is to focus on what makes the ping-pong ball special and different from other balls.

7,8,9. "RIDER" PROBLEMS

The following three tasks form a series of "Rider" Problems which are presented to the patient in sequence.

7. HORSE-AND-RIDER PROBLEM

Materials

The problem is composed of three pieces. One is a picture of a rider seated on the midsection of a horse; the same figure is duplicated upside down on the opposite end of the same piece. The other two pieces consist of pictures of two identical horses. The figures are printed on heavy cardboard so that they are not visible from the reverse side.

Task

Fit the three pieces together so that the two riders sit on top of the horses as they normally do, without bending, folding or tearing any of the pieces.

Commentary

An analytical perceptual attitude is essential for the solution of the Horse-and-Rider Problem. Patients typically attempt to place each rider on top of each horse and discover that the riders and the horses do not fit together in the expected manner. Clues to the solution are derived from seeing the incongruity between the greater width of the

 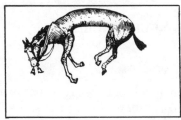 

Horse-and-Rider Problem

horse's body on the rider piece compared to the horse piece; that the contours of the horse's body and saddle on the rider piece curve upwards, whereas the neck on the horse piece curves downwards; and that the rider piece cannot possibly be placed over the horse piece because it would cover the horse's legs. The solution requires building a new configuration by integrating the contours of compatible parts from the different pieces rather than vainly and impulsively trying to force incongruous parts from each whole piece into a quick, easy solution.

To facilitate the solution, the therapist can help the patient to become more aware of the perceptual qualities of the parts and the contradictions obtained when he attempts to integrate the whole horse piece with the whole rider piece. The patient has to overcome a global and undifferentiated view of the figures. By adopting a part-whole, analytical attitude, the patient can separate the whole pieces into their parts, and part-by-part juxtapose and integrate different parts from the different pieces to form a unified whole.

For example, the reins from the horse's bridle can be fitted in a continuous line to the reins shown just in front of the rider's saddle. Moreover, by carefully piecing the upward-moving part in front of the rider's saddle so that it continues in an upward direction when connected to the horse's mane, the patient is forced to rotate the horse piece and rider piece so that the front of the horse's legs are raised into a gallop. At the same time, the upward-moving rear part of the saddle of the rider piece is juxtaposed with the rear of the other horse so that the rear legs are also raised into a gallop. When the rider is properly integrated with the front of one of the horse pieces and the rear of the other horse piece, the other rider and horse pieces automatically fall into place because they are integrated in the same manner.

Throughout the patient's problem-solving attempts, the therapist can assist him by pointing out the contradictions and incongruities which are blocking effective part-whole integrations.

8. COWBOY-AND-BULL PROBLEM

Materials

The problem is composed of two pieces: one piece consists of a picture of a cowboy mounted on the midsection of a bull; the same figure is duplicated upside down on the same piece. The second piece consists of pictures of two identical bulls, each upside down from the other. The pictures are printed on 20-lb. paper so that they can be seen from the reverse side.

Task

Fit the two pieces together so that the cowboys sit on top of the bulls as they normally do without bending, folding, or tearing any of the pieces.

Commentary

The basic design of this task is the same as the Horse-and-Rider Problem except that trying simply to repeat the solution which was effective with the Horse-and-Rider Problem actually interferes with the solution to this new problem. The solution requires the patient to break out of the old pattern and adopt a fresh perspective, while at the same time applying some elements of the old solution to the new context.

Even though the two puzzles are superficially similar, the task is not solvable in the old way because when the cowboys are placed over the bulls in the previously effective way, the patient finds that the cowboys, unlike the riders, face in the wrong direction, i.e., they face to the rear of the bulls. Consequently, the patient must give up the repetition of the old pattern and adopt a new approach. He is required

Cowboy-and-Bull Problem

to discover how the direction of the cowboys can be reversed and integrated with the front of the bulls. A reversal of direction of the cowboys can be accomplished by flipping the figures of the cowboys over to the reverse side and, while holding both the cowboys and the bulls up to the light, superimposing and integrating the parts into the whole figure. Thus, although a critical part of the old Horse-and-Rider solution is essential for the solution of this new task, to be effectively used the old solution must be applied in a new way. The patient must perceptually shift his orientation and view the pieces from a new perspective. Instead of conceiving of the pieces as parts that can simply be moved around on the table, the patient has to break out of the limitations of the flat plane.

The patient can be helped by focusing on how one can reverse the direction of a printed figure. He can be encouraged to experiment with and manipulate the pieces and view them from various perspectives.

9. CLOWN-AND-DONKEY PROBLEM

Materials

Two identical sets of printed pictures. Each set is composed of three parts: two donkeys which are mirror images of each other and a picture with two clowns on it. Each set can be cut into three parts with a scissors with which the patient is provided.

Task

The therapist first hands the patient only one set and a pair of scissors, and says: "Here are two donkeys and two clowns. Cut them

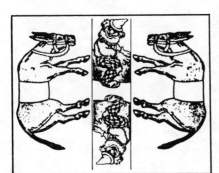

Clown-and-Donkey Problem

along the lines into three parts and then fit the parts together so that the clowns sit on top of the donkeys as they normally do." Then the therapist hands the patient the second set and says, "And here's a set you can keep." Both sets are presented with the heads of the donkeys at the top.

The problem must be solved without turning over any of the parts to the reverse side. If the patient tries this alternative, the therapist says: "This problem has to be solved without turning over any of the parts."

Commentary

Since neither of the former "rider" solutions are applicable or acceptable for this problem, the therapist focuses on the patient's ability to break out of restrictive repetition of old, inappropriate ways and take a fresh perspective. For example, when the therapist says, "And here's a set you can keep," the instructions can be misinterpreted to imply that the second set is irrelevant and simply a "gift" outside of the problem-solving context. In fact, it is essential to the solution. Since the donkeys in each set are *mirror images* of one another, and since the problem can only be solved with two *identical* donkeys, the patient must cut off one of the donkeys from the second set which is identical to one of the donkeys in the first set to complete the solution in the manner of the original Horse-and-Rider Problem.

Solution of the problem requires using resources from an unexpected context—an often vital ingredient in problem solving. The patient must go beyond the narrow confines of the "problem set" and overcome the false assumption that "Here's a set you can keep" excludes its use in the solution.

When the patient encounters difficulty with the task, the therapist can help him to focus first on what is missing to solve the problem and second on perceiving the problem from a wider viewpoint so as to discover the missing parts outside of the limited context of the "problem set."

10. RULER PROBLEM

Materials

A transparent plastic ruler which looks like an ordinary 12″ ruler with standard inch and centimeter markings. In actuality, it is a specially made ruler that has been proportionately reduced to 11¹¹⁄₁₆″. To solve the problem, two objective comparison standards are unobtrusively provided: (1) a standard box of facial tissues, which has the dimensions of the tissues printed on the box, is placed to one side of the therapy table; and (2) a standard 8½″ × 11″ sheet of paper with printing on it is either tacked to a bulletin board on the opposite side of the room or placed on a table adjacent to the therapy table.

Task

What is wrong with this ruler?

Commentary

First, the patient has to differentiate the essential from the non-essential qualities of the ruler and grasp that it is the measuring

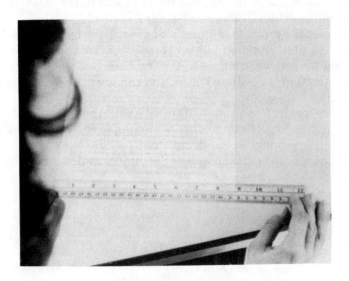

Ruler Problem

qualities of a ruler which are fundamental. For example, slight imperfections in the manufacture of the ruler, such as minute irregularities in the printing of the numbers, should be considered as irrelevant. The patient must, therefore, identify the real fault in the ruler's measuring qualities. Because the ruler is only ⁵⁄₁₆″ shorter than a real ruler, it is impossible to distinguish it from a real ruler simply by using one's visual senses. Therefore, one must determine the objective length of the ruler by testing it against reality. One can obtain consensual validation by comparing it with an objective, reliable standard known to represent true lengths. To solve the problem, the patient has to search for and discover one of the objective reality standards which are provided and test the ruler against it.

The solution to the problem can be facilitated by helping the patient to learn how to test reality. He must develop an awareness that things are not always what they appear to be, but can be evaluated when they are compared with reliable standards. The patient can be helped to develop effective ways of using his senses in combination with the resources in the environment to provide feedback and consensual validation.

11. T-PROBLEM

Materials

Four irregularly shaped pieces of yellow cardboard.

Task

Fit the pieces together so that they form the letter "T."

Commentary

The solution to this problem is blocked if one conceives of the T simply as an orthogonal figure composed only of vertical and horizontal units. To solve the problem, the patient needs to break out of the orthogonal structure of the T and apprehend that verticals and horizontals can be formed with irregular diagonals. The patient is then enabled to use the large notched piece as a diagonal with one section serving as part of the horizontal top of the T and the other section serving as part of the vertical stem.

To help the patient in this differentiating process, the therapist can suggest that the patient draw a figure of a T and rotate it so that it lies on its side or is upside down. This new perspective enables the patient to see the figure not as an orthogonal letter, but as just another geometrical figure which more readily can be broken down into non-orthogonal parts. The differentiating process also can be implemented by helping the patient to dissect the T into irregular parts. He is asked

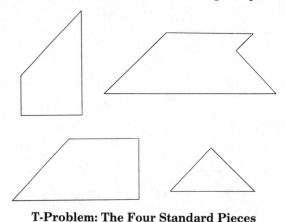

T-Problem: The Four Standard Pieces

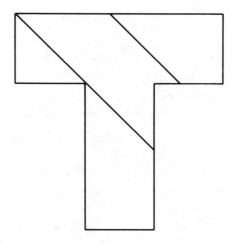

T-Problem

to draw a solid T and then to divide it up using the shapes of the pieces as guidelines for the analytical process. Finally, an effective method for assisting the patient to assume the analytic-synthetic attitude necessary for the solution is to ask him to feel and describe the pieces with his eyes closed. Experiencing the pieces on a concrete, sensory-tactile-kinesthetic level enables the patient more fully to focus on and perceive each piece as an independent unit so that it can be used and integrated into the whole figure in new, adaptive ways.

12. TANGRAMS

Materials

Seven geometrically shaped pieces of red-colored cardboard. A variety of figures resembling human beings, animals and objects are used during different stages of therapy. A skating figure is the first in the series.

Task

Combine the seven pieces to make this figure.

Commentary

The task requires an ability to differentiate a whole into its component parts and to engage in analytic-synthetic cognitive functioning.

Tangrams

13. TRIANGLES PROBLEM

Materials

Six narrow sticks, each 3″ in length.

Task

Make four equilateral triangles with the six sticks, without bending, breaking, or splitting any of the sticks, with all of the ends fitting perfectly together, no parts left over and without any of the sticks crossing over one another.

Commentary

The problem is insoluble as long as one limits one's perspective to the flat plane of the table. Mastery of the task requires the patient to take an active role not only in experimenting with different configurations, but in breaking out of the plane and constructing the triangles in the third dimension. Even then, to consummate the solution, the patient has to participate in the task actively by using his hands to grasp and support the sticks in an upright position while forming a pyramid.

References

Adler, A. *What Life Should Mean To You.* Boston: Little, Brown, 1931.

Alexander, F. The Principle of Corrective Emotional Experience. In F. Alexander and T. M. French et al., *Psychoanalytic Therapy.* New York: Ronald Press, 1946.

Anthony, E. J. The Significance of Jean Piaget for Child Psychiatry. *British Journal of Medical Psychology,* 1956, *29,* 20-34.

Anthony, E. J. Freud, Piaget and Human Knowledge: Some Comparisons and Contrasts. *The Annual of Psychoanalysis, 4,* 253-277. New York: International Universities Press, 1976.

Arieti, S. Psychotherapy of Severe Depression. In S. Arieti and J. Bemporad, *Severe and Mild Depression.* New York: Basic Books, 1978.

Basch, M. F. Developmental Psychology and Explanatory Theory in Psychoanalysis. *The Annual of Psychoanalysis, 5,* 229-263. New York: International Universities Press, 1977.

Beck, A. T. *Cognitive Therapy and the Emotional Disorders.* New York: International Universities Press, 1976.

Beck, A. T., Rush, A. J., Shaw, B., and Emery, G. *Cognitive Therapy of Depression.* New York: Guilford Press, 1979.

Bettelheim, B. *The Empty Fortress.* New York: Free Press, 1967.

Bieber, I. *Cognitive Psychoanalysis.* New York: Jason Aronson, 1980.

Blum, H. P. On the Conception and the Development of the Transference Neurosis. *Journal of the American Psychoanalytic Association,* 1971, *19,* 41-53.

Cowan, P. A. *Piaget: With Feeling.* New York: Holt, Rinehart and Winston, 1978.

Ellis, A. *Humanistic Psychotherapy: The Rational-Emotive Approach.* New York: Julian Press, 1973.

Erikson, E. H. Personal Communication, 29 January 1983.

221

Feuerstein, R. *Instrumental Enrichment: An Intervention Program for Cognitive Modifiability*. Baltimore: University Park Press, 1980.

Frank, J. D. Therapeutic Factors in Psychotherapy. *American Journal of Psychotherapy*, 1971, *25*, 350-361.

Freud, A. *The Ego and the Mechanisms of Defense* (Rev. Ed.). New York: International Universities Press, 1966. (Originally published, 1936.)

Freud, S. Fragment of an Analysis of a Case of Hysteria. *Standard Edition*, 7, 7-122. London: Hogarth Press, 1953. (Originally published, 1905.)

Freud, S. On Beginning the Treatment (Further Recommendations on the Technique of Psycho-Analysis I). *Standard Edition, 12*, 123-144. London: Hogarth Press, 1958. (Originally published, 1913.)

Freud, S. Remembering, Repeating and Working-Through (Further Recommendations on the Technique of Psycho-Analysis II). *Standard Edition, 12*, 147-156. London: Hogarth Press, 1958. (Originally published, 1914.)

Freud, S. Lines of Advance in Psycho-Analytic Therapy. *Standard Edition, 17*, 159-168. London: Hogarth Press, 1955. (Originally published, 1919.)

Friedman, L. Piaget and Psychotherapy. *Journal of the American Academy of Psychoanalysis*, 1978, *6*, 175-192.

Gill, M. M. *Analysis of Transference*. Psychological Issues Monograph 53. New York: International Universities Press, 1982.

Glover, E. *The Technique of Psycho-Analysis*. New York: International Universities Press, 1955.

Goldfried, M. R. and Goldfried, A. P. Cognitive Change Methods. In F. H. Kanfer and A. P. Goldstein (Eds.), *Helping People Change* (2nd ed.). New York: Pergamon Press, 1980.

Gouin-Décarie, T. *Intelligence and Affectivity in Early Childhood*. New York: International Universities Press, 1965. (Originally published, 1962.)

Greenson, R. R. *The Technique and Practice of Psychoanalysis*. New York: International Universities Press, 1967.

Greenspan, S. I. *Intelligence and Adaptation: An Integration of Psychoanalytic and Piagetian Developmental Psychology*. Psychological Issues Monograph 47/48. New York: International Universities Press, 1979.

Gruber, H. E. and Vonèche, J. J. (Eds.). *The Essential Piaget*. New York: Basic Books, 1977.

Inhelder, B., Sinclair, H., and Bovet, M. *Learning and the Development of Cognition*. Cambridge, Mass.: Harvard University Press, 1974.

Jones, E. *The Life and Work of Sigmund Freud* (Vol. 3). New York: Basic Books, 1957.

Kanzer, M. Verbal and Nonverbal Aspects of Free Association. *Psychoanalytic Quarterly*, 1961, *30*, 327-350.

Kuhn, D. Mechanisms of Change in the Development of Cognitive Structures. *Child Development*, 1972, *43*, 833-844.

Loewald, H. On the Therapeutic Action of Psycho-Analysis. *International Journal of Psycho-Analysis*, 1960, *41*, 16-33.

Loewald, H. Some Considerations on Repetition and Repetition Compulsion. *International Journal of Psycho-Analysis*, 1971, *52*, 59-66.

Luborsky, L. Clinicians' Judgments of Mental Health: Specimen Case Descriptions and Forms for the Health-Sickness Rating Scale. *Bulletin of the Menninger Clinic*, 1975, *39*, 448-480.

Luborsky, L. Helping Alliances in Psychotherapy. In J. L. Claghorn (Ed.), *Successful Psychotherapy*. New York: Brunner/Mazel, 1976.

Luborsky, L. *Principles of Psychoanalytic Psychotherapy*. New York: Basic Books, 1984.

Mahoney, M. J. *Cognition and Behavior Modification*. Cambridge, Mass.: Ballinger, 1974.

Meichenbaum, D. *Cognitive-Behavior Modification*. New York: Plenum Press, 1977.

Piaget, J. *The Origins of Intelligence in Children*. (M. Cook, Trans.) New York: International Universities Press, 1952. (Originally published, 1936.)

Piaget, J. *The Construction of Reality in the Child*. (M. Cook, Trans.) New York: Basic Books, 1954. (Originally published, 1937.)

Piaget, J. *Play, Dreams and Imitation in Childhood*. (C. Gattegno and F. M. Hodgson, Trans.) New York: Norton, 1951. (Originally published, 1945.)

Piaget, J. *The Psychology of Intelligence*. (M. Piercy and D. E. Berlyne, Trans.) London: Routledge & Kegan Paul, 1950. (Originally published, 1947.)

Piaget, J. *Intelligence and Affectivity: Their Relationship During Child Development*. (T. A. Brown and C. E. Kaegi, Trans.) Palo Alto: Annual Reviews, 1981. (Originally published, 1954.)

Piaget, J. Development and Learning. In S. F. Campbell (Ed.), *Piaget Sampler*. New York: John Wiley, 1976. (Originally published, 1964.)

Piaget, J. *The Development of Thought: Equilibration of Cognitive Structures*. (A. Rosin, Trans.) New York: Viking Press, 1977. (Originally published, 1975.)

Piaget, J. What is Psychology? *American Psychologist*, 1978, *33*, 648-652.

Piaget, J. and Weiner, M. L. Recherches sur le Développement des Perceptions (Vol. 35). Quelques Interférences entre la Perception de la Vitesse et la Causalité Perceptive. *Archives de Psychologie*, 1957-1958, *36*, 236-252.

Rapaport, D. *Collected Papers*. New York: Basic Books, 1967.

Rosen, J. The Treatment of Schizophrenic Psychosis by Direct Analytic Therapy. *Psychiatric Quarterly*, 1947, *21*, 3-25.

Sandler, A. M. Comments on the Significance of Piaget's Work for Psychoanalysis. *International Review of Psycho-Analysis*, 1975, *2*, 365-377.

Schafer, R. *Psychoanalytic Interpretation in Rorschach Testing*. New York: Grune & Stratton, 1954.

Schmid-Kitsikis, E. Piagetian Theory and Its Approach to Psychopathology. *American Journal of Mental Deficiency*, 1973, *77*, 694-705.

Sechehaye, M. A. *Symbolic Realization*. New York: International Universities Press, 1951.

Sherman, A. R. *In Vivo* Therapies for Phobic Reactions, Instrumental Behavior Problems, and Interpersonal and Communication Problems. In A. P. Goldstein and F. H. Kanfer (Eds.), *Maximizing Treatment Gains: Transfer Enhancement in Psychotherapy*. New York: Academic, 1979.

Sherman, A. R. and Levine, M. P. *In Vivo* Therapies for Compulsive Habits, Sexual Difficulties, and Severe Adjustment Problems. In A. P. Goldstein and F. H. Kanfer (Eds.), *Maximizing Treatment Gains: Transfer Enhancement in Psychotherapy*. New York: Academic, 1979.

Strupp, H. H. Success and Failure in Time-Limited Psychotherapy: Further Evidence (Comparison 4). *Archives of General Psychiatry*, 1980, *37*, 947-954.

Turiel, E. An Experimental Test of the Sequentiality of Developmental Stages in the Child's Moral Judgments. *Journal of Personality and Social Psychology*, 1966, *3*, 611-618.

Wachtel, P. L. Transference, Schema, and Assimilation: The Relevance of

Piaget to the Psychoanalytic Theory of Transference. *The Annual of Psychoanalysis*, *8*, 59-76. New York: International Universities Press, 1981.

Weiner, M. L. The Illusion of Normality. In M. L. Weiner, *The Cognitive Unconscious: A Piagetian Approach to Psychotherapy.* Davis, Calif.: International Psychological Press, 1975. (Original unpublished manuscript, 1951.)

Weiner, M. L. Perceptual Sensitization. In M. L. Weiner, *The Cognitive Unconscious: A Piagetian Approach to Psychotherapy.* Davis, Calif.: International Psychological Press, 1975. (Original unpublished manuscript, 1952.)

Weiner, M. L. The Development of Veridicality. In M. L. Weiner, *The Cognitive Unconscious: A Piagetian Approach to Psychotherapy.* Davis, Calif.: International Psychological Press, 1975. (Original unpublished manuscript, 1954.)

Weiner, M. L. The Effects of Differently Structured Visual Fields on the Perception of Verticality. *American Journal of Psychology*, 1955a, *68*, 291-293.

Weiner, M. L. Effects of Training in Space Orientation on Perception of the Upright. *Journal of Experimental Psychology*, 1955b, *49*, 367-373.

Weiner, M. L. Perceptual Development in a Distorted Room: A Phenomenological Study. *Psychological Monographs*, 1956, *70*, No. 423.

Weiner, M. L. *The Cognitive Unconscious: A Piagetian Approach to Psychotherapy.* Davis, Calif.: International Psychological Press, 1975.

Weiner, M. L. A Freudian and Piagetian Rapprochement in Psychotherapy. *Bulletin of the Menninger Clinic*, 1979, *43*, 443-462.

Weiner, M. L. The Ego Activation Method: Therapeutic Laboratory for Adaptation. *Psychoanalysis and Contemporary Thought*, 1980a, *3*, 569-600.

Weiner, M. L. Dynamic Cognitive Therapy. In R. Herink (Ed.), *The Psychotherapy Handbook*. New York: New American Library, 1980b.

Weiner, M. L. Equilibration of Structures in Psychotherapy. In S. Modgil and C. Modgil (Eds.), *Toward a Theory of Psychological Development*. Windsor, England: NFER Publishing Co., 1980c.

Weiner, M. L. Ego Activation in the Treatment of Acutely Depressed Outpatients. *Journal of the American Academy of Psychoanalysis*, 1982, *10*, 493-513.

Weiner, M. L. The Ego Activation Method: An *In Vivo* Cognitive Therapy Integrating Behavioral and Psychodynamic Approaches. *Cognitive Therapy and Research*, 1983, *7*, 11-16.

Weiner, M. L. The Efficacy of Cognitive-Experiential Therapy. *Abstracts of the Society for Psychotherapy Research*, 1984. (Paper presented at the 15th Annual Meeting, Lake Louise, Alberta, Canada, June, 1984.)

Weiner, M. L. Treatment of Acute Schizophrenic Episodes with Cognitive-Experiential Therapy. *British Journal of Cognitive Psychotherapy*, 1985, *3*, in press.

Werner, H. *Comparative Psychology of Mental Development* (3rd ed.). New York: International Universities Press, 1957.

Witkin, H. A. *The Effects of Training and of Structural Aids on Performance in Three Tests of Space Orientation*. Washington, D. C.: Division of Research, Civil Aeronautics Administration, Report No. 80, 1948.

Witkin, H. A. et al. *Personality Through Perception*. New York: Harper & Row, 1954.

Witkin, H. A. et al. *Psychological Differentiation*. New York: Wiley, 1962.

Wolff, P. H. *The Developmental Psychologies of Jean Piaget and Psychoanalysis.*
Psychological Issues Monograph 5. New York: International Universities
Press, 1960.

Index